WORDSWORTH LITERARY LIVES

General Editor: Keith Carabine

SHAKESPEARE

& His Tragic Life

TO THE READER

This figure, that thou here seest put,
It was for gentle Shakespeare cut;
Wherein the graver had a strife
With nature to out-do the life:
O, could he but have drawn his wit
As well in brass as he hath hit
His face, the print would then surpass
All that was ever writ in brass.
But, since he cannot, reader, look
Not on his picture, but his book.

BEN JONSON

Shakespeare

& His Tragic Life

A BIOGRAPHY BY
FRANK HARRIS

Introduction by
J. H. STAPE

WORDSWORTH EDITIONS

In loving memory of
MICHAEL TRAYLER
the founder of Wordsworth Editions

1

Readers who are interested in other titles from
Wordsworth Editions are invited to visit our website at
www.wordsworth-editions.com

For our latest list and a full mail-order service, contact
Bibliophile Books, 5 Datapoint, South Crescent, London E16 4TL
TEL: +44 (0)20 7474 2474 FAX: +44 (0)20 7474 8589
ORDERS: orders@bibliophilebooks.com
WEBSITE: www.bibliophilebooks.com

First published as *The Man Shakespeare and His Tragic Life Story* in 1909.
First published as *Shakespeare & His Tragic Life* in 2008
by Wordsworth Editions Limited
8B East Street, Ware, Hertfordshire SG12 9HJ

ISBN 978 1 84022 563 1

Text © Wordsworth Editions Limited 2008
Introduction © J. H. Stape 2008

Wordsworth® is a registered trademark of
Wordsworth Editions Limited

Typeset in Great Britain by Antony Gray
Printed and bound by Clays Ltd, St Ives plc

Contents

Introduction

Shakespearean biography has always attracted more than its fair share of cranks. It seems as if the very paucity of documents about the life of England's – and arguably the world's – greatest playwright has encouraged speculation ranging from the sensible to the ridiculous. Such staggering genius must, it has been felt, be explained by more than mere reading, however brilliant; by more than inspired imitation from Classical and contemporary Italian models; and by more than first-hand experience on the stage. The works themselves in their dazzling insight, variety and poetic achievement demand, it seems, that their author have an extraordinarily rich life and an unusually wide and deep education. With the few firm and verifiable biographical facts that have come down about the playwright from the Elizabethan period, 'Shakespeare the man' is inevitably an enigmatic, almost wholly inaccessible figure, with the result that myth and supposition have tended to take over where fact peters out.

Asked by a Parisian literary magazine to comment on the Baconian controversy (the school of thought that contends that Sir Francis Bacon was, in fact, the author of Shakespeare's plays), Joseph Conrad, taking an almost disarmingly commonsensical view of the subject, first commented, 'The Bacon controversy has never interested me because what does it matter to us who wrote Shakespeare's works?' He then went on to recount that he

> once knew a kind of hermit (he lived in a wooden hut in a small wood) who affirmed absolutely that Shakespeare's works were written by a supernatural being to whom he gave a name I no longer remember. As he seemed greatly attached to this theory, I told him I wished him well but that in the end I was wholly indifferent to the question. Straightaway he told me I was an idiot. Thus ended our relations. [25 September 1922, *Collected Letters*, 7: 526]

Absurd as that story is designed to be, there has been no lack of real-life contenders: others to whom the authorship of Shakespeare's works has been attributed include the 17th Earl of Oxford, Sir Walter Raleigh and even Queen Elizabeth I.

An ardent and serious Shakespearean, during a period of marked Bardolatry, Frank Harris is happy to neglect the absurdly speculative. Harris's boundless enthusiasm for the dramatist – Oscar Wilde remembered him as 'upstairs, thinking of Shakespeare at the top of his voice' – was one fully shared with his time, and Harris, a man who had cut his literary teeth in the hurly-burly of daily journalism as editor of the *Evening News* before moving on to the editorship of serious monthlies, was supremely skilled at sniffing out and exploiting popular interests. Theatrical troupes specialising in Shakespeare's works, notably the F. R. Benson Company, flourished in the capital as well as at Stratford-upon-Avon, the poet's birthplace, where the first Shakespeare Memorial Theatre opened in 1879. The plays were also dragged up and down the provinces season in, season out, by actor-knights and travelling players. The talents of the day's great actors and actresses – Herbert Beerbohm Tree, Ellen Terry, Sir Henry Irving, and Harley Granville Barker – ensured that the theatres were full, while the poet's memory was kept ever green by the National Shakespeare Memorial Committee and the highly active London Shakespeare League. The latter, patronised by celebrated professors as well as by members of the aristocracy, fêted the poet's birthday with the Lord Mayor at Mansion House.

More significantly, the age saw technological changes that began to affect productions, with more elaborate lighting and technical effects than ever before. Still quite near its late-Victorian peak (Tennyson was histrionically placed in his grave with a copy of *Cymbeline*), Bardolatry was at the time a firm fixture of the English identity. Conrad's fictional Lord Jim carries 'a thick green-and-gold volume – a half-crown complete Shakespeare' (Chapter 23) with him into the jungles of the Malay Archipelago; he had many real-life counterparts. During this period, A. C. Bradley, Professor of Poetry in Oxford University, produced his highly influential *Shakespearean Tragedy* (1904), while Professor Walter Raleigh, Chair of English Literature in Oxford, wrote his biography, *Shakespeare* (1907), in the 'English Men of Letters' series. In 1909, enter Frank Harris with his strong views on the playwright, poet and the man. Nothing if not sure of himself, Harris followed up his subjective study of the poet's life with, first, a play, *Shakespeare and his Love* (1910; written 1904?), and two years later *The Women of Shakespeare's Plays*, a compilation of his essays written for the *English Review* during 1910–11. In the latter year, such was Harris's reputation as a critic – and the general interest in Shakespeare – that he could attract an audience to fashionable Claridge's Hotel to hear him speak on Shakespeare's love life (*The Times*, 20 November 1911, p. 10).

And yet as E. M. Forster, who found Harris's *The Man Shakespeare and his Tragic Life Story*** 'amusing' and 'stimulating', said: it contained 'some truth, though far from true as a whole' (*Selected Letters*, I, p. 99). Harris, who famously courted controversy in several biographies and more often than not sought out the 'truth' of his impressions rather than the truth of fact, might not have been wholly displeased by Forster's encomium, guarded as it is. But warmer praise had come for his book: the popular novelist Arnold Bennett was unsparingly enthusiastic, describing it as 'a masterpiece on Shakespeare', and going so far as to assert that it was 'the best way to make Shakespeare's acquaintance'. Only somewhat less eager in his acclaim was Bernard Shaw, a friend of Harris, who reviewed the drama for him when he edited the *Saturday Review*: 'Nobody has discovered, or divined, more interesting and suggestive references.' The *New York Times* reviewer went much further, offering unstinting commendation of a kind that would please any writer: 'This is the book for which we have waited a lifetime.'

Academic critics, however, did not share these opinions. They rejected the thesis that Shakespeare revealed himself intimately in all his works under the guise of his characters and seem also to have been provoked by the contention that the playwright-poet's life was 'tragic' – an eye-catching but somewhat misleading word in Harris's title. The 'tragedy', a word used in its loose and popular sense, amounts to Shakespeare's having been unhappy in love, both in his marriage and in his choice of a beloved in Mary Fitton: 'for I have to tell here the story of his passion and his soul's wreck . . . And this more intimate under-standing of the man will enable us to reconstruct, partially at least, the happenings of his . . . life's journey from his school days in 1575 till he crept home to Stratford to die nearly forty years later' (Chapter 1). Despite Harris's determined efforts, the contours of Shakespeare's 'intimate' life remain a matter of speculation and only that.

* The present Wordsworth edition has been retitled *Shakespeare & His Tragic Life*.

One of the day's leading Shakespeare scholars, the influential Danish critic Georg Brandes (1847–1927), lashed out at Harris's arguments in a well-attended lecture in New York City, objecting to the proposition that anyone who had read the dramatist's works would find it impossible to admire Shakespeare. He declared that he himself, *pace* Harris, had 'accomplished the impossible' (*New York Times*, 8 June 1914, p. 7). In his review of Harris's life for *Munsey's Magazine*, Matthew Brander (1852–1929), first Professor of Dramatic Literature at Columbia University, attacked the work as outright 'nonsense':

> Mr Harris discovers that Shakespeare put himself into every one of his plays . . . Mr Harris is emboldened to put forth an utterly fanciful theory. It isn't more absurd than other theories about Shakespeare which have been proclaimed with equally blatant blasts on the trumpet of self-advertisement . . . It is nonsense, nothing more nor less.   [cited in the *New York Times Book Review*, 6 July 1913, p. 390]

Never one to shy from controversy, Harris eagerly rose to the proffered bait. Addressing none of Brander's specific objections to his portrait, he launched a gloves-off *ad hominem* attack that was partly undignified name-calling. The assault was certainly calculated to keep Harris's name in the news. Proclaiming Brander 'armored in stupidity', which he later qualified as 'insolent and provincial', Harris kicked as low as he could: 'a few hours after his death his only chance of being remembered by men of letters is as "the pedantic American professor, Maunders Bathos" ' (an allusion to a hostile portrayal of the academic in a novel). Harris recalled his own dramatic successes, pitting the practitioner against the mere critic, and also loudly sang his own praises as well as publicising the warm approval accorded his work by the novelists George Meredith and Arnold Bennett.

However that may be, the book pushed its way into public notice, even if it failed to win over academic critics. Like so many other works by Harris before and after it, *The Man Shakespeare* was enmeshed in lively controversy from the day it was published. Harris had perhaps courted this in cocking a snook at all past critics: his introduction boasts that he alone in some four centuries of criticism had sniffed out the essential individual behind the plays and sonnets: 'Without a single exception, the commentators have missed out the man and his story.' The eminent late-twentieth-century Shakespeare critic Stanley Wells calls the study 'sensational', a tribute to its iconoclastic treatment of the much loved 'Bard' as a flesh-and-blood man, who, perhaps un-surprisingly, resembles Frank Harris in certain important ways.

Harris's central thesis, summed up in his Introduction, is plainly put: ' . . . it is possible from Shakespeare's writings to establish beyond doubt the main features of his character and the chief incidents of his life.' The forensic energy, the aim expressed in the forceful and authoritative language of scientific and legal discourse ('beyond doubt') and the investigative method, on their surface, appear reasonable. As a man whose passions found their reflection everywhere in his own work, Harris applies a rule that he found appropriate to him, but 'there's the rub', for to seek out the writer in the work is, by our later lights and for that matter by some of Harris's day, a naïve and futile task. With its origins in speculation, it ends all too often in overstatement. The principal and irrefutable objection to such a quest is that it denies the writer the chameleon-like ability – the 'negative capability' of Keats or the 'myriad-mindedness' of Coleridge – to don masks, adopt poses and disappear entirely into his or her art. Harris's stance was even in his day an old-fashioned one, running contrary to the theory of the artist's impersonality, espoused by the French novelist Gustave Flaubert in the mid-nineteenth century and destined to flower both in the work and theoretical statements of James Joyce and T. S. Eliot.

Harris's critical assumptions and methods were, then, somewhat dated and not especially sharp. Possessing a keen eye for the telling detail and self-educated in close observation, he possessed analytical instincts. These do not, however, constitute a method of scientific inquiry and examination. Moreover, his study sometimes suggests its origins, being, in part, a patchwork of Harris's articles written for the *Saturday Review*, the joins of which tend to show. A lawyer by training, Harris un-doubtedly possessed a canny sense of human foible and motive, but his strong impulse towards biography – a form that repeatedly attracted his pen – found its outlet in the indistinct and generalised. Eschewing facts and dates, of which in the case of Shakespeare there were few available anyway, and mainly indifferent to scholarly protocols such as footnotes and sources, *The Man Shakespeare and his Tragic Life Story* is a record of intense, sometimes provocative, reading, thought and feeling about Shakespeare's output and the response to him by selected critics, notably Coleridge, Hazlitt and Goethe. It is also testimony to a life-long passion. And it is unsurprising that Harris, himself a man of intense emotions and artistic temperament, found himself reflected, in part, in Shakespeare: 'the Swan of Avon', to invoke a dated phrase, was, thus, an artist in the thrall of deep desires, hedged in by societal constraints and frustrated in love.

Having taken on the task of convincing the reader of the one-to-one and exact relationship between Shakespeare's work and life, Harris carefully shapes his style to his persuasive purpose, peppering his insistent prose with rhetorical questions, transitional devices and apt quotations. The style often seeks to compel – and, perhaps more rarely, to seduce – the reader: 'It may be well to add here a couple of portraits of Shakespeare in later life in order *to establish beyond question* the chief features of his character' (Book One, Chapter 3). The opening gambit's deliberate informality and casualness are immediately dropped for the language of law and logic, for, as Harris well realised, his argument required acceptance in its entirety, no half measures being available either to him or his reader. Thus the words 'proof' and 'evidence' recur, and Harris transfers his legal training and well-honed persuasive skills to literary criticism – and to an inherently elusive subject.

Throughout, the book's tone is forceful and argumentative; on rare occasions, it seems almost bullying. The latter tendency perhaps suggests both Harris's conscious awareness of the difficulty of his task and an unconscious recognition of its inevitable failure, for inference, however intelligent, and taste, however well informed, cannot make up for the fatal absence of documentary evidence. The rhetorical strategies used in making his case are typical and revealing (italics added in the below examples):

> The object of *this inquiry* is to show him [Shakespeare] as he lived and loved and suffered, and *the proofs* of this and of that trait *shall be so heaped up as to stifle doubt and reach absolute conviction*.
>
>   [Book One, Chapter 1]

> The sextet of this sonnet *absolutely disproves* guilty intimacy, and is, I believe, intended to disprove it.   [Book Two, Chapter 5]

> I assume the identity of Brutus with Shakespeare before I have *absolutely proved* it because *it furnishes the solution* to the difficulties of the play.   [Book Two, Chapter 6]

Harris, who is so given to absolutes, must at times hedge his bets when doubt cannot decently be denied, and a vocabulary of hesitancy also peppers his arguments; thus some of his assertions are wisely qualified as 'probable' or even 'very probable'. But, on the whole, subtlety in argument is not Harris's strong suit. Although generally aware, and even hyper-aware, that a case must be patiently built in order to convince the presumed sceptic, he sometimes succumbs to emotion, and his appeal to logic is not always impeccable: 'These admonitions are so far-fetched and so emphatic that they *plainly* discover personal feeling . . . The known facts, too, all corroborate this inference' (Book Two, Chapter 14; italics added). The cards seem laid openly on the table, but one must agree with the initial premises to grant the conclusion and, as all too often happens, speculation quickly hardens into 'fact'.

Unsurprisingly, then, the neutral language occasionally reveals the ardent believer rather than the painstaking logician. The language, in fact, is sometimes not that of a wholly temperate man, something Harris would never have claimed or wished to be. The brash pushiness, even when intermittent throughout several hundred pages, tends to cloy. And as with the frame, so with the smaller picture, as propositions are repeatedly 'clearly' this or 'certainly' this, or 'plainly' or 'evidently' that, a rhetorical strategy aimed less at convincing the reader than at staving off possible dissent (italics added in the below examples):

Biron is supposed to be young in the play [*Love's Labours Lost*], and he has never been distinguished for his gravity, but for his wit and humour: the Princess calls him 'quick Biron'. The two lines are *clearly* Shakespeare's criticism of himself. [Book Two, Chapter 4]

The drinking episode of Cassio [in *Othello*] was not found by Shakespeare in Cinthio, and is, I think, *clearly* the confession of Shakespeare himself, for though aptly invented to explain Cassio's dismissal it is unduly prolonged, and thus constitutes perhaps the most important fault in the construction of the play. [Book Two, Chapter 8]

The first scene of the second act shows us how Shakespeare, the dramatist, worked. Cassio is *plainly* Shakespeare the poet; any of his speeches taken at haphazard proves it. [Book Two, Chapter 8]

The despair is wholly unexpected and out of place, as was the story of his weakness and infirmity, his 'beating mind'. It is *evidently* Shakespeare's own confession. [Book Two, Chapter 13]

Concurrent with this muscular coercion is a conversational, leisurely style of considerable poise, showing Harris in a less anxious, more relaxed light. As he reveals his personal tastes, insights and sensations, his manner becomes less overwrought, even if still emphatic: 'I am inclined to accept', 'I can see him talking, talking with extreme fluency in a high tenor voice', 'In his native air, I imagine, his health gradually improved.' Here the rhetorical tactic – one of concession and possibility – has arguably greater impact than the more assertive tone sometimes adopted.

In addition to these styles is a belletristic one, wholly typical of Harris and his age. To the modern reader, the welding of that style to a broadly 'scientific' aim, where proof and evidence are central, may seem both odd and dated, but the marriage of the two is not lacking in period interest, and Harris's writing style, however far distant from the spare and pliable qualities of the English currently in vogue, largely suits his purposes:

> It is time to speak of him frankly; he was gentle, and witty; gay, and sweet-mannered, very studious, too, and fair of mind; but at the same time he was weak in body and irresolute, hasty and wordy, and took habitually the easiest way out of difficulties; he was ill-endowed in the virile virtues and virile vices. When he showed arrogance it was always of intellect and not of character; he was a parasite by nature. But none of these faults would have brought him to ruin; he was snared again in full manhood by his master-quality, his overpowering sensuality, and thrown in the mire.   [Book Two, Chapter 14]

This says little, as, after all, it intends. Here the 'impression' alone counts, and Harris multiplies adjectives in a knowing, craftsmanlike way so as to put the reader off the scent of specifics and, even, meaning. What, for instance, allows him to deduce that Shakespeare was 'a parasite by nature'? However that may be, the vague wave of the hand seems all the more impressive because of the writing's easy confidence and assumed casualness, which hints at an intimate relationship with its audience. The balanced, sinuous sentences pause in such a way as to give a sense of proper weight while, on the other hand, avoiding portentousness. The tone seeks to be weighty without being pedantic. The vocabulary and tone are close to those of the everyday educated speech of the period (another device aimed at disarming the critical or sceptical reader), while the rhythms, in their obvious calculation, and even staginess, are distant from it. Depending upon one's viewpoint, these are either faults or virtues.

For the modern reader, this method can rapidly descend into facile, even arch, mannerism:

> How Shakespeare delights in making love! It reminds one of the first flutings of a thrush in early spring; over and over again he tries the notes with delighted iteration till he becomes a master of his music and charms the copses to silence with his song: and so Shakespeare sings of love again and again till at length we get the liquid notes of passion and the trills of joy all perfected in *Romeo and Juliet*; but the voice is the voice we heard before in *Venus and Adonis* and *The Comedy of Errors*. [Book Two, Chapter 1]

Constructed out of the metaphor of Shakespeare as 'the Swan of Avon' and the more general tradition of Orpheus the singer charming nature, this exclamatory effusion seems little more than 'fine writing', an accumulation of the most conventional poetic effects. Firmly grounded in the stylistic and rhetorical protocols of the time, the extract reveals the writer eagerly seeking out *la belle page*, a prose not of statement but of self-aware beauty. Harris's assertions are thus boldly and simply just that, subject neither to microscopic inspection nor even to the burden of proof: he worships 'his' Shakespeare (for all the writer's personal flaws), with the reader invited to become a fellow worshipper, joining in his Bardolatry. As we have seen, academic critics baulked at Harris's propositions, but his style, aimed squarely at a popular market, won that audience over.

For us, this performative prose has a certain period interest and even charm; through it Shakespeare at times seems to become a social type, that of the late-Victorian gentleman, emerging less from his own time than from the pages of a John Galsworthy novel. There is, however, a crucial difference: Harris grants to the experience of overwhelming love and desire primacy of place, finding that experience to be the inner core of Shakespeare's being, as it was for himself. It is not coincidental that Harris's four-volume tell-all autobiographical outpouring (1922–7) bears the title *My Life and Loves*. To contextualise this portrait, one need also recall how in the early twentieth century and in the wake of the Victorian period, D. H. Lawrence, like Harris, makes claims for the 'vital' and erotic as the core human experience.

It is, perhaps naturally enough, precisely here that Harris most egregiously wanders off into ambitious speculation. Pronouncing Shakespeare's marriage to Anne Hathaway 'unfortunate', because she was eight years his senior, he states that *The Comedy of Errors* establishes her as 'spitefully jealous, and a bitter scold'. Having made that leap, it is but a short step to assert that Shakespeare nursed a persistent 'enmity' (later characterised as 'hatred' and 'loathing') towards the wife to whom his 'sensuality and rashness' had impelled him in his reckless youth, and from whom, in due course, he escaped to London – and to world fame. In 1597 (one of the book's very few dates), the situation changed: now established on the theatrical scene, Shakespeare again found himself shaken by passion, remaining for a dozen years in the thrall of a maid of honour, one Mary Fitton (*c.*1578–1647), presumed by some to be the woman behind 'the dark lady' of the sonnets: 'The story of his idolatrous passion for Mary Fitton is the story of his life' (Book Two, Chapter 4).

But this patent exaggeration is not all: Shakespeare, an inveterate sensualist in Harris's view, on his annual visits to Stratford simply could not resist Mrs D'Avenant, who, Stratford gossip had it, bore him a son, William D'Avenant, eventually to become a playwright. Never overly cautious when it comes to the erotic, Harris is pleased to accept the story as true: 'There is every reason to accept the story as it has been handed down' (Book Two, Chapter 15). The statement betrays excessive naïvety about fame's perils: individuals have been happy to lay hold of the famous even to the extent of claiming illegitimate descent from them. Harris falls in readily with this probable fiction because it suits his willingness to fly in the face of convention. For Harris, adultery counts for little, and in being so strongly motivated by sexual passion, Shakespeare becomes more thoroughly a modern, a man motivated by sentiment and one mainly indifferent, or even insouciant, to societal *fiat*.

As to the real-life Mistress Mary Fitton, the little known of her establishes that she was no stranger to fleshly passions. She was the mistress of the Earl of Pembroke and of the married Vice-Admiral Sir Richard Levenson, but her authenticated biography contains not even a hint that she was acquainted with Shakespeare, a fact that seems to have little hindered speculation and perhaps even fomented it. Before Harris vigorously championed her claims – and advanced the further ones that the poet-playwright retired to Stratford-upon-Avon after her second marriage to Captain William Polewhele and died there of a broken heart – the literary scholar Thomas Tyler (1826–1902), also a theological scholar, had done so at a meeting of the 'New Shakspere Society' in June 1884, elaborating this case in his influential 1890 edition of *The Sonnets*.

Detractors quickly arose following its publication, and Tyler answered his critics in *The Herbert–Fitton Theory: A Reply* (1898). William Archer, an important dramatic critic of the day, came to Tyler's defence in 1897 in the *Fortnightly Review*, a serious journal that Frank Harris had edited in the 1880s. For his part, Sydney Lee (perhaps Harris's nemesis 'Dryasdust') refuted the Fitton theory in his *Life of William Shakespeare* (1898) as well as in the *Dictionary of National Biography*, which he sub-edited with Virginia Woolf's father, the critic and biographer Leslie Stephen. His grounds were naïvely literalist: the 'dark lady', it turns out, was fair – at least if certain alleged portraits of her were indeed she. Wedded to his theory, Tyler predictably mounted a case against their being so. Bernard Shaw, who dismissed the attribution of identity as bogus, none the less took advantage of the controversy, stoked into vigorous life again by Harris's work, making Mary Fitton the title-character of his 1910 play *The Dark Lady of the Sonnets*.

If Harris's account of Shakepeare's 'tragic love' is especially excited and urgent, it also reveals another of his blind spots: he shows scant interest in the playwright's attraction for the dedicatee of the sonnets and the inspiration of nearly half of them, Mr W. H., the 'fair youth' variously identified as Henry Wriothesley, the third Earl of South-ampton (1563–1614), or the third Earl of Pembroke, William Herbert (1580–1630), and made much of by Oscar Wilde, under the fictitious name 'Willie Hughes', in his famous story 'The Portrait of Mr W. H.' (1889). Hostile to the notion that Shakespeare may have felt more than warm affection for a young man, Harris dismisses the traditional identifications as mere speculation, and then, on supposed literary grounds, rules out sexual passion: 'the woman is characterised by a terrible veracity of passion, whereas those addressed to the youth are rather conventional than convincing' (Book Two, Chapter 5). The degree to which Harris is merely asserting himself as the confirmed heterosexual indifferent to – or repelled by – 'unnatural' passion, or whether fresh memories of his friend Oscar Wilde's rise and fall or the period's general silencing of discourse on male love influences his treatment cannot be gauged, but on this topic Harris remains guarded, even tight-lipped. As the obituary for Frank Harris in *Time Magazine* jibed of a man who was an unabashed self-promoter, fascinated by himself to a degree well beyond the confines of normal self-preoccupation: 'He wrote always of Frank Harris, even when his subject was another man' (7 September 1931). This limitation applies to Harris's Shakespeare, with the writer seemingly unable to recognise that the poet may have been moved deeply by impulses inimical to, or at odds with, his own. Outside this book, however, Harris was seemingly open to wider, more sophisticated views, reputedly quipping that had Shakespeare needed his services, he would simply have had no choice but to submit, a *bon mot* Max Beerbohm turned into a witty sketch titled '*Had Shakespeare asked me . . .*' (1896).

Whatever the flaws of Harris's *The Man Shakespeare* – the overstated allegiance to the Mary Fitton theory, the failure seriously to engage with the homoerotic elements of *The Sonnets*, the moulding of the playwright in his own image, to name but a few – the work importantly contributes to the growing debate about biographical form getting under way at the turn of the twentieth century. For one thing, at a time when the genre largely consisted of stodgy multi-volume tomes of life and letters and the formal air-brushed portraits of that great late-Victorian enterprise the *Dictionary of National Biography*, Harris's impressionistic method is strikingly original. Succumbing to the traditional tyranny of chronology, Harris nevertheless presents Shakespeare's life through a highly individual prism. Documents are invoked now and then, as is selective reading, but Harris's 'personal' experience of the plays and poetry remains at the forefront: Shakespeare can be known, the book asserts, by those whose sensibilities are fully open to the implications of the work. A creative temperament himself, Harris thus responds to a fellow artist as only an artist can, and he makes his insights available to the critic and general reader, necessarily at one remove from creative endeavour. Harris further develops his method in his biographies of his friends Oscar Wilde (1916; written 1910) and Bernard Shaw (1931), as well as in his four-volume series of *Contemporary Portraits* (1915–24) and his auto-biography. And it would be wise to remember that Lytton Strachey's path-breaking *Eminent Victorians* (1918), published as the Great War neared its close, not only re-evaluated the Victorians but also ushered in a new, more sceptical age, wary of old dogmas, inheritances and long-established hierarchies. Although they have not weathered the test of time as well as Strachey's biographies, Harris's partake in this demolition work, sometimes overtly, but at other times, and with no less revolutionary force, in their questioning attitudes and in bridling against 'authorities' of one kind or another.

The Shakespeare who emerges from his study is undeniably a deeply flawed human being, unable to dominate his impulses and hence the victim of his flawed decisions. While no lion-taming biographer, Harris, who treats his subject with enormous and clear-eyed respect, does not flinch from criticising or finding fault and, in this, he presents a Shakespeare less sentimentalised than did many at his period. He is also more intensely human – Shakespeare the man, indeed, as Harris's title directs – than he is in the work of several of Harris's more learned contemporaries whose eyes were firmly fixed on interpreting the documentary record and in maintaining a whitewashed view of an artist, who, whatever little we really know of him, must have been emotionally complex. If this humanity is partly concocted out of Harris's 'feelings' more than from the recorded facts, it none the less serves Harris's purpose: instinct and insight are the traditional domain of the imaginative writer, hard facts the territory of the nugget-gathering historian and scholar. It must, of course, be admitted that Harris made no lasting contribution to the study of Shakespeare's life: he discovered no documents, brought forward no new hard evidence; rather, he pinned his colours to a theory that in the main has the character of a will o' the wisp, and reshuffled what was already known. But to adapt what Joseph Conrad said about the authorship of Shakespeare's work, 'Who cares if Shakespeare was in love with Mary Fitton, one of the four children of Sir Edward Fitton of Cheshire, wife of So-and-So and mistress of Such-and-Such?' The only thing beyond doubt is that the writer knew how to speak of love in all its varieties and moods, and, however he may have gathered this knowledge, put it to work in supremely moving plays and poems that still speak to us four centuries after their creation. Following several commentators, Harris insists on pinpointing historical models where doing so with certainty, given the unsatisfactory state of the evidence, is impossible. Like them, he is reduced to speculation, a game that once begun can be played and replayed because an endgame is not part of its rules.

Harris's main accomplishment was to have produced for his day a highly readable, if decidedly idiosyncratic, portrait of the playwright who, as Ben Jonson claimed, was 'for all time'. In doing so, Harris may also have influenced a considerably more important writer than himself:

his method surely anticipates Virginia Woolf's biographical *jeu d'esprit*, *Orlando* (1928), which asserts that the imagination, as articulated in fiction, can illuminate the deeper wellsprings of a life more accurately and truly than the hard facts gathered through drudgery, however meticulous.

J. H. STAPE
Research Fellow in St Mary's University College,
Strawberry Hill, London

Biography

Born in Galway in about 1856, 'Frank' (in fact, James Thomas) Harris was the son of a seaman father of stern temperament. After his education in Armagh and Denbighshire, Harris in 1871 joined in the vast Irish exodus to the United States, where he studied law at the recently opened University of Kansas. Arriving in England in 1875, he tutored French at Brighton, and then turned to journalism, being appointed editor of the *Evening News* in 1883, a post in which he developed a keen nose for gossip and a tendency for audacious self-promotion. Named head of the *Fortnightly Review* in 1886, Harris embarked on an editorial career that involved sensationalism, contentious political views and canny choices (Bernard Shaw and Max Beerbohm served as his drama critics). On the *Saturday Review* in 1894, which he purchased and then ran for four years, he mingled brilliant editorial skills with an over-pronounced search for controversy. In 1898, Harris established himself in France and from then on led a bohemian life there and in London, until 1915, when he left for New York, editing *Pearson's Magazine* there from 1916 to 1922. Under his editorship, it took a hostile attitude towards Britain's war effort, and earned Harris the title of 'traitor', while his increasingly extravagant views saw him in trouble with American censorship. His personal conduct was of an unconventional and *outré* character and is described lavishly and at length in his autobiography, *My Life and Loves* (1922–27). Harris, who became a naturalised American in 1921, left the country for France in 1923, settling permanently in Nice where, impoverished, he died of heart failure in 1931. Among his works are plays, short fiction and biographies of Oscar Wilde, Shakespeare and Bernard Shaw. Married three times, he also had a long-term mistress. Colourful and reckless, Harris, who though he made many enemies also made loyal friends, served as the model for several fictional characters. The *Oxford Dictionary of National of Biography* remembers him as 'journalist and rogue'.

SHAKESPEARE
& His Tragic Life

I DEDICATE THIS BOOK TO MY FRIEND,
ERNEST BECKETT (NOW LORD GRIMTHORPE),
A MAN OF MOST EXCELLENT DIFFERENCES
WHO UNITES TO A GENIUS FOR PRACTICAL THINGS
A PASSIONATE SYMPATHY FOR ALL
HIGH ENDEAVOUR IN LITERATURE AND ART

Author's Preface

This book has grown out of a series of articles contributed to *The Saturday Review* some ten or twelve years ago. As they appeared they were talked of and criticised in the usual way; a minority of readers thought 'the stuff' interesting; many held that my view of Shakespeare was purely arbitrary; others said I had used a concordance to such purpose that out of the mass of words I had managed, by virtue of some unknown formula, to recreate the character of the man.

The truth is much simpler: I read Shakespeare's plays in boyhood, chiefly for the stories; every few years later I was fain to reread them; for as I grew I always found new beauties in them which I had formerly missed, and again and again I was lured back by tantalising hints and suggestions of a certain unity underlying the diversity of characters. These suggestions gradually became more definite till at length, out of the myriad voices in the plays, I began to hear more and more insistent the accents of one voice, and out of the crowd of faces, began to distinguish more and more clearly the features of the writer; for all the world like some lovelorn girl, who, gazing with her soul in her eyes, finds in the witch's cauldron the face of the beloved.

I have tried in this book to trace the way I followed, step by step; for I found it effective to rough in the chief features of the man first, and afterwards, taking the plays in succession, to show how Shakespeare painted himself at full-length not once, but twenty times, at as many different periods of his life. This is one reason why he is more interesting to us than the greatest men of the past, than Dante even, or Homer; for Dante and Homer worked only at their best in the flower of manhood. Shakespeare, on the other hand, has painted himself for us in his green youth with hardly any knowledge of life or art, and then in his eventful maturity, with growing experience and new powers, in masterpiece after masterpiece; and at length in his decline with weakened grasp and fading colours, so that in him we can study the growth and fruiting and decay of the finest spirit that has yet been born among men. This tragedy of tragedies, in which *Lear* is only one scene – this rise to intensest life and widest vision and fall through abysms of despair and madness to exhaustion and death – can be followed experience by experience, from Stratford to London and its thirty years of passionate living, and then from London to village Stratford again, and the eternal shrouding silence.

As soon as this astonishing drama discovered itself to me in its tragic completeness I jumped to the conclusion that it must have been set forth long ago in detail by Shakespeare's commentators, and so, for the first time, I turned to their works. I do not wish to rail at my fore-runners as Carlyle railed at the historians of Cromwell, or I should talk, as he talked, about 'libraries of inanities . . . conceited dilettantism and pedantry . . . prurient stupidity', and so forth. The fact is, I found all this, and worse; I waded through tons of talk to no result. Without a single exception the commentators have all missed the man and the story; they have turned the poet into a tradesman, and the unimagi-nable tragedy of his life into the commonplace record of a successful tradesman's career. Even to explain this astounding misadventure of the host of critics is a little difficult. The mistake, of course, arose from the fact that his contemporaries told very little about Shakespeare; they left his appearance and even the incidents of his life rather vague. Being without a guide, and having no clear idea of Shakespeare's character, the critics created him in their own image, and, whenever they were in doubt, idealised him according to the national type.

Still, there was at least one exception. Some Frenchman, I think it is Joubert, says that no great man is born into the world without another man being born about the same time, who understands and can inter-pret him, and Shakespeare was of necessity singularly fortunate in his interpreter. Ben Jonson was big enough to see him fairly, and to give excellent-true testimony concerning him. Jonson's view of Shakespeare is astonishingly accurate and trustworthy so far as it goes; even his attitude of superiority to Shakespeare is fraught with meaning. Two hundred years later, the rising tide of international criticism produced two men, Goethe and Coleridge, who also saw Shakespeare, if only by glimpses, or rather by divination of kindred genius, recognising certain indubitable traits. Goethe's criticism of *Hamlet* has been vastly over-praised; but now and then he used words about Shakespeare which, in due course, we shall see were illuminating words, the words of one who guessed something of the truth. Coleridge, too, with his curious, com-plex endowment of philosopher and poet, resembled Shakespeare, saw him, therefore, by flashes, and might have written greatly about him;

but, alas, Coleridge, a Puritan born, was brought up in epicene hypocrisies, and determined to see Shakespeare – that child of the Renascence – as a Puritan, too, and consequently mis-saw him far oftener than he saw him; misjudged him hideously, and had no inkling of his tragic history.

There is a famous passage in Coleridge's *Essays on Shakespeare* which illustrates what I mean. It begins: 'In Shakespeare all the elements of womanhood are holy'; and goes on to eulogise the instinct of chastity which all his women possess, and this in spite of Doll Tearsheet, Tamora, Cressida, Goneril, Regan, Cleopatra, the Dark Lady of the Sonnets, and many other frail and fascinating figures. Yet whatever gleam of light has fallen on Shakespeare since Coleridge's day has come chiefly from that dark lantern which he now and then flashed upon the master.

In one solitary respect, our latter-day criticism has been successful; it has established with very considerable accuracy the chronology of the plays, and so the life-story of the poet is set forth in due order for those to read who can.

This then is what I found – a host of commentators who saw men as trees walking, and mistook plain facts, and among them one authentic witness, Jonson, and two interesting though not trustworthy witnesses, Goethe and Coleridge – and nothing more in three centuries. The mere fact may well give us pause, pointing as it does to a truth which is still insufficiently understood. It is the puzzle of criticism, at once the despair and wonder of readers, that the greatest men of letters usually pass through life without being remarked or understood by their contemporaries. The men of Elizabeth's time were more interested in Jonson than in Shakespeare, and have told us much more about the younger than the greater master; just as Spaniards of the same age were more interested in Lope de Vega than in Cervantes, and have left a better picture of the second-rate playwright than of the world-poet. Attempting to solve this problem Emerson coolly assumed that the men of the Elizabethan age were so great that Shakespeare himself walked about among them unnoticed as a giant among giants. This reading of the riddle is purely transcendental. We know that Shakespeare's worst plays were far oftener acted than his best; that *Titus Andronicus* by popular favour was more esteemed than *Hamlet*. The majority of contemporary poets and critics regarded Shakespeare rather as a singer of 'sugred' verses than as a dramatist. The truth is that

Shakespeare passed through life unnoticed because he was so much greater than his contemporaries that they could not see him at all in his true proportions. It was Jonson, the nearest to him in greatness, who alone saw him at all fairly and appreciated his astonishing genius.

Nothing illustrates more perfectly the unconscious wisdom of the English race than the old saying that 'a man must be judged by his peers'. One's peers, in fact, are the only persons capable of judging one, and the truth seems to be that three centuries have only produced three men at all capable of judging Shakespeare. The jury is still being collected. But from the quality of the first three, and of their praise, it is already plain that his place will be among the highest. From various indications, too, it looks as if the time for judging him had come: *Hamlet* is perhaps his most characteristic creation, and Hamlet, in his intellectual unrest, morbid brooding, cynical self-analysis and dislike of bloodshed, is much more typical of the nineteenth or twentieth century than of the sixteenth. Evidently the time for classifying the creator of Hamlet is at hand.

And this work of description and classification should be done as a scientist would do it: for criticism itself has at length bent to the Time-spirit and become scientific. And just as in science, analysis for the moment has yielded pride of place to synthesis, so the critical move-ment in literature has in our time become creative. The chemist, who resolves any substance into its elements, is not satisfied till by synthesis he can recreate the substance out of its elements: this is the final proof that his knowledge is complete. And so we care little or nothing today for critical analyses or appreciations which are not creative present-ments of the person. 'Paint him for us,' we say, 'in his habit as he lived, and we will take it that you know something about him.'

One of the chief attempts at creative criticism in English literature, or, perhaps it would be fairer to say, the only memorable attempt, is Carlyle's *Cromwell*. He has managed to build up the man for us quite credibly out of Cromwell's letters and speeches, showing us the under-lying sincerity and passionate resolution of the great Puritan once for all. But unfortunately Carlyle was too romantic an artist, too persuaded in his hero-worship to discover for us Cromwell's faults and failings. In his book we find nothing of the fanatic who ordered the Irish massacres, nothing of the neuropath who lived in hourly dread of assassination. Carlyle has painted his subject all in lights, so to speak; the shadows are not even indicated, and yet he ought to have known that in proportion to the brilliancy of the light the shadows must of necessity be dark. It is not for me to point out that this romantic painting of great men, like all other make-believes and hypocrisies, has its drawbacks and shortcomings: it is enough that it has had its day and produced its pictures of giant-heroes and their worshippers for those who love such childish toys.

The wonderful age in which we live – this twentieth century with its X-rays that enable us to see through the skin and flesh of men, and to study the working of their organs and muscles and nerves – has brought a new spirit into the world, a spirit of fidelity to fact, and with it a new and higher ideal of life and of art, which must of necessity change and transform all the conditions of existence, and in time modify the almost immutable nature of man. For this new spirit, this love of the fact and of truth, this passion for reality will do away with the foolish fears and futile hopes which have fretted the childhood of our race, and will slowly but surely establish on broad foundations the Kingdom of Man upon Earth. For that is the meaning and purpose of the change which is now coming over the world. The faiths and convictions of twenty centuries are passing away and the forms and institutions of a hundred generations of men are dissolving before us like the baseless fabric of a dream. A new morality is already shaping itself in the spirit; a morality based not on guesswork and on fancies; but on ascertained laws of moral health; a scientific morality belonging not to statics, like the morality of the Jews, but to dynamics, and so fitting the nature of each individual person. Even now conscience with its prohibitions is fading out of life, evolving into a more profound consciousness of ourselves and others, with multiplied incitements to wise living. The old religious asceticism with its hatred of the body is dead; the servile acceptance of conditions of life and even of natural laws is seen to be vicious; it is of the nobility of man to be insatiate in desire and to rebel against limiting conditions; it is the property of his intelligence to constrain even the laws of nature to the attainment of his ideal.

Already we are proud of being students, investigators, servants of truth, and we leave the great names of demigods and heroes a little contemptuously to the men of bygone times. As student-artists we are no longer content with the outward presentment and form of men: we want to discover the protean vanities, greeds and aspirations of men, and to lay bare, as with a scalpel, the hidden motives and springs of action. We dream of an art that shall take into account the natural daily decay and up-building of cell-life; the wars that go on in the blood; the fevers of the brain; the creeping paralysis of nerve-exhaustion; above all, we must be able even now from a few bare facts, to recreate a man and make him live and love again for the reader, just as the biologist from a few scattered bones can reconstruct some prehistoric bird or fish or mammal.

And we student-artists have no desire to paint our subject as better or nobler or smaller or meaner than he was in reality; we study his limitations as we study his gifts, his virtues with as keen an interest as his vices; for it is in some excess of desire, or in some extravagance of mentality, that we look for the secret of his achievement, just as we begin to wonder when we see hands constantly outstretched in pious supplication, whether a foot is not thrust out behind in some secret shame, for the biped, man, must keep a balance.

I intend first of all to prove from Shakespeare's works that he has painted himself twenty times from youth till age at full length: I shall consider and compare these portraits till the outlines of his character are clear and certain; afterwards I shall show how his little vanities and shames idealised the picture, and so present him as he really was, with his imperial intellect and small snobberies; his giant vices and paltry self-deceptions; his sweet gentleness and long martyrdom. I cannot but think that his portrait will thus gain more in truth than it can lose in ideal beauty. Or let me come nearer to my purpose by means of a simile. Talking with Sir David Gill one evening on shipboard about the fixed stars, he pointed one out which is so distant that we cannot measure how far it is away from us and can form no idea of its magnitude. 'But surely,' I exclaimed, 'the great modern telescopes must bring the star nearer and magnify it?' 'No,' he replied, 'no; the best instruments make the star clearer to us, but certainly not larger.' This is what I wish to do in regard to Shakespeare; make him clearer to men, even if I do not make him larger.

And if I were asked why I do this, why I take the trouble to recreate a man now three centuries dead, it is first of all, of course, because he is worth it – the most complex and passionate personality in the world, whether of life or letters – because, too, there are certain lessons which the English will learn from Shakespeare more quickly and easily than from any living man, and a little because I want to get rid of Shakespeare by assimilating all that was fine in him, while giving all that was common and vicious in him as spoil to oblivion. He is like the

Old-Man-of-the-Sea on the shoulders of our youth; he has become an obsession to the critic, a weapon to the pedant, a nuisance to the man of genius. True, he has painted great pictures in a superb, romantic fashion; he is the Titian of dramatic art: but is there to be no Rembrandt, no Balzac, no greater Tolstoy in English letters? I want to liberate Englishmen so far as I can from the tyranny of Shakespeare's greatness. For the new time is upon us, with its new knowledge and new claims, and we English are all too willing to live in the past, and so lose our inherited place as leader of the nations.

The French have profited by their glorious Revolution: they trusted reason and have had their reward; no such leap forward has ever been made as France made in that one decade, and the effects are still potent. In the last hundred years the language of Molière has grown fourfold; the slang of the studios and the gutter and the laboratory, of the engineering school and the dissecting table, has been ransacked for special terms to enrich and strengthen the language in order that it may deal easily with the new thoughts. French is now a superb instrument, while English is positively poorer than it was in the time of Shake-speare, thanks to the prudery of our illiterate middle class. Divorced from reality, with its activities all fettered in baby-linen, our literature has atrophied and dwindled into a babble of nursery rhymes, tragedies of Little Marys, tales of Babes in a Wood. The example of Shakespeare may yet teach us the value of free speech; he could say what he liked as he liked: he was not afraid of the naked truth and the naked word, and through his greatness a Low Dutch dialect has become the chiefest instrument of civilisation, the world-speech of humanity at large.

FRANK HARRIS
London, 1909

BOOK ONE

Shakespeare Painted by Himself

I

Hamlet: Romeo–Jaques

'As I passed by . . . I found an altar with this inscription, To THE UNKNOWN GOD. Whom therefore ye ignorantly worship, him declare I unto you.' This work of Paul – the discovery and proclaiming of an unknown god – is in every age the main function of the critic.

An unknown god this Shakespeare of ours, whom all are agreed it would be well to know, if in any way possible. As to the possibility, however, the authorities are at loggerheads. Hallam, 'the judicious', declared that it was impossible to learn anything certain about 'the man, Shakespeare'. Wordsworth, on the other hand (without a nickname to show a close connection with the common), held that Shakespeare unlocked his heart with the sonnets for key. Browning jeered at this belief, to be in turn contradicted by Swinburne. Matthew Arnold gave us in a sonnet 'the best opinion of his time':

> Others abide our question. Thou art free.
> We ask and ask – Thou smilest and art still,
> Out-topping knowledge.

But alas! the best opinion of one generation is in these matters often flat unreason to the next, and it may be that in this instance neither the opinion of Hallam nor Browning nor Arnold will be allowed to count.

As it is the object of a general to win battles so it is the life-work of the artist to show himself to us, and the completeness with which he reveals his own individuality is perhaps the best measure of his genius. One does this like Montaigne, simply, garrulously, telling us his height and make, his tastes and distastes, his loves and fears and habits, till gradually the seeming-artless talk brings the man before us, a sun-warmed fruit of humanity, with uncouth rind of stiff manners and sweet kindly juices, not perfect in any way, shrivelled on this side by early frost-bite, and on that softened to corruption through too much heat, marred here by the bitter-black cicatrice of an ancient injury and there fortune-spotted, but on the whole healthy, grateful, of a most pleasant

ripeness. Another, like Shakespeare, with passionate conflicting sympathies and curious impartial intellect cannot discover himself so simply;
needs, like the diamond, many facets to show all the light in him, and so
proceeds to cut them one after the other as Falstaff or Hamlet, to the
dazzling of the purblind.

Yet Shakespeare's purpose is surely the same as Montaigne's, to reveal
himself to us, and it would be hasty to decide that his skill is inferior.
For while Montaigne had nothing but prose at his command, and not
too rich a prose, as he himself complains, Shakespeare in magic of
expression has had no equal in recorded time, and he used the lyric as
well as the dramatic form, poetry as well as prose, to give his soul
utterance.

We are doing Shakespeare wrong by trying to believe that he hides
himself behind his work; the suspicion is as unworthy as the old suspicion dissipated by Carlyle that Cromwell was an ambitious hypocrite.
Sincerity is the birthmark of genius, and we can be sure that Shakespeare has depicted himself for us with singular fidelity; we can see him
in his works, if we will take the trouble, 'in his habit as he lived'.

We are doing ourselves wrong, too, by pretending that Shakespeare
'out-tops knowledge'. He did not fill the world even in his own time:
there was room beside him in the days of Elizabeth for Marlowe and
Spenser, Ben Jonson and Bacon, and since then the spiritual outlook,
like the material outlook, has widened to infinity. There is space in life
now for a dozen ideals undreamed-of in the sixteenth century. Let us
have done with this pretence of doglike humility; we, too, are men, and
there is on earth no higher title, and in the universe nothing beyond our
comprehending. It will be well for us to know Shakespeare and all his
high qualities and do him reverence; it will be well for us, too, to see his
limitations and his faults, for after all it is the human frailties in a man
that call forth our sympathy and endear him to us, and without love
there is no virtue in worship, no attraction in example.

The doubt as to the personality of Shakespeare, and the subsequent
confusion and contradictions are in the main, I think, due to Coleridge.
He was the first modern critic to have glimpses of the real Shakespeare,
and the vision lent his words a singular authority. But Coleridge was a
hero-worshipper by nature and carried reverence to lyric heights. He
used all his powers to persuade men that Shakespeare was μυριόνους
ἀνήρ – 'the myriad-minded man'; a sort of demigod who was everyone
and no one, a Proteus without individuality of his own. The theory has

held the field for nearly a century, probably because it flatters our national vanity; for in itself it is fantastically absurd and leads to most ridiculous conclusions. For instance, when Coleridge had to deal with the fact that Shakespeare never drew a miser, instead of accepting the omission as characteristic, for it is confirmed by Ben Jonson's testimony that he was 'of an open and free nature', Coleridge proceeded to argue that avarice is not a permanent passion in humanity, and that Shakespeare probably for that reason chose to leave it undescribed. This is an example of the ecstasy of hero-worship; it is begging the question to assume that whatever Shakespeare did was perfect; humanity cannot be penned up even in Shakespeare's brain. Like every other man of genius Shakespeare must have shown himself in his qualities and defects, in his preferences and prejudices; 'a fallible being', as stout old Dr Johnson knew, 'will fail somewhere'.

Even had Shakespeare tried to hide himself in his work, he could not have succeeded. Now that the print of a man's hand or foot or ear is enough to distinguish him from all other men, it is impossible to believe that the mask of his mind, the very imprint, form and pressure of his soul should be less distinctive. Just as Monsieur Bertillon's whorl-pictures of a thumb afford overwhelming proofs of a man's identity, so it is possible from Shakespeare's writings to establish beyond doubt the main features of his character and the chief incidents of his life. The time for random assertion about Shakespeare and unlimited eulogy of him has passed away for ever: the object of this enquiry is to show him as he lived and loved and suffered, and the proofs of this and of that trait shall be so heaped up as to stifle doubt and reach absolute conviction. For not only is the circumstantial evidence overwhelming and conclusive, but we have also the testimony of eyewitnesses with which to confirm it, and one of these witnesses, Ben Jonson, is of rare credibility and singularly well equipped.

Let us begin, then, by treating Shakespeare as we would treat any other writer, and ask simply how a dramatic author is most apt to reveal himself. A great dramatist may not paint himself for us at any time in his career with all his faults and vices; but when he goes deepest into human nature, we may be sure that self-knowledge is his guide; as Hamlet said, 'To know a man well, were to know himself' (oneself), so far justifying the paradox that dramatic writing is merely a form of autobiography. We may take then as a guide this first criterion that, in his masterpiece of psychology, the dramatist will reveal most of his own nature.

If a dozen lovers of Shakespeare were asked to name the most profound and most complex character in all his dramas it is probable that everyone without hesitation would answer Hamlet. The current of cultivated opinion has long set in this direction. With the intuition of a kindred genius, Goethe was the first to put Hamlet on a pedestal: 'the incomparable', he called him, and devoted pages to an analysis of the character. Coleridge followed with the confession whose truth we shall see later: 'I have a smack of Hamlet myself, if I may say so.' But even if it be admitted that Hamlet is the most complex and profound of Shakespeare's creations, and therefore probably the character in which Shakespeare revealed most of himself, the question of degree still remains to be determined. Is it possible to show certainly that even the broad outlines of Hamlet's character are those of the master-poet?

There are various ways in which this might be proved. For instance, if one could show that whenever Shakespeare fell out of a character he was drawing, he unconsciously dropped into the Hamlet vein, one's suspicion as to the identity of Hamlet and the poet would be enormously strengthened. There is another piece of evidence still more convincing. Suppose that Shakespeare in painting another character did nothing but paint Hamlet over again trait by trait – virtue by virtue, fault by fault – our assurance would be almost complete; for a dramatist only makes this mistake when he is speaking unconsciously in his proper person. But if both these kinds of proof were forthcoming, and not once but a dozen times, then surely our conviction as to the essential identity of Hamlet and Shakespeare would amount to practical certitude.

Of course it would be foolish, even in this event, to pretend that Hamlet exhausts Shakespeare; art does little more than embroider the fringe of the garment of life, and the most complex character in drama or even in fiction is simple indeed when compared with even the simplest of living men or women. Shakespeare included in himself Falstaff and Cleopatra, beside the author of the sonnets, and knowledge drawn from all these must be used to fill out and perhaps to modify the outlines given in Hamlet before one can feel sure that the portrait is a re-presentment of reality. But when this study is completed, it will be seen that with many necessary limitations, Hamlet is indeed a revelation of some of the most characteristic traits of Shakespeare.

To come to the point quickly, I will take Hamlet's character as analysed by Coleridge and Professor Dowden.

Coleridge says: 'Hamlet's character is the prevalence of the abstracting and generalising habit over the practical. He does not want courage, skill, will or opportunity; but every incident sets him thinking: and it is curious, and at the same time strictly natural, that Hamlet, who all the play seems reason itself, should be impelled at last by mere accident to effect his object.' Again he says: 'in Hamlet we see a great, an almost enormous intellectual activity and a proportionate aversion to real action consequent upon it.'

Professor Dowden's analysis is more careful but hardly as complete. He calls Hamlet 'the meditative son' of a strong-willed father, and adds, 'he has slipped on into years of full manhood still a haunter of the university, a student of philosophies, an amateur in art, a ponderer on the things of life and death who has never formed a resolution or executed a deed. This long course of thinking apart from action has destroyed Hamlet's very capacity for belief . . . In presence of the spirit he is himself "a spirit", and believes in the immortality of the soul. When left to his private thoughts he wavers uncertainly to and fro; death is a sleep; a sleep, it may be, troubled with dreams . . . He is incapable of certitude . . . After his fashion (that of one who relieves himself by speech rather than by deeds) he unpacks his heart in words.'

Now what other personage is there in Shakespeare who shows these traits or some of them? He should be bookish and irresolute, a lover of thought and not of action, of melancholy temper too, and prone to unpack his heart with words. Almost everyone who has followed the argument thus far will be inclined to think of Romeo. Hazlitt declared that 'Romeo is Hamlet in love. There is the same rich exuberance of passion and sentiment in the one, that there is of thought and sentiment in the other. Both are absent and self-involved; both live out of them- selves in a world of imagination.' Much of this is true and affords a noteworthy example of Hazlitt's occasional insight into character, yet for reasons that will appear later it is not possible to insist, as Hazlitt does, upon the identity of Romeo and Hamlet. The most that can be said is that Romeo is a younger brother of Hamlet, whose character is much less mature and less complex than that of the student-prince. Moreover, the characterisation in Romeo – the mere drawing and painting – is very inferior to that put to use in Hamlet. Romeo is half hidden from us in the rose-mist of passion, and after he is banished from Juliet's arms we only see him for a moment as he rushes madly by into never-ending night, and all the while Shakespeare is thinking more of the poetry of the theme than of his hero's character. Romeo is crude and immature when compared with a profound psychological study like *Hamlet*. In *Hamlet* the action often stands still while incidents are invented for the mere purpose of displaying the peculiarities of the protagonist. *Hamlet*, too, is the longest of Shakespeare's plays with the exception of *Antony and Cleopatra*, and 'the total length of Hamlet's speeches,' says Dryasdust, 'far exceeds that of those allotted by Shakespeare to any other of his characters.' The important point, however, is that Romeo has a more than family likeness to Hamlet. Even in the heat and heyday of his passion Romeo plays thinker; Juliet says, 'Goodnight' and disappears, but he finds time to give us the abstract truth:

> Love goes towards love, as schoolboys from their books,
> But love from love, toward school with heavy looks.

Juliet appears again unexpectedly, and again Hamlet's generalising habit asserts itself in Romeo:

> How silver-sweet sound lovers' tongues by night,
> Like softest music to attending ears.

We may be certain that Juliet would have preferred more pointed praise. He is indeed so lost in his ill-timed reverie that Juliet has to call him again and again by name before he attends to her.

Romeo has Hamlet's peculiar habit of talking to himself. He falls into a soliloquy on his way to Juliet in Capulet's orchard, when his heart must have been beating so loudly that it would have prevented him from hearing himself talk, and into another when hurrying to the apothecary. In this latter monologue, too, when all his thoughts must have been of Juliet and their star-crossed fates, and love-devouring Death, he is able to picture for us the apothecary and his shop with a wealth of detail that says more for Shakespeare's painstaking and memory than for his insight into character. The fault, however, is not so grave as it would be if Romeo were a different kind of man; but like Hamlet he is always ready to unpack his heart with words, and if they are not the best words sometimes, sometimes even very inappropriate words, it only shows that in his first tragedy Shakespeare was not the master of his art that he afterwards became.

In the churchyard scene of the fifth act Romeo's likeness to Hamlet comes into clearest light.

Hamlet says to Laertes:

> I pr'ythee, take thy fingers from my throat;
> For though I am not splenitive and rash
> Yet have I something in me dangerous
> Which let thy wisdom fear.

In precisely the same temper, Romeo says to Paris:

> Good, gentle youth, tempt not a desperate man;
> Fly hence and leave me; think upon these gone,
> Let them affright thee.

This magnanimity is so rare that its existence would almost of itself be sufficient to establish a close relationship between Romeo and Hamlet. Romeo's last speech, too, is characteristic of Hamlet: on the very threshold of death he generalises:

> How oft when men are at the point of death,
> Have they been merry? which their keepers call
> A lightening before death.

There is in Romeo, too, that peculiar mixture of pensive sadness and loving sympathy which is the very vesture of Hamlet's soul; he says to 'Noble County Paris':

> O, give me thy hand,
> One writ with me in sour misfortune's book.

And finally Shakespeare's supreme lyrical gift is used by Romeo as unconstrainedly as by Hamlet himself. The beauty in the last soliloquy is of passion rather than of intellect, but in sheer triumphant beauty some lines of it have never been surpassed:

> Here, here will I remain
> With worms that are thy chambermaids; O, here
> Will I set up my everlasting rest
> And shake the yoke of inauspicious stars
> From this world-wearied flesh.

The whole soliloquy and especially the superb epithet 'world-wearied' are at least as suitable to Hamlet as to Romeo. Passion, it is true, is more accentuated in Romeo, just as there is greater irresolution combined with intenser self-consciousness in Hamlet, yet all the qualities of the youthful lover are to be found in the student-prince. Hamlet is evidently the later finished picture of which Romeo was merely the charming sketch.

Hamlet says he is revengeful and ambitious, although he is nothing of the kind, and in much the same way Romeo says:

> I'll be a candle-holder and look on,

whereas he plays the chief part and a very active part in the drama. If he were more of a 'candle-holder' and onlooker, he would more resemble Hamlet. Then too, though he generalises, he does not search the darkness with aching eyeballs as Hamlet does; the problems of life do not as yet lie heavy on his soul; he is too young to have felt their mystery and terror; he is only just within the shadow of that melancholy which to Hamlet discolours the world.

Seven or eight years after writing *Romeo and Juliet*, Shakespeare growing conscious of these changes in his own temperament embodied them in another character, the melancholy Jaques in *As You Like It*. Everyone knows that Jaques is Shakespeare's creation; he is not to be found in Lodge's *Rosalynde*, whence Shakespeare took the story and most of the characters of his play. Jaques is only sketched in with light strokes, but all his traits are peculiarly Hamlet's traits. For Jaques is a melancholy student of life as Hamlet is, with lightning-quick intelligence and heavy heart, and these are the Hamlet qualities which were not brought into prominence in the youthful Romeo. Passages taken at haphazard will suffice to establish my contention. 'Motley's the only wear,' says Jaques, as if longing to assume the cap and bells, and Hamlet plays the fool's part with little better reason. Jaques exclaims:

> Give me leave
> To speak my mind, and I will through and through
> Cleanse the foul body of the infected world,
> If they will patiently receive my medicine.

And Hamlet cries:

> The time is out of joint; O cursed spite
> That ever I was born to set it right.

The famous speech of Jaques, 'All the world's a stage', might have been said by Hamlet, indeed belongs of right to the person who gave the exquisite counsel to the players. Jaques' confession of melancholy, too, both in manner and matter is characteristic of Hamlet. How often Shakespeare must have thought it over before he was able to bring the peculiar nature of his own malady into such relief:

> I have neither the scholar's melancholy, which is emulation; nor the musician's, which is fantastical; nor the courtier's, which is proud; nor the soldier's, which is ambitious; nor the lawyer's, which is politic; nor the lady's, which is nice; nor the lover's, which is all these; but it is a melancholy of mine own, compounded of many simples, extracted from many objects, and, indeed, the sundry contemplation of my travels; which, by often rumination, wraps me in, a most humorous sadness.

This 'humorous sadness', the child of contemplation, was indeed Shakespeare's most constant mood. Jaques, too, loves solitude and the country as Hamlet loved them – and above all the last trait recorded of Jaques, his eagerness to see the reformed Duke and learn from the convert, is a perfect example of that intellectual curiosity which is one of Hamlet's most attaching characteristics. Yet another trait is attributed to Jaques, which we must on no account forget. The Duke accuses him of lewdness though lewdness seems out of place in Jaques's character, and is certainly not shown in the course of the action. If we combine the characters of Romeo, the poet-lover, and Jaques, the pensive-sad philosopher, we have almost the complete Hamlet.

It is conceivable that even a fair-minded reader of the plays will admit all I have urged about the likeness of Romeo and Jaques to Hamlet without concluding that these preliminary studies, so to speak, for the great portrait render it at all certain that the masterpiece of portraiture is a likeness of Shakespeare himself. The impartial critic will probably say, 'You have raised a suspicion in my mind; a strong suspicion it may be, but still a suspicion that is far from certitude.' Fortunately the evidence still to be offered is a thousand times more convincing than any inferences that can properly be drawn from Romeo or from Jaques, or even from both together.

2
Hamlet–Macbeth

There is a later drama of Shakespeare's, a drama which comes between *Othello* and *Lear*, and belongs, therefore, to the topmost height of the poet's achievement, whose principal character is Hamlet, Hamlet over again, with every peculiarity and every fault; a Hamlet, too, entangled in an action which is utterly unsuited to his nature. Surely if this statement can be proved, it will be admitted by all competent judges that the identity of Hamlet and his creator has been established. For Shakespeare must have painted this second Hamlet unconsciously. Think of it. In totally new circumstances the poet speaks with Hamlet's voice in Hamlet's words. The only possible explanation is that he is speaking from his own heart, and for that reason is unaware of the mistake. The drama I refer to is *Macbeth*. No one, so far as I know, has yet thought of showing that there is any likeness between the character of Hamlet and that of Macbeth, much less identity; nevertheless, it seems to me easy to prove that Macbeth, 'the rugged Macbeth', as Hazlitt and Brandes call him, is merely our gentle ir-resolute, humanist, philosopher Hamlet masquerading in galligaskins as a Scottish thane.

Let us take the first appearance of Macbeth, and we are forced to remark at once that he acts and speaks exactly as Hamlet in like circum-stances would act and speak. The honest but slow Banquo is amazed when Macbeth starts and seems to fear the fair promises of the witches; he does not see what the nimble Hamlet-intellect has seen in a flash – the dread means by which alone the promises can be brought to fulfil-ment. As soon as Macbeth is hailed 'Thane of Cawdor' Banquo warns him, but Macbeth, in spite of the presence of others, falls at once, as Hamlet surely would have fallen, into a soliloquy: a thing, considering the circumstances, most false to general human nature, for what he says must excite Banquo's suspicion, and is only true to the Hamlet-mind, that in and out of season loses itself in meditation. The soliloquy, too, is startlingly characteristic of Hamlet. After giving expression to the merely natural uplifting of his hope, Macbeth begins to weigh the for and against like a student-thinker:

> This supernatural soliciting
> Cannot be ill; cannot be good; if ill,
> Why hath it given me earnest of success,
> Commencing in a truth? I am thane of Cawdor:
> If good, why do I yield to that suggestion
> Whose horrid image . . .
>   function
> Is smothered in surmise and nothing is
> But what is not –

When Banquo draws attention to him as 'rapt', Macbeth still goes on talking to himself, for at length he has found arguments against action:

> If chance will have me King, why chance may crown me,
> Without my stir, –

all in the true Hamlet vein. At the end of the act, Macbeth when excusing himself to his companions becomes the student of Wittenberg in proper person. The courteous kindliness of the words is almost as characteristic as the bookish illustration:

> Kind gentlemen, your pains
> Are registered where every day I turn
> The leaf to read them.

If this is not Hamlet's very tone, manner and phrase, then individuality of nature has no peculiar voice.

I have laid such stress upon this, the first scene in which Macbeth appears, because the first appearance is by far the most important for the purpose of establishing the main outlines of a character; first impressions in a drama being exceedingly difficult to modify and almost impossible to change.

Macbeth, however, acts Hamlet from one end of the play to the other; and Lady Macbeth's first appearance (a personage almost as important to the drama as Macbeth himself) is used by Shakespeare to confirm this view of Macbeth's character. After reading her husband's letter almost her first words are:

> Yet do I fear thy nature.

> It is too full o' the milk of human kindness
> To catch the nearest way.

What is this but a more perfect expression of Hamlet's nature than Hamlet himself gives? Hamlet declares bitterly that he is 'pigeon livered', and lacks 'gall to make oppression bitter'; he says to Laertes, 'I loved you ever', and to his mother:

> I must be cruel only to be kind,

and she tells the King that he wept for Polonius' death. But the best phrase for his gentle-heartedness is what Lady Macbeth gives here: he is 'too full o' the milk of human kindness'. The words are as true of the Scottish chieftain as of the Wittenberg student; in heart they are one and the same person.

Though excited to action by his wife, Macbeth's last words in this scene are to postpone decision. 'We will speak further', he says, whereupon the woman takes the lead, warns him to dissemble, and adds, 'leave all the rest to me'. Macbeth's doubting, irresolution, and dislike of action could hardly be more forcibly portrayed.

The seventh scene of the first act begins with another long soliloquy by Macbeth, and this soliloquy shows us not only Hamlet's irresolution and untimely love of meditation, but also the peculiar pendulum-swing of Hamlet's thought:

> If it were done when 'tis done, then 'twere well
> It were done quickly: if the assassination
> Could trammel up the consequence, and catch
> With his surcease success: that but this blow
> Might be the be-all and the end-all; here,
> But here upon this bank and shoal of time
> We'd jump the life to come . . .

Is not this the same soul which also in a soliloquy questions fate? – 'Whether 'tis better in the mind . . . '

Macbeth, too, has Hamlet's peculiar and exquisite intellectual fairness – a quality, be it remarked in passing, seldom found in a ruthless murderer. He sees even the King's good points:

> this Duncan
> Hath borne his faculties so meek, hath been
> So clear in his great office, that his virtues

> Will plead like angels, trumpet-tongued, against
> The deep damnation of his taking off.

Is it not like Hamlet to be able to condemn himself in this way beforehand? Macbeth ends this soliloquy with words which come from the inmost of Hamlet's heart:

> I have no spur
> To prick the sides of my intent, but only
> Vaulting ambition, which o'erleaps itself,
> And falls on the other.

Hamlet, too, has no spur to prick the sides of his intent, and Hamlet, too, would be sure to see how apt ambition is to overleap itself, and so would blunt the sting of the desire. This monologue alone should have been sufficient to reveal to all critics the essential identity of Hamlet and Macbeth. Lady Macbeth, too, tells us that Macbeth left the supper table where he was entertaining the King, in order to indulge himself in this long monologue, and when he hears that his absence has excited comment, that he has been asked for even by the King, he does not attempt to excuse his strange conduct, he merely says, 'We will proceed no further in this business', showing in true Hamlet fashion how resolution has been 'sicklied o'er with the pale cast of thought'. In fact, as his wife says to him, he lets ' "I dare not" wait upon "I would" like the poor cat i' the adage'. Even when whipped to action by Lady Macbeth's preternatural eagerness, he asks:

> If we should fail?

whereupon she tells him to screw his courage to the sticking place, and describes the deed itself. Infected by her masculine resolution, Macbeth at length consents to what he calls the 'terrible feat'. The word 'terrible' here is surely more characteristic of the humane poet-thinker than of the chieftain-murderer. Even at this crisis, too, of his fate Macbeth cannot cheat himself; like Hamlet he is compelled to see himself as he is:

> False face must hide what the false heart doth know.

I have now considered nearly every word used by Macbeth in this first act: I have neither picked passages nor omitted anything that might make against my argument; yet every impartial reader must acknowledge that Hamlet is far more clearly sketched in this first act of *Macbeth* than in the first act of *Hamlet*. Macbeth appears in it as an irresolute dreamer, courteous, and gentle-hearted, of perfect intellectual fairness and bookish phrase; and in especial his love of thought and dislike of action are insisted upon again and again.

In spite of the fact that the second act is one chiefly of incident, filled indeed with the murder and its discovery, Shakespeare uses Macbeth as the mouthpiece of his marvellous lyrical faculty as freely as he uses Hamlet. A greater singer even than Romeo, Hamlet is a poet by nature, and turns every possible occasion to account, charming the ear with subtle harmonies. With a father's murder to avenge, he postpones action and sings to himself of life and death and the undiscovered country in words of such magical spirit-beauty that they can be compared to nothing in the world's literature save perhaps to the last chapter of Ecclesiastes. From the beginning to the end of the drama Hamlet is a great lyric poet, and this supreme personal gift is so natural to him that it is hardly mentioned by the critics. This gift, however, is possessed by Macbeth in at least equal degree and excites just as little notice. It is credible that Shakespeare used the drama sometimes as a means of reaching the highest lyrical utterance.

Without pressing this point further let us now take up the second act of the play. Banquo and Fleance enter; Macbeth has a few words with them; they depart, and after giving a servant an order, Macbeth begins another long soliloquy. He thinks he sees a dagger before him, and immediately falls to philosophising:

> Come let me clutch thee:
> I have thee not and yet I see thee still.
> Art thou not, fatal vision, sensible
> To feeling as to sight? or art thou but
> A dagger of the mind, a false creation
> Proceeding from the heat-oppressed brain?
> I see thee yet in form as palpable
> As that which now I draw
> [. . .]
> Mine eyes are made the fools o' the other senses.
> Or else worth all the rest: I see thee still;
> And on thy blade and dudgeon gouts of blood
> Which was not so before. – There's no such thing.

What is all this but an illustration of Hamlet's assertion:

> There is nothing either good or bad
> But thinking makes it so.

Just too as Hamlet swings on his mental balance, so that it is still a debated question among academic critics whether his madness was feigned or real, so here Shakespeare shows us how Macbeth loses his foothold on reality and falls into the void.

The lyrical effusion that follows is not very successful, and probably on that account Macbeth breaks off abruptly:

> Whiles I threat he lives,
> Words to the heat of deeds too cold breath gives,

which is, of course, precisely Hamlet's complaint:

> This is most brave;
> That I, the son of a dear father murdered,
> Prompted to my revenge by heaven and hell,
> Must, like a whore, unpack my heart with words.

After this Lady Macbeth enters, and the murder is committed, and now wrought to the highest tension Macbeth must speak from the depths of his nature with perfect sincerity. Will he exult, as the ambitious man would, at having taken successfully the longest step towards his goal? Or will he, like a prudent man, do his utmost to hide the traces of his crime, and hatch plans to cast suspicion on others? It is Lady Macbeth who plays this part; she tells Macbeth to 'get some water',

> And wash this filthy witness from your hand,

while he, brainsick, rehearses past fears and shows himself the sensitive poet-dreamer inclined to piety: here is the incredible scene:

LADY M. There are two lodged together.

MACBETH One cried, 'God bless us!' and 'Amen' the other,
As they had seen me with these hangman's hands.
Listening their fear, I could not say 'Amen',
When they did say 'God bless us'.

LADY M.   Consider it not so deeply.

MACBETH But wherefore could not I pronounce 'Amen'?

> I had most need of blessing, and 'Amen'
> Stuck in my throat.

This religious tinge colouring the weakness of self-pity is to be found again and again in *Hamlet*; Hamlet, too, is religious-minded; he begs Ophelia to remember his sins in her orisons. When he first sees his father's ghost he cries:

> Angels and ministers of grace defend us,

and when the ghost leaves him his word is, 'I'll go pray'. This new trait, most intimate and distinctive, is therefore the most conclusive proof of the identity of the two characters. The whole passage in the mouth of a murderer is utterly unexpected and out of place; no wonder Lady Macbeth exclaims:

> These deeds must not be thought
> After these ways: so, it will make us mad.

But nothing can restrain Macbeth; he gives rein to his poetic imagination, and breaks out in an exquisite lyric, a lyric which has hardly any closer relation to the circumstances than its truth to Shakespeare's nature:

> Methought I heard a voice cry, 'Sleep no more!
> Macbeth does murder sleep', – the innocent sleep:
> Sleep, that knits up the ravelled sleave of care,

and so forth – the poet in love with his own imaginings.

Again Lady Macbeth tries to bring him back to a sense of reality; tells him his thinking unbends his strength, and finally urges him to take the daggers back and

> smear
> The sleepy grooms with the blood.

But Macbeth's nerve is gone; he is physically broken now as well as mentally o'erwrought; he cries:

> I'll go no more;
> I am afraid to think what I have done.
> Look on't again I dare not.

All this is exquisitely characteristic of the nervous student who has been screwed up to a feat beyond his strength, 'a terrible feat', and who has broken down over it, but the words are altogether absurd in the mouth of an ambitious, half-barbarous chieftain.

His wife chides him as fanciful, childish – 'infirm of purpose' – she'll put the daggers back herself; but nothing can hearten Macbeth; every household noise sets his heart thumping:

> Whence is that knocking?
> How is't with me when every noise appals me?

His mind rocks; he even imagines he is being tortured:

> What hands are here? Ha!
> They pluck out my eyes.

And then he swings into another incomparable lyric:

> Will all great Neptune's ocean wash this blood
> Clean from my hand? No, this my hand will rather
> The multitudinous seas incarnadine,
> Making the green one red.

There is a great deal of the poet-neuropath and very little of the murderer for ambition's sake in this lyrical hysteria. No wonder Lady Macbeth declares she would be ashamed 'to wear a heart so white'. It is all Hamlet over again, Hamlet wrought up to a higher pitch of intensity. And here it should be remembered that *Macbeth* was written three years after *Hamlet* and probably just before *Lear*; one would therefore expect a greater intensity and a deeper pessimism in Macbeth than in Hamlet.

The character-drawing in the next scene is necessarily slight. The discovery of the murder impels everyone save the protagonist to action, but Macbeth finds time even at the climax of excitement to coin Hamlet-words that can never be forgotten:

> There's nothing serious in mortality;

and the description of Duncan:

> His silver skin laced with his golden blood

– as sugar'd sweet as any line in the sonnets, and here completely out of place.

In these first two acts the character of Macbeth is outlined so firmly that no after-touches can efface the impression.

Now comes a period in the drama in which deed follows so fast upon deed, that there is scarcely any opportunity for characterisation. To the casual view Macbeth seems almost to change his nature, passing from murder to murder quickly if not easily. He not only arranges for Banquo's assassination, but leaves Lady Macbeth innocent of the knowledge. The explanation of this seeming change of character is at hand. Shakespeare took the history of Macbeth from Holinshed's *Chronicle*, and there it is recorded that Macbeth murdered Banquo and many others, as well as Macduff's wife and children. Holinshed makes Duncan have 'too much of clemencie', and Macbeth 'too much of crueltie'. Macbeth's actions correspond with his nature in Holinshed; but Shakespeare first made Macbeth in his own image – gentle, bookish and irresolute – and then found himself fettered by the historical fact that Macbeth murdered Banquo and the rest. He was therefore forced to explain in some way or other why his Macbeth strode from crime to crime. It must be noted as most characteristic of gentle Shakespeare that even when confronted with this difficulty he did not think of lending Macbeth any tinge of cruelty, harshness, or ambition. His Macbeth commits murder for the same reason that the timorous deer fights – out of fear.

> To be thus is nothing;
> But to be safely thus. Our fears in Banquo
> Stick deep, and in his royalty of nature
> Reigns that which would be feared:

And again:

> There is none but he
> Whose being I do fear:

This proves, as nothing else could prove, the all-pervading, attaching kindness of Shakespeare's nature. Again and again Lady Macbeth saves the situation and tries to shame her husband into stern resolve, but in vain; he's 'quite unmann'd in folly'.

Had Macbeth been made ambitious, as the commentators assume, there would have been a sufficient motive for his later actions. But ambition is foreign to the Shakespeare-Hamlet nature, so the poet does not employ it. Again and again he returns to the explanation that the timid grow dangerous when 'frighted out of fear'. Macbeth says:

> But let the frame of things disjoint, both the worlds suffer
> Ere we will eat our meal in fear, and sleep
> In the affliction of these terrible dreams
> That shake us nightly.

In passing I may remark that Hamlet, too, complains of 'bad dreams'.

In deep Hamlet melancholy, Macbeth now begins to contrast his state with Duncan's:

> After life's fitful fever he sleeps well.
> Treason has done his worst: nor steel nor poison,
> Malice domestic, foreign levy, nothing,
> Can touch him further.

Lady Macbeth begs him to sleek o'er his rugged looks, be bright and jovial. He promises obedience; but soon falls into the dark mood again and predicts 'a deed of dreadful note'. Naturally his wife questions him, and he replies:

> Be innocent of the knowledge, dearest chuck,
> Till thou applaud the deed. Come, seeling night,
> Scarf up the tender eye of pityful day,
> And with thy bloody and invisible hand
> Cancel and tear to pieces that great bond
> Which keeps me pale.

No other motive for murder is possible to Shakespeare-Macbeth but fear.

Banquo is murdered, but still Macbeth cries:

> I am cabined, cribbed, confined, bound in
> To saucy doubts and fears.

The scene with the ghost of Banquo follows, wherein Macbeth again shows the nervous imaginative Hamlet nature. His next speech is mere reflection, and again Hamlet might have framed it:

> the time has been
> That when the brains were out the man would die
> And there an end:

But while fear may be an adequate motive for Banquo's murder, it can hardly explain the murder of Macduff's wife and children. Shakespeare feels this, too, and therefore finds other reasons natural enough; but the first of these reasons, 'his own good', is not especially characteristic of Macbeth, and the second, while perhaps characteristic, is absurdly inadequate: men don't murder out of tediousness:

> For mine own good
> All causes shall give way: I am in blood*
> Stepped in so far, that, should I wade no more,
> Returning were as tedious as go o'er.

Take it all in all, this latter reason is as poor a motive for cold-blooded murder as was ever given, and Shakespeare again feels this, for he brings in the witches once more to predict safety to Macbeth and adjure him to be 'bloody, bold and resolute'. When they have thus screwed his courage to the sticking place as his wife did before, Macbeth resolves on Macduff's murder, but he immediately recurs to the old explanation; he does not do it for his 'own good' nor because 'returning is tedious'; he does it

> That I may tell pale-hearted fear it lies,
> And sleep in spite of thunder.

It is fair to say that Shakespeare's Macbeth is so gentle-kind, that he can find no motive in himself for murder, save fear. The words Shakespeare puts into Hubert's mouth in *King John* are really his own confession:

> Within this bosom never enter'd yet
> The dreadful motion of a murderous thought.

The murders take place and the silly scenes in England between Malcolm and Macduff follow, and then come Lady Macbeth's illness, and the characteristic end. The servant tells Macbeth of the approach of the English force, and he begins the wonderful monologue:

---

* It seems to me probable that Shakespeare, unable to find an adequate motive for murder, borrowed this one from *Richard III*. Richard says:

> But I am in
> So far in blood that sin will pluck on sin –

This is an explanation following the fact rather than a cause producing it – an explanation, moreover, which may be true in the case of a fiendlike Richard, but is not true of a Macbeth.

> my May of life
> Is fall'n into the sear, the yellow leaf;
> And that which should accompany old age,
> As honour, love, obedience, troops of friends,
> I must not look to have; but in their stead
> Curses, not loud, but deep, mouth-honour, breath
> Which the poor heart would fain deny, and dare not.

Truly this is a strange murderer who longs for 'troops of friends', and who at the last push of fate can find in himself kindness enough towards others to sympathise with the 'poor heart'. All this is pure Hamlet; one might better say, pure Shakespeare.

We are next led into the field with Malcolm and Macduff, and immediately back to the castle again. While the women break into cries, Macbeth soliloquises in the very spirit of bookish Hamlet:

> I have almost forgot the taste of fears.
> The time has been, my senses would have cooled
> To hear a night-shriek; and my fell of hair
> Would at a dismal treatise rouse and stir
> As life were in 't.

The whole passage, and especially the 'dismal treatise', recalls the Wittenberg student with a magic of representment.

The death of the Queen is announced, and wrings from Macbeth a speech full of despairing pessimism, a bitterer mood than ever Hamlet knew; a speech, moreover, that shows the student as well as the incomparable lyric poet:

> She should have died hereafter:
> There would have been a time for such a word. –
> Tomorrow, and tomorrow, and tomorrow,
> Creeps in this petty pace from day to day,
> To the last syllable of recorded time;
> And all our yesterdays have lighted fools
> The way to dusty death. Out, out, brief candle!
> Life's but a walking shadow; a poor player,
> That struts and frets his hour upon the stage,
> And then is heard no more: it is a tale
> Told by an idiot, full of sound and fury,
> Signifying nothing.

Macbeth's philosophy, like Hamlet's, ends in utter doubt, in a passion of contempt for life, deeper than anything in Dante. The word 'syllable' in this lyric outburst is as characteristic as the 'dismal treatise' in the previous one, and more characteristic still of Hamlet is the likening of life to 'a poor player'.

The messenger tells Macbeth that Birnam Wood has begun to move, and he sees that the witches have cheated him. He can only say, as Hamlet might have said:

> I 'gin to be aweary of the sun,
> And wish the estate o' the world were now undone. –
> Ring the alarum bell! Blow wind! Come, wrack!
> At least we'll die with harness on our back.

And later he cries:

> They have tied me to a stake; I cannot fly,
> But bear-like I must fight the course.

This seems to me intensely characteristic of Hamlet; the brutal side of action was never more contemptuously described, and Macbeth's next soliloquy makes the identity apparent to everyone; it is in the true thinker-sceptic vein:

> Why should I play the Roman* fool and die
> On mine own sword?

Macbeth then meets Macduff, and there follows the confession of pity and remorse, which must be compared to the gentle-kindness with which Hamlet treats Laertes and Romeo treats Paris. Macbeth says to Macduff:

> Of all men else I have avoided thee:
> But get thee back, my soul is too much charged
> With blood of thine already.

---

* About the year 1600 Shakespeare seems to have steeped himself in Plutarch. For the next five or six years, whenever he thinks of suicide, the Roman way of looking at it occurs to him. Having made up his mind to kill himself, Laertes cries:

> I am more an antique Roman than a Dane,

and, in like case, Cleopatra talks of dying 'after the high Roman fashion'.

Then comes the 'something desperate' in him that Hamlet boasted of – and the end.

Here we have every characteristic of Hamlet without exception. The crying difference of situation only brings out the essential identity of the two characters. The two portraits are of the same person and finished to the fingertips. The slight shades of difference between Macbeth and Hamlet only strengthen our contention that both are portraits of the poet; for the differences are manifestly changes in the same character, and changes due merely to age. Just as Romeo is younger than Hamlet, showing passion where Hamlet shows thought, so Macbeth is older than Hamlet; in Macbeth the melancholy has grown deeper, the tone more pessimistic, and the heart gentler.* I venture, therefore, to assert that the portrait we find in Romeo and Jaques first, and then in Hamlet, and afterwards in Macbeth, is the portrait of Shakespeare himself, and we can trace his personal development through these three stages.

---

* Immediately after the publication of these first two essays, Sir Henry Irving seized the opportunity and lectured before a distinguished audience on the character of Macbeth. He gave it as his opinion that 'Shakespeare has presented Macbeth as one of the most blood-thirsty, most hypocritical villains in his long gallery of men, instinct with the virtues and vices of their kind (*sic*).' Sir Henry Irving also took the occasion to praise the simile of pity:

> And pity, like a naked new-born babe,
> Striding the blast.

This ridiculous fustian seemed to him 'very beautiful'. All this was perfectly gratuitous: no one needed to be informed that a man might have merit as an actor and yet be without any understanding of psychology or any taste in letters.

3

Duke Vincentio–Posthumus

It may be well to add here a couple of portraits of Shakespeare in later life in order to establish beyond question the chief features of his character. With this purpose in mind I shall take a portrait that is a mere sketch of him, Duke Vincentio in *Measure for Measure*, and a portrait that is minutely finished and perfect, though consciously idealised, Posthumus, in *Cymbeline*. And the reason I take this careless, wavering sketch, and contrast it with a highly-finished portrait, is that, though the sketch is here and there hardly recognisable, the outline being all too thin and hesitating, yet now and then a characteristic trait is over-emphasised, as we should expect in careless work. And this sketch in lines now faint, now all too heavy, is curiously convincing when put side by side with a careful and elaborate portrait in which the same traits are reproduced, but harmoniously, and with a perfect sense of the relative value of each feature. No critic, so far as I am aware, not Hazlitt, not Brandes, not even Coleridge, has yet thought of identifying either Duke Vincentio or Posthumus with Hamlet, much less with Shakespeare himself. The two plays are very unlike each other in tone and temper; *Measure for Measure* being a sort of tract for the times, while *Cymbeline* is a purely romantic drama. Moreover, *Measure for Measure* was probably written a couple of years after *Hamlet*, towards the end of 1603, while *Cymbeline* belongs to the last period of the poet's activity, and could hardly have been completed before 1610 or 1611. The dissimilarity of the plays only accentuates the likeness of the two protagonists.

Measure for Measure is one of the best examples of Shakespeare's contempt for stagecraft. Not only is the mechanism of the play, as we shall see later, astonishingly slipshod, but the ostensible purpose of the play, which is to make the laws respected in Vienna, is not only not attained, but seems at the end to be rather despised than forgotten. This indifference to logical consistency is characteristic of Shakespeare; Hamlet speaks of 'the undiscovered country from whose bourne no traveller returns' just after he has been talking with his dead father. The poetic dreamer cannot take the trouble to tie up the loose ends of a story: the real purpose of *Measure for Measure*, which is the confusion of the pretended ascetic Angelo, is fulfilled, and that is sufficient for the thinker, who has thus shown what 'our seemers be'. It is no less characteristic of Shakespeare that Duke Vincentio, his *alter ego*, should order another to punish loose livers – a task which his kindly nature found too disagreeable. But, leaving these general considerations, let us come to the first scene of the first act: the second long speech of the Duke should have awakened the suspicion that Vincentio is but another mask for Shakespeare. The whole speech proclaims the poet; the Duke begins:

> Angelo
> There is a kind of character in thy life,

Hamlet says to Rosencrantz and Guildenstern in what is supposed to be prose:

> There is a kind of confession in your looks.

A little later the line:

> Spirits are not finely touched
> But to fine issues,

is so characteristic of Hamlet-Shakespeare that it should have put every reader on the track.

The speeches of the Duke in the fourth scene of the first act are also characteristic of Shakespeare. But the four lines,

> My holy sir, none better knows than you
> How I have ever loved the life removed,
> And held in idle price to haunt assemblies,
> Where youth and cost and witless bravery keep,

are to me an intimate, personal confession; a fuller rendering indeed of Hamlet's 'Man delights not me; no, nor woman neither'. In any case it will be admitted that a dislike of assemblies and cost and witless bravery is peculiar in a reigning monarch, so peculiar indeed that it reminds me of the exiled Duke in *As You Like It*, or of Duke Prospero in *The Tempest* (two other incarnations of Shakespeare), rather than of anyone in real life. A love of solitude; a keen contempt for shows and the 'witless bravery' of court-life were, as we shall see, characteristics of Shakespeare from youth to old age.

In the first scene of the third act the Duke as a friar speaks to the condemned Claudio. He argues as Hamlet would argue, but with, I think, a more convinced hopelessness. The deepening scepticism would of itself force us to place *Measure for Measure* a little later than *Hamlet*:

> Reason thus with life:
> If I do lose thee, I do lose a thing
> That none but fools would keep; a breath thou art,
> [. . .]
>   The best of rest is sleep,
> And that thou oft provok'st, yet grossly fear'st
> Thy death, which is no more. Thou'rt not thyself;
> For thou exist'st on many a thousand grains
> That issue out of dust. Happy thou art not;
> For what thou hast not, still thou striv'st to get,
> And what thou hast, forgett'st.
> [. . .]
>   What's in this,
> That bears the name of life? Yet in this life
> Lie hid more thousand deaths; yet death we fear,
> That makes these odds all even.

That this scepticism of Vincentio is Shakespeare's scepticism appears from the fact that the whole speech is worse than out of place when addressed to a person under sentence of death. Were we to take it seriously, it would show the Duke to be curiously callous to the sufferings of the condemned Claudio; but callous the Duke is not, he is merely a pensive poet-philosopher talking in order to lighten his own heart. Claudio makes unconscious fun of the Duke's argument:

> To sue to live, I find I seek to die,
> And seeking death, find life: let it come on.

This scepticism of Shakespeare which shows itself out of place in Angelo and again most naturally in Claudio's famous speech, is one of the salient traits of his character which is altogether over-emphasised in this play. It is a trait, moreover, which finds expression in almost everything he wrote. Like nearly all the great spirits of the Renaissance, Shakespeare was perpetually occupied with the heavy problems of man's life and man's destiny. Was there any meaning or purpose in life, any result of the striving? Was Death to be feared or a Hereafter to be desired? – incessantly he beat straining wings in the void. But even in early manhood he never sought to deceive himself. His Richard II had sounded the shallow vanity of man's desires, the futility of man's hopes; he knew that man

> With nothing shall be pleased, till he be eased
> With being nothing.

And this sad knowledge darkened all Shakespeare's later thinking. Naturally, when youth passed from him and disillusionment put an end to dreaming, his melancholy deepened, his sadness became despairing; we can see the shadows thickening round him into night. Brutus takes an 'everlasting farewell' of his friend, and goes willingly to his rest. Hamlet dreads 'the undiscovered country'; but unsentient death is to him 'a consummation devoutly to be wished'. Vincentio's mood is half-contemptuous, but the melancholy persists; death is no 'more than sleep', he says, and life a series of deceptions; while Claudio in this same play shudders away from death as from annihilation, or worse, in words which one cannot help regarding as Shakespeare's:

CLAUDIUS   Ay, but to die, and go we know not where;
> To lie in cold obstruction and to rot . . .

A little later and Macbeth's soul cries to us from the outer darkness: 'there's nothing serious in mortality'; life's

>   a tale
> Told by an idiot, full of sound and fury,
> Signifying nothing.

And from this despairing gloom come Lear's shrieks of pain and pitiful ravings, and in the heavy intervals the gibberings of the fool. Even when the calmer mood of age came upon Shakespeare and took away the bitterness, he never recanted; Posthumus speaks of life and death in almost the words used by Vincentio, and Prospero has nothing to add save that 'our little life is rounded with a sleep'.

It is noteworthy that Shakespeare always gives these philosophic questionings to those characters whom I regard as his impersonations,*

---

* One of my correspondents, Mr Theodore Watts-Dunton, has been kind enough to send me an article contributed to *Colbourn's Magazine* in 1873, in which he declares that 'Shakespeare seems to have kept a sort of Hamlet and when he breaks this rule, he breaks it in favour of some Claudio who is not a character at all, but the mere mouthpiece of one of his moods.

I now come to a point in the drama which at once demands and defies explanation. In the first scene of the third act the Duke, after listening to the terrible discussion between Isabella and Claudio, first of all tells Claudio that 'Angelo had never the purpose to corrupt' Isabella, and then assures Claudio that tomorrow he must die. The explanation of these two falsehoods would be far to seek, unless we take it that they were invented simply in order to prolong our interest in the drama. But this assumption, though probable, does not increase our sympathy with the protagonist – the lies seem to be too carelessly uttered to be even characteristic – nor yet our admiration of the structure of a play that needs to be supported by such flimsy buttresses. Still this very carelessness of fact, as I have said, is Shakespearean; the philosophic dreamer paid little attention to the mere incidents of the story.

The talk between the Duke and Isabella follows. The form of the Duke's speech, with its touch of euphuistic conceit, is one which Hamlet-Shakespeare affects:

> The hand that hath made you fair hath made you good: the goodness that is cheap in beauty makes beauty brief in goodness; but grace, being the soul of your complexion, shall keep the body of it ever fair.

This Duke plays philosopher, too, in and out of season as Hamlet did: he says to Isabella:

> Virtue is bold, and goodness never fearful,

generalising his praise even to a woman.

---

notebook, full of Hamlet thoughts, of which "To be or not to be" may be taken as the type. These he was burdened with. These did he cram into Hamlet as far as he could, and then he tossed the others indiscriminately into other plays, tragedies and histories, perfectly regardless of the character who uttered them.' Though Mr Watts-Dunton sees that some of these 'Hamlet thoughts' are to be found in Macbeth and Prospero and Claudio, he evidently lacks the key to Shakespeare's personality, or he would never have said that Shakespeare tossed these reflections 'indiscriminately into other plays'. Nevertheless the statement itself is interesting, and deserves more notice than has been accorded to it.

Again, when Pompey is arrested, he passes from the individual to the general, exclaiming:

> That we were all as some would seem to be,
> Free from our faults, as from faults seeming free.

Then follows the interesting talk with Lucio, who awakens the slightly pompous Duke to natural life with his contempt. When Lucio tells the Duke, who is disguised as a friar, that he (the Duke) was a notorious loose-liver – 'he had some feeling of the sport; he knew the service' – the Duke merely denies the soft impeachment; but when Lucio tells him that the Duke is not wise, but 'a very superficial, ignorant, unweighing fellow', the Duke bursts out, 'either this is envy in you, folly, or mistaking: . . . Let him but be testimonied in his own bringings-forth, and he shall appear to the envious a scholar, a statesman, and a soldier', which recalls Hamlet's 'Friends, scholars, and soldiers', and Ophelia's praise of Hamlet as 'courtier, soldier, scholar'. Lucio goes off, and the Duke 'moralises' the incident in Hamlet's very accent:

> No might nor greatness in mortality
> Can censure 'scape; backwounding calumny
> The whitest virtue strikes. What king so strong
> Can tie the gall up in the slanderous tongue?

Hamlet says to Ophelia:

> Be thou as chaste as ice, as pure as snow, thou shall not escape
> calumny.

And Laertes says that 'virtue itself' cannot escape calumny.

The reflection is manifestly Shakespeare's own, and here the form, too, is characteristic. It may be as well to recall now that Shakespeare himself was calumniated in his lifetime; the fact is admitted in Sonnet 36, where he fears his 'guilt' will 'shame' his friend.

In his talk with Escalus the Duke's speech becomes almost obscure from excessive condensation of thought – a habit which grew upon Shakespeare.

Escalus asks:

> What news abroad in the world?

The Duke answers:

None, but that there is so great a fever on goodness, that the dissolution of it must cure it: novelty is only in request. . . . There is scarce truth enough alive to make societies secure, but security enough to make fellowships accursed.

Escalus then tells us of the Duke's temperament in words which would fit Hamlet perfectly; for, curiously enough, they furnish us with the best description of Shakespeare's melancholy:

Rather rejoicing to see another merry, than merry at anything which professed to make him rejoice.

And, lastly, the curious rhymed soliloquy of Vincentio which closes this third act, must be compared with the epilogue to *The Tempest*:

> He who the sword of Heaven will bear
> Should be as holy as severe;
> Pattern in himself to know,
> Grace to stand and virtue go;
> [. . .]
> Shame to him whose cruel striking
> Kills for faults of his own liking!
> Twice treble shame on Angelo,
> To weed my vice and let his grow!
> [. . .]

In the fifth act the Duke, freed from making plots and plans, speaks without constraint and reveals his nature ingenuously. He uses words to Angelo that recall the sonnets:

> O, your desert speaks loud; and I should wrong it,
> To lock it in the wards of covered bosom,
> When it deserves, with characters of brass,
> A forted residence 'gainst the tooth of time
> And razure of oblivion.*

Again, the Duke argues in gentle Shakespeare's fashion for Angelo and against Isabella:

> If he had so offended,
> He would have weighed thy brother by himself
> And not have cut him off.

---

* Cf. Sonnet 122 with its 'full character'd' and 'razed oblivion'.

It seems impossible for Shakespeare to believe that the sinner can punish sin. It reminds one of the sacred 'he that is without sin among you let him first cast a stone'. The detections and forgivings of the last act follow.

It will be admitted, I think, on all hands that Duke Vincentio speaks throughout the play with Shakespeare's voice. From the point of view of literary art his character is very far from being as complex or as deeply realised as that of Hamlet or Macbeth, or even as that of Romeo or of Jaques, and yet one other trait besides that of sceptical brooding is so over-accentuated that it can never be forgotten. In the last scene the Duke orders Barnardine to the block and the next moment respites him; he condemns

An Angelo for Claudio; death for death,

then pardons Angelo, and at once begins to chat with him in kindly intimacy; he asserts that he cannot forgive Lucio, Lucio who has traduced him, shall be whipped and hanged, and in the same breath he remits the heavy penalty. Truly he is 'an unhurtful opposite'* whose anger has no steadfastness; but the gentle forgivingness of disposition that is so marked in Vincentio is a trait we found emphasised in Romeo, and again in Hamlet and again in Macbeth. It is, indeed, one of the most permanent characteristics of Shakespeare. From the begin-

---

* The critics are at variance over this ending, and, indeed, over the whole play. Coleridge says that 'our feelings of justice are grossly wounded in Angelo's escape'; for 'cruelty with lust and damnable baseness cannot be forgiven.' Mr Swinburne, too, regrets the miscarriage of justice; the play to him is a tragedy, and should end tragically with the punishment of the 'autotype of the huge national vice of England'. Perhaps, however, Puritan hypocrisy was not so widespread or so powerful in the time of Shakespeare as it is nowadays; perhaps, too, Shakespeare was not so good a hater as Mr Swinburne, nor so strenuous a moralist as Coleridge was, at least in theory. In any case it is evident that Shakespeare found it harder to forgive Lucio, who had hurt his vanity, than Angelo, who pushed lust to outrage and murder, which strange, yet characteristic, fact I leave to the mercy of future commentators. Mr Sidney Lee regards *Measure for Measure* as 'one of Shakespeare's greatest plays'. Coleridge, however, thought it 'a hateful work'; it is also a poor work, badly constructed, and for the most part carelessly written. In essence it is a mere tract against Puritanism, and in form a sort of Arabian Nights' Entertainment in which the hero plays the part of Haroun-al-Raschid.

ning to the end of the play, Duke Vincentio is weakly-kind in act and swayed by fitful impulses; his assumed austerity of conduct is the thin varnish of vanity that will not take on such soft material. The Hamlet weakness is so exaggerated in him, and so unmotived, that I am inclined to think Shakespeare was even more irresolute and indisposed to action than Hamlet himself.

In the character of Posthumus, the hero of *Cymbeline*, Shakespeare has painted himself with extraordinary care; has, in fact, given us as deliberate and almost as complete a picture of himself as he did in Hamlet. Unluckily his hand had grown weaker in the ten years' interval, and he gave such loose rein to his idealising habit that the portrait is neither so veracious nor so lifelike. The explanation of all this will be given later; it is enough for the moment to state that as Posthumus is perhaps the completest portrait of him that we have after his mental shipwreck, we must note the traits of it carefully, and see what manner of man Shakespeare took himself to be towards the end of his career.

It is difficult to understand how the commentators have been able to read *Cymbeline* without seeing the likeness between Posthumus and Hamlet. The wager which is the theme of the play may have hindered them a little, but as they found it easy to excuse its coarseness by attributing lewdness to the time, there seems to have been no reason for not recognising Posthumus. Posthumus is simply a staider Hamlet considerably idealised. I am not at all sure that the subject of the play was void of offence in the time of Elizabeth; all finer spirits must even then have found it puerile and coarse. What would Spenser have said about it? Shakespeare used the wager because of the opportunities it gave him of painting himself and an ideal woman. His view of it is just indicated; Iachimo says:

> I make my wager rather against your confidence than her reputation: and, to bar your offence herein too, I durst attempt it against any lady in the world.

But in spite of the fact that Iachimo makes his insult general, Posthumus warns him that:

> If she remain unseduced . . . for your ill opinion, and the assault you have made to her chastity, you shall answer me with your sword.

From this it appears that the bet was distasteful to Posthumus; it is not so offenceful to him as it should have been according to our modern temper; but this shortcoming, an unconscious shortcoming, is the only fault which Shakespeare will allow in his hero. In the first scene of the first act Posthumus is praised as men never praise the absent without a personal motive; the First Gentleman says of him:

>   I do not think
> So fair an outward and such stuff within
> Endows a man but he.

The Second Gentleman replies:

>   You speak him far;

and the First Gentleman continues:

> I do extend him, sir, within himself;
> Crush him together, rather than unfold
> His measure duly.

And as if this were not enough, this gentleman-eulogist goes on to tell us that Posthumus has sucked in 'all the learnings' of his time 'as we do air', and further:

>   He lived in court –
> Which rare it is to do – most praised, most loved;
> A sample to the young'st, to the more mature
> A glass that feated them; and to the graver
> A child that guided dotards.

This gross praise is ridiculously unnatural, and outrages our knowledge of life; men are much more apt to criticise than to praise the absent; but it shows a prepossession on Shakespeare's part in favour of Posthumus which can only be explained by the fact that in Posthumus he was depicting himself. Every word is significant to us, for Shakespeare evidently tells us here what he thought about himself, or rather what he wished to think, towards the end of his life. It is impossible to believe that he was 'most praised, most loved'; men do not love or praise their superiors in looks, or intellect.

The first words which Posthumus in this same scene addresses to Imogen, show the gentle Shakespeare nature:

> O lady, weep no more, lest I give cause

> To be suspected of more tenderness
> Than doth become a man.

And when Imogen gives him the ring and tells him to wear it till he
woos another wife, he talks to her exactly as Romeo would have talked:

> How! how! another? –
> You gentle gods, give me but this I have,
> And sear up my embracements from a next
> With bonds of death! [*putting on the ring*]
>   Remain, remain thou here
> While sense can keep it on.

And he concludes as self-depreciating Hamlet would have concluded:

> And sweetest, fairest,
> As I my poor self did exchange for you,
> To your so infinite loss, so in our trifles
> I still win of you; for my sake wear this:
> It is a manacle of love; I'll place it
> Upon this fairest prisoner. [*putting a bracelet on her arm*]

In his fight with Cloten he is depicted as a rare swordsman of wonderful magnanimity. Pisanio says:

> My master rather played than fought,
> And had no help of anger.

I call this gentle kindness which Posthumus displays, the birthmark of
Shakespeare; he had 'no help of anger'. As the play goes on we find
Shakespeare's other peculiarities, or Hamlet's. Iachimo represents
Posthumus as 'merry', 'gamesome', 'the Briton reveller'; but curiously
enough Imogen answers as Ophelia might have answered about
Hamlet:

> When he was here,
> He did incline to sadness; and ofttimes
> Not knowing why.

This uncaused melancholy that distinguishes Romeo, Jaques, Hamlet,
Macbeth, and Vincentio is not more characteristic of the Hamlet-
Shakespeare nature than the way Posthumus behaves when Iachimo
tries to make him believe that he has won the wager. Posthumus is

convinced almost at once; jumps to the conclusion, indeed, with the heedless rapidity of the naive, sensitive, quick-thinking man who has cultivated his emotions and thoughts by writing in solitude, and not the suspicions and distrust of others which are developed in the market-place. One is reminded of Goethe's famous couplet:

> Es bildet ein Talent sich in der Stille,
> Sich ein Charakter in dem Strom der Welt.

Posthumus is all in fitful extremes; not satisfied with believing the lie, he gives Iachimo Imogen's ring as well, and bursts into a diatribe:

> Let there be no honour
> Where there's beauty; truth, where semblance; love,
> Where there's another man,

and so forth. Even Philario, who has no stake in the matter, is infinitely harder to convince:

> Have patience, sir,
> And take your ring again; 'tis not yet won:
> It may be probable she lost it.

Then this 'unstable opposite', Posthumus, demands his ring back again, but as soon as Iachimo swears that he had the bracelet from her arm, Posthumus swings round again to belief from sheer rapidity of thought. Again Philario will not be convinced. He says:

> Sir, be patient,
> This is not strong enough to be believed
> Of one persuaded well of –

But Posthumus will not await the proof for which he has asked. He is convinced upon suspicion, as Othello was, and the very nimbleness of his Hamlet-intellect, seeing that probabilities are against him, entangles him in the snare. Even his servant Pisanio will not believe in Imogen's guilt though his master assures him of it. Shakespeare does not notice this peculiar imprudent haste of his hero, as he notices, for example, the hasty speech of Hotspur by letting Harry of England imitate it, simply because the quick-thinking was his own; while the hurried stuttering speech was foreign to him. Posthumus goes on to rave against women as Hamlet did; as all men do who do not understand them:

> For even to vice
> They are not constant, but are changing still.

And Posthumus betrays as clearly as ever Hamlet did that he is merely
Shakespeare masquerading:

> I'll write against them,
> Detest them, curse them – yet 'tis greater skill
> In a true hate, to pray they have their will:
> The very devils cannot plague them better.

'Write against them' indeed! This is the same threat which Shakespeare uses against his dark mistress in Sonnet 140, and everyone will
admit that it is more in the character of the poet and man of letters than
in that of the warrior son-in-law of a half-barbarous king. The last line
here, because it is a little superfluous, a little emphatic, seems to me
likely to have a personal application. When Shakespeare's mistress had
her will, did she fall to misery, I wonder?

I may be allowed to notice here how intensely characteristic all this
play is of Shakespeare. In the third scene of the third act, life in the
country is contrasted to its advantage with life at Court; and then gold
is treated as dirt by the princely brothers – both these, the love of
country life, and the contempt of gold, are, as we shall see later, abiding
peculiarities of Shakespeare.

When we come to Posthumus again almost at the end of the play we
find that his anger with Imogen has burned itself out. He is angry now
with Pisanio for having executed his order and murdered her; he should
have 'saved the noble Imogen to repent'. Surely the poet Shakespeare
and not the outraged lover speaks in this epithet, 'noble'.

Posthumus describes the battle in which he took so gallant a part in
Shakespeare's usual manner. He falls into rhyme; he shows the cheap
modesty of the conventional hero; he tells of what others did, and
nothing of his own feats; Belarius and the two striplings, he says:

> With their own nobleness . . . gilded pale looks.

Unfortunately one is reminded of the exquisite sonnet line:

> Gilding pale streams with heavenly alchemy.

'Gild' is one of Shakespeare's favourite words; he uses it very often,
sometimes indeed as in this case, ineffectively.

But the scene which reveals the character of Posthumus beyond all doubt is the prison scene in the fifth act. His soliloquy which begins:

> Most welcome, bondage, for thou art a way,
> I think, to liberty –

is all pure Shakespeare. When he determines to give up life, he says:

> O Imogen! I'll speak to thee in silence,

and Hamlet at his death comes to the selfsame word:

> The rest is silence.

The scene with the gaoler is from Hamlet's soul; Posthumus jests with his keeper as Hamlet with the gravedigger:

> So, if I prove a good repast to the spectators, the ship pays the shot;

and the Hamlet melancholy:

> I am merrier to die than thou art to live;

and the Hamlet riddle still unsolved:

> I tell thee, fellow, there are none want eyes to direct them the way I am going; but such as wink, and will not use them.

When the messenger comes to bring him to the king, Posthumus cries:

> Thou bringest good news, I am called to be made free,

for there are 'no bolts for the dead'.

Those who wish to see how Shakespeare's mind worked will compare Posthumus' speech to Iachimo, when he has learned the truth, with Othello's words when he is convinced of his own fatal error and of Desdemona's chastity. The two speeches are twins; though the persons uttering them should be of totally different characters. The explanation of this astounding similarity will be given when we come to *Othello*.

It is characteristic of Posthumus that he should strike Imogen in her page's dress, not recognising her; he is ever too quick – a mere creature of impulse. More characteristic still is the way he forgives Iachimo, just as Vincentio forgave Angelo:

> Kneel not to me:
> The power that I have on you, is to spare you,

> The malice towards you, to forgive you. Live,
> And deal with others better.

In judging his fellow-men this is Shakespeare's harshest word. Posthumus, then, is presented to us in the beginning of the play as perfect, a model to young and old, of irreproachable virtue and of all wonderful qualities. In the course of the play, however, he shows himself very nimble-witted, credulous, and impulsive, quick to anger and quicker still to forgive; with thoughts all turned to sadness and to musing; a poet – ever in extremes; now hating his own rash errors to the point of demanding the heaviest punishment for them; now swearing that he will revenge himself on women by writing against them; a philosopher – he jests with his gaoler and consoles himself with despairing speculation in the very presence of the Arch-Fear. All these are manifestly characteristics of Hamlet, and Posthumus possesses no others.

So far, then, from finding that Shakespeare never revealed himself in his dramas, I have shown that he pictured himself as the hero* of six plays written at widely different times; in fact that, like Rembrandt, he painted his own portrait in all the critical periods of life: as a sensuous youth given over to love and poetry in Romeo; a few years later as a melancholy onlooker at life's pageant in Jaques; in middle age as the passionate, melancholy, aesthete-philosopher of kindliest nature in Hamlet and Macbeth; as the fitful Duke incapable of severity in *Measure for Measure*, and finally, when standing within the shadow, as Posthumus, an idealised yet feebler replica of Hamlet.

---

* A hypercritic might contend that Jaques was not the hero of *As You Like It*; but the objection really strengthens my argument. Shakespeare makes of Jaques, who is merely a secondary character without influence on the action, the principal person in the play simply because in Jaques he satisfied his own need of self-revealing.

4

Shakespeare's Men of Action: the Bastard, Arthur and King Richard II

It is time now, I think, to test my theory by considering the converse of it. In any case, the attempt to see the other side is pretty sure to make for enlightenment, and may thus justify itself. In the mirror which Shakespeare held up to human nature, we not only see Romeo, and Jaques, Hamlet, Macbeth and Posthumus; but also the leonine, frank face of the Bastard, the fiery, lean, impatient mask of Hotspur, and the cynical, bold eyes of Richard III. Even if it were admitted that Shakespeare preferred the type of the poet-philosopher, he was certainly able, one would say, to depict the man of action with extraordinary vigour and success. He himself then must have possessed a certain strength of character, certain qualities of decision and courage; he must have had, at least, 'a good stroke in him', as Carlyle phrased it. This is the universal belief, a belief sanctioned by Coleridge and Goethe, and founded apparently on plain facts, and yet, I think, it is mistaken, demonstrably untrue. It might even be put more plausibly than any of its defenders has put it. One might point out that Shakespeare's men of action are nearly all to be found in the historical plays which he wrote in early manhood, while the portrait of the philosopher-poet is the favourite study of his riper years. It would then be possible to suggest that Shakespeare grew from a bold roistering youth into a melancholy, thoughtful old age, touching both extremes of manhood in his own development. But even this comforting explanation will not stand: his earliest impersonations are all thinkers.

Let us consider, again, how preference in a writer is established. Everyone feels that Sophocles prefers Antigone to Ismene; Ismene is a mere sketch of gentle feminine weakness; while Antigone is a great portrait of the *revoltée* , the first appearance indeed in literature of the 'new woman', and the place she fills in the drama, and the ideal qualities attributed to her girlhood – alike betray the personal admiration of the poet. In the same way Shakespeare's men of action are mere sketches in comparison with the intimate detailed portrait of the aesthete-philosopher-poet with his sensuous, gentle, melancholy temperament. Moreover, and this should be decisive, Shakespeare's men of action are all taken from history, or tradition, or story, and not from imagination, and their characteristics were supplied by the chroniclers and not invented by the dramatist. To see how far this is true I must examine Shakespeare's historical plays at some length Such an examination did not form a part of my original purpose. It is very difficult, not to say impossible, to ascertain exactly how far history and verbal tradition helped Shakespeare in his historical portraits of English worthies. Jaques, for instance, is his own creation from top to toe; every word given to him therefore deserves careful study; but how much of Hotspur is Shakespeare's, and how much of the Bastard? Without pretending, however, to define exactly the sources or the limits of the master's inspiration, there are certain indications in the historical plays which throw a flood of light on the poet's nature, and certain plain inferences from his methods which it would be folly not to draw.

Let us begin with *King John*, as one of the easiest and most helpful to us at this stage, and remembering that Shakespeare's drama was evidently founded on the old play entitled *The Troublesome Raigne of King John*, let us from our knowledge of Shakespeare's character forecast what his part in the work must have been. A believer in the theory I have set forth would guess at once that the strong, manly character of the Bastard was vigorously sketched even in the old play, and just as surely one would attribute the gentle, feminine, pathetic character of Arthur to Shakespeare. And this is precisely what we find: Philip Fauconbridge is excellently depicted in the old play; he is called:

> A hardy wildehead, tough and venturous,

and he talks and acts the character to the life. In *The Troublesome Raigne*, as in *King John*, he is proud of his true father, the lion-hearted Richard, and careless of the stain of his illegitimate birth; he cries:

> The world's in my debt,
> There's something owing to Plantaginet.
> I, marrie Sir, let me alone for game
> Ile act some wonders now I know my name;

> By blessed Marie Ile not sell that pride
> For England's wealth and all the world beside.

Who does not feel the leaping courage and hardihood of the Bastard in these lines? Shakespeare seizes the spirit of the character and renders it, but his emendations are all by way of emphasis: he does not add a new quality; his Bastard is the Bastard of *The Troublesome Raigne*. But the gentle, pathetic character of Arthur is all Shakespeare's. In the old play Arthur is presented as a prematurely wise youth who now urges the claims of his descent and speaks boldly for his rights, and now begs his vixenish mother to

> Wisely winke at all
> Least further harmes ensue our hasty speech.

Again, he consoles her with the same prudence:

> Seasons will change and so our present griefe
> May change with them and all to our reliefe.

This Arthur is certainly nothing like Shakespeare's Arthur. Shakespeare, who had just lost his only son Hamnet,* in his twelfth year, turns Arthur from a young man into a child, and draws all the pathos possible from his weakness and suffering; Arthur's first words are of 'his powerless hand', and his advice to his mother reaches the very fount of tears:

> Good my mother, peace!
> I would that I were low laid in my grave;
> I am not worth this coil that's made for me.

When taken prisoner his thought is not of himself:

> O, this will make my mother die with grief.

He is a woman-child in unselfish sympathy.

The whole of the exquisitely pathetic scene between Hubert and Arthur belongs, as one might have guessed, to Shakespeare, that is, the whole pathos of it belongs to him.

In the old play Arthur thanks Hubert for his care, calls him 'courteous keeper', and, in fact, behaves as the conventional prince. He has no

---

* Some months before writing *King John* Shakespeare had visited Stratford for the first time after ten years absence and had then perhaps learned to know and love young Hamnet.

words of such affecting appeal as Shakespeare puts into Arthur's mouth:

> I would to heaven
> I were your son, so you would love me, Hubert.

This love and longing for love is the characteristic of Shakespeare's Arthur; he goes on:

> Are you sick, Hubert? You look pale today.
> In sooth, I would you were a little sick,
> That I might sit all night and watch with you:
> I warrant, I love you more than you do me.

A girl could not be more tender, more anxious for love's assurance. In *The Troublesome Raigne*, when Hubert tells Arthur that he has bad news for him, tidings of 'more hate than death', Arthur faces the unknown with a man's courage; he asks:

> What is it, man? if needes be don,
> Act it, and end it, that the paine were gon.

It might be the Bastard speaking, so hardy-reckless are the words. When this Arthur pleads for his eyesight, he does it in this way:

> I speake not only for eyes priviledge,
> The chiefe exterior that I would enjoy:
> But for thy perill, farre beyond my paine,
> Thy sweete soules losse more than my eyes vaine lack.

Again at the end he says:

> Delay not, Hubert, my orisons are ended,
> Begin I pray thee, reave me of my sight'.

And when Hubert relents because his 'conscience bids him desist', Arthur says:

> Hubert, if ever Arthur be in state
> Looke for amends of this received gift.

In all this there is neither realisation of character nor even sincere emotion. But Shakespeare's Arthur is a masterpiece of soul-revealing, and moves us to pity at every word:

> Will you put out mine eyes?

> These eyes that never did, nor never shall,
> So much as frown on you?

And then the child's imaginative horror of being bound:

> For heaven's sake, Hubert, let me not be bound.
> Nay, hear me, Hubert: drive these men away,
> And I will sit as quiet as a lamb;
> I will not stir, nor wince, nor speak a word.

When Hubert relents, Shakespeare's Arthur does not promise reward, he simply breathes a sigh of exquisite affection:

> O, now you look like Hubert: all this while
> You were disguised.

And finally, when Hubert promises never to hurt him, his words are:

> O heaven! I thank you, Hubert.

Arthur's character we owe entirely to Shakespeare, there is no hint of his weakness and tenderness in the original, no hint either of the pathos of his appeal – these are the inventions of gentle Shakespeare, who has manifestly revealed his own exceeding tenderness and sweetness of heart in the person of the child Prince. Of course, there are faults in the work; faults of affectation and word-conceit hardly to be endured. When Hubert says he will burn out his eyes with hot irons, Arthur replies:

> Ah, none, but in this iron age, would do it!
> The iron of itself, though heat red-hot,

and so forth . . . Nor does this passage of tinsel stand alone. When the iron cools and Hubert says he can revive it, Arthur replies with pinch-beck conceits:

> An if you do you will but make it blush,
> And glow with shame at your proceedings,

and so forth. The faults are bad enough; but the heavenly virtues carry them all off triumphantly. There is no creation like Arthur in the whole realm of poetry; he is all angelic love and gentleness, and yet neither mawkish nor unnatural; his fears make him real to us, and the horror of his situation allows us to accept his exquisite pleading as possible. We need only think of Tennyson's May Queen, or of his unspeakable Arthur, or of Thackeray's prig Esmond, in order to understand how difficult it is in literature to make goodness attractive or even credible. Yet Shakespeare's art triumphs where no one else save Balzac and Turgenev has achieved even a half-success.

I cannot leave this play without noticing that Shakespeare has shown in it a hatred of murder just as emphatically as he has revealed his love of gentleness and pity in the creation of Arthur. In spite of the loyalty which the English nobles avow in the second scene of the fourth act, which is a quality that always commends itself to Shakespeare, Pembroke is merely their mouthpiece in requesting the King to 'enfranchise Arthur'. As soon as John tells them that Arthur is dead they throw off their allegiance and insult the monarch to his face. Even John is startled by their indignation, and brought as near remorse as is possible for him:

> I repent;
> There is no sure foundation set on blood;
> No certain life achieved by others' death –

– which reads like a reflection of Shakespeare himself. When the Bastard asks the nobles to return to their allegiance, Salisbury finds an astonishing phrase to express their loathing of the crime:

> The King hath dispossess'd himself of us;
> We will not line his thin bestained cloak
> With our pure honours, *nor attend the foot*
> *That leaves the print of blood where'er it walks.*

In all literature there is no more terrible image: Shakespeare's horror of bloodshed has more than Aeschylean intensity. When the dead body of Arthur is found each of the nobles in turn expresses his abhorrence of the deed, and all join in vowing instant revenge. Even the Bastard calls it

> A damned and bloody work,
> The graceless action of a heavy hand,

and a little later the thought of the crime brings even this tough adventurer to weakness:

> I am amazed, methinks, and lose my way
> Among the thorns and dangers of this world.

– a phrase that suits the weakness of Richard II or Henry VI or Shakespeare himself better than it suits the hardy Bastard. Even as a young man Shakespeare hated the cruelty of ambition and the savagery of war as much as he loved all the ceremonies of chivalry and observances of gentle courtesy.

Very similar inferences are to be drawn from a study of Shakespeare's *King Richard II*, which in some respects is his most important historical creation. Coleridge says: 'I know of no character drawn by our great poet with such unequalled skill as that of *Richard II*.' Such praise is extravagant; but it would have been true to say that up to 1593 or 1594, when Shakespeare wrote *King Richard II*, he had given us no character so complex and so interesting as this Richard. Coleridge overpraised the character-drawing probably because the study of Richard's weakness and irresolution, and the pathos resulting from such helplessness, must have seemed very like an analysis of his own nature.

Let us now examine *Richard II*, and see what light it casts on Shakespeare's qualities. There was an old play of the same title, a play which is now lost, but we can form some idea of what it was like from the description in Forman's Diary. Like most of the old history-plays it ranged over twenty years of Richard's reign, whereas Shakespeare's tragedy is confined to the last year of Richard's life. It is probable that the old play presented King Richard as more wicked and more deceitful than Shakespeare imagines him. We know that in the *Confessio Amantis*, Gower, the poet, cast off his allegiance to Richard: for he cancelled the dedication of the poem to Richard, and dedicated it instead to Henry. William Langland, too, the author of the *Vision of Piers Plowman*, turned from Richard at the last, and used his deposition as a warning to ill-advised youth. It may be assumed, then, that tradition pictured Richard as a vile creature in whom weakness nourished crime. Shakespeare took his story partly from Holinshed's narrative, and partly either from the old play or from the traditional view of Richard's character. When he began to write the play he evidently intended to portray Richard as even more detestable than history and tradition had presented him. In Holinshed Richard is not accused of the murder of Gloster, whereas Shakespeare directly charges him with it, or rather makes Gaunt do so, and the accusation is not denied, much less disproved. At the close of the first act we are astonished by the revelation of Richard's devilish heartlessness. The King hearing that his uncle, John of Gaunt, is 'grievous sick', cries out:

Now put it, God, in his physician's mind,

> To help him to his grave immediately!
> The lining of his coffers shall make coats
> To deck our soldiers for these Irish wars.
> Come, gentlemen, let's all go visit him:
> Pray God we may make haste and come too late.

This mixture of greed and cold cruelty decked out with blasphemous phrase is viler, I think, than anything attributed by Shakespeare to the worst of his villains. But surely some hint of Richard's incredible vileness should have come earlier in the play, should have preceded at least his banishment of Bolingbroke, if Shakespeare had really meant to present him to us in this light.

In the first scene of the second act, when Gaunt reproves him, Richard turns on him in a rage, threatening. In the very same scene York reproves Richard for seizing Gaunt's money and land, and Richard retorts:

> Think what you will: we seize into our hands
> His plate, his goods, his money, and his lands.

But when York blames him to his face and predicts that evil will befall him and leaves him, Richard in spite of this at once creates:

> Our uncle York, Lord Governor of England;
> For he is just, and always loved us well.

This Richard of Shakespeare is so far, I submit, almost incomprehensible. When reproved by Gaunt and warned, Richard rages and threatens; when blamed by York much more severely, Richard rewards York: the two scenes contradict each other. Moreover, though his callous selfishness, greed and cruelty are apparently established, in the very next scene of this act our sympathy with Richard is called forth by the praise his queen gives him. She says:

> I know no cause
> Why I should welcome such a guest as grief,
> Save bidding farewell to so sweet a guest
> As my sweet Richard.

And from this scene to the end of the play Shakespeare enlists all our sympathy for Richard. Now, what is the reason of this right-about-face on the part of the poet?

It appears to me that Shakespeare began the play intending to present the vile and cruel Richard of tradition. But midway in the play he saw that there was no emotion, no pathos, to be got out of the traditional view. If Richard were a vile, scheming, heartless murderer, the loss of his crown and life would merely satisfy our sense of justice, but this outcome did not satisfy Shakespeare's desire for emotion, and particularly his desire for pathos,* and accordingly he veers round, says nothing more of Richard's vileness, lays stress upon his weakness and sufferings, discovers, too, all manner of amiable qualities in him, and so draws pity from us for his dethronement and murder.

The curious thing is that while Shakespeare is depicting Richard's heartlessness, he does his work badly; the traits, as I have shown, are crudely extravagant and even contradictory; but when he paints Richard's gentleness and amiability, he works like a master, every touch is infallible: he is painting himself.

It was natural for Shakespeare to sympathise deeply with Richard; he was still young when he wrote the play, young enough to remember vividly how he himself had been led astray by loose companions, and this formed a bond between them. At this time of his life this was Shakespeare's favourite subject: he treated it again in *Henry IV*, which is at once the epilogue to *Richard II* and a companion picture to it; for the theme of both plays is the same – youth yielding to unworthy companions – though the treatment in the earlier play is incomparably feebler than it became in *King Henry IV*. Bushy, Bagot, and Green, the favourites of Richard, are not painted as Shakespeare afterwards painted Falstaff and his followers. But partly because he had not yet attained to such objective treatment of character, Shakespeare identified himself peculiarly with Richard; and his painting of Richard is more intimate, more subtle, more self-revealing and pathetic than anything in *Henry IV*.

As I have already said, from the time when Richard appoints York as Regent, and leaves England, Shakespeare begins to think of himself as Richard, and from this moment to the end no one can help sympathising with the unhappy King. At this point, too, the character-drawing becomes, of a sudden, excellent. When Richard lands in England, he is given speech after speech, and all he says and does afterwards throws light, it seems to me, on Shakespeare's own nature. Let us mark each

---

* In the last scene of the last act of *Lear*, Albany says:

> This judgement of the heavens, that makes us tremble
> Touches us not with pity.

trait. First of all Richard is intensely, frankly emotional: he 'weeps for joy' to be in England again; 'weeping, smiling', he greets the earth of England, and is full of hope. 'The thief, the traitor', Bolingbroke, will not dare to face the light of the sun; for 'every man that Bolingbroke has in his pay', he cries exultantly, God hath given Richard a 'glorious angel; . . . Heaven still guards the right'. A moment later he hears from Salisbury that the Welshmen whom he had relied upon as allies are dispersed and fled. At once he becomes 'pale and dead'. From the height of pride and confidence he falls to utter hopelessness.

> All souls that will be safe fly from my side;
> For time hath set a blot upon my pride.

Aumerle asks him to remember who he is, and at once he springs from dejection to confidence again. He cries:

> Awake, thou sluggard majesty! thou sleepest.
> Is not the king's name forty thousand names?

The next moment Scroop speaks of cares, and forthwith fitful Richard is in the dumps once more. But this time his weakness is turned to resignation and sadness, and the pathos of this is brought out by the poet:

> Strives Bolingbroke to be as great as we?
> Greater he shall not be; if he serve God
> We'll serve him, too, and be his fellow so.
> Revolt our subjects? that we cannot mend;
> They break their faith to God, as well as us.
> Cry woe, destruction, ruin, loss, decay;
> The worst is death, and death will have his day.

Who does not hear Hamlet speaking in this memorable last line? Like Hamlet, too, this Richard is quick to suspect even his friends' loyalty. He guesses that Bagot, Bushy, and Green have made peace with Bolingbroke, and when Scroop seems to admit this, Richard is as quick as Hamlet to unpack his heart with words:

> O villains, vipers, damned without redemption!
> Dogs, easily won to fawn on any man!
> Snakes,

and so forth.

But as soon as he learns that his friends are dead he breaks out in a long lament for them which ranges over everything from worms to kings, and in its melancholy pessimism is the prototype of those meditations which Shakespeare has put in the mouth of nearly all his favourite characters. Who is not reminded of Hamlet's great monologue when he reads:

> For within the hollow crown,
> That rounds the mortal temples of a king,
> Keeps Death his court: and there the antic sits
> Scoffing his state, and grinning at his pomp;
> Allowing him a breath, a little scene
> To monarchise, be fear'd and kill with looks;
> Infusing him with self and vain conceit,
> As if this flesh, which walls about our life,
> Were brass impregnable; and, humour'd thus,
> Comes at the last, and with a little pin*
> Bores through his castle wall, and – farewell, King!

Let us take another two lines of this soliloquy:

> For God's sake, let us sit upon the ground
> And tell sad stories of the death of kings.

In the second scene of the third act of *Titus Andronicus* we find Titus saying to his daughter:

> I'll to thy closet; and go read with thee
> Sad stories chanced in the times of old.

Again, in the *Comedy of Errors*, Aegeon tells us that his life was prolonged:

> To tell sad stories of my own mishaps.

The similarity of these passages shows that in the very spring of life and heyday of the blood Shakespeare had in him a certain romantic melancholy which was developed later by the disappointments of life into the despairing of Macbeth and Lear.

When the Bishop calls upon Richard to act, the King's weathercock mind veers round again, and he cries:

* In Hamlet's famous soliloquy the pin is a 'bodkin'.

> This ague fit of fear is over-blown,
> An easy task it is to win our own.

But when Scroop tells him that York has joined with Bolingbroke, he believes him at once, gives up hope finally, and turns as if for comfort to his own melancholy fate:

> Beshrew thee, cousin, which didst lead me forth
> Of that sweet way I was in to despair!

That 'sweet way' of despair is Romeo's way, Hamlet's, Macbeth's and Shakespeare's way.

In the next scene Richard meets his foes, and at first plays the king. Shakespeare tells us that he looks like a king, that his eyes are as 'bright as an eagle's'; and this poetic admiration of state and place seems to have got into Richard's blood, for at first he declares that Bolingbroke is guilty of treason, and asserts that:

> My master, God omnipotent,
> Is mustering in his clouds, on our behalf,
> Armies of pestilence.

Of course, he gives in with fair words the next moment, and the next rages against Bolingbroke; and then comes the great speech in which the poet reveals himself so ingenuously that at the end of it the King he pretends to be, has to admit that he has talked but idly. I cannot help transcribing the whole of the passage, for it shows how easily Shakespeare falls out of this King's character into his own:

> What must the King do now? Must he submit?
> The King shall do it. Must he be depos'd?
> The King shall be contented: must he lose
> The name of king? O! God's name, let it go:
> I'll give my jewels for a set of beads;
> My gorgeous palace for a hermitage;
> My gay apparel for an alms-man's gown;
> My figur'd goblets for a dish of wood;
> My sceptre for a palmer's walking staff;
> My subjects for a pair of carved saints;
> And my large kingdom for a little grave,
> A little, little grave, an obscure grave: –
> Or I'll be buried in the King's highway,

> Some way of common trade, where subjects' feet
> May hourly trample on their sovereign's head:
> For on my heart they tread, now whilst I live;
> And, buried once, why not upon my head? –
> Aumerle, thou weep'st; my tender-hearted cousin! –
> We'll make foul weather with despised tears;
> Our sighs, and they, shall lodge the summer corn,
> And make a dearth in this revolting land.
> Or shall we play the wantons with our woes,
> And make some pretty match with shedding tears?
> As thus: – To drop them still upon one place,
> Till they have fretted us a pair of graves
> Within the earth; and, therein laid, – There lies
> Two kinsmen digg'd their graves with weeping eyes.
> Would not this ill do well? – Well, well, I see
> I talk but idly, and you mock at me. –
> Most mighty prince, my lord Northumberland,
> What says King Bolingbroke? will his majesty
> Give Richard leave to live till Richard die?
> You make a leg, and Bolingbroke says ay.

Everyone will admit that the poet himself speaks here, at least, from the words 'I'll give my jewels' to the words 'Would not this ill do well?' But the melancholy mood, the pathetic acceptance of the inevitable, the tender poetic embroidery now suit the King who is fashioned in the poet's likeness.

The next moment Richard revolts once more against his fate:

> Base court, where kings grow base,
> To come at traitors' calls, and do them grace.

And when Bolingbroke kneels to him he plays upon words, as Gaunt did a little earlier in the play, misery making sport to mock itself. He says:

> Up, cousin, up; your heart is up, I know,
> Thus high at least, although your knee be low –

and then he abandons himself to do 'what force will have us do'.

The Queen's wretchedness is next used to heighten our sympathy with Richard, and immediately afterwards we have that curious scene between the gardener and his servant which is merely youthful Shakespeare, for such a gardener and such a servant never yet existed. The scene* shows the extravagance of Shakespeare's love of hierarchy, and shows also that his power of realising character is as yet but slight. The abdication follows, when Richard in exquisite speech after speech unpacks his heavy heart. To the very last his irresolution comes to show as often as his melancholy. Bolingbroke is sharply practical:

> Are you contented to resign the crown?

Richard answers:

> Ay, no; no, ay; – for I must nothing be;
> Therefore, no, no, for I resign to thee.

When he is asked to confess his sins in public, he moves us all to pity:

> Must I do so? and must I ravel out
> My weaved up follies? Gentle Northumberland,
> If thy offences were upon record,
> Would it not shame thee, in so fair a troop,
> To read a lecture of them?

His eyes are too full of tears to read his own faults, and sympathy brings tears to our eyes also. Richard calls for a glass wherein to see his sins, and we are reminded of Hamlet, who advises the players to hold the mirror up to nature. He jests with his grief, too, in quick-witted retort, as Hamlet jests:

RICHARD　　　　　　　　　　　　Say that again.
> The shadow of my sorrow? Ha! let's see: –
> 'Tis very true, my grief lies all within;
> And these external manners of lament

---

* Coleridge gives this scene as an instance of Shakespeare's 'wonderful judgement'; the introduction of the gardener, he says, 'realises the thing', and, indeed, the introduction of a gardener would have this tendency, but not the introduction of this pompous, priggish philosopher togged out in old Adam's likeness. Here is the way this gardener criticises the King:

> All superfluous branches
> We lop away, that bearing boughs may live;
> Had he done so, himself had borne the crown,
> Which waste of idle hours hath quite thrown down.

> Are merely shadows to the unseen grief,
> That swells with silence in the tortur'd soul.

Hamlet touches the selfsame note:

> 'Tis not alone my inky cloak, good mother,
> Nor customary suits of solemn black,
> [. . .]
> But I have that within which passeth show;
> These but the trappings and the suits of woe.

In the fifth act, the scene between the Queen and Richard is used simply to move our pity. She says he is 'most beauteous', but all too mild, and he answers her:

> I am sworn brother, sweet,
> To grim necessity; and he and I
> Will keep a league till death.

He bids her take,

> As from my death-bed, my last living leave,

and for her consolation he turns again to the telling of romantic melancholy stories:

> In winter's tedious nights, sit by the fire
> With good old folks; and let them tell thee tales
> Of woeful ages long ago betid:
> And, ere thou bid good-night, to quit their grief,
> Tell thou the lamentable fall of me,
> And send the hearers weeping to their beds,
> For why; the senseless brands will sympathise
> The heavy accent of thy moving tongue.

I cannot copy this passage without drawing attention to the haunting music of the third line.

The scene in which York betrays his son to Bolingbroke and prays the king not to pardon but 'cut off' the offending member, is merely a proof, if proof were wanted, of Shakespeare's admiration of kingship and loyalty, which in youth, at least, often led him to silliest extravagance.

The dungeon scene and Richard's monologue in it are as characteristic

of Shakespeare as the similar scene in *Cymbeline* and the soliloquy of
Posthumus:

> RICHARD I have been studying how I may compare
> This prison where I live unto the world:
> And for because the world is populous,
> And here is not a creature but myself,
> I cannot do it; yet I'll hammer it out,
> My brain I'll prove the female to my soul
> My soul the father; and these two beget
> A generation of still breeding thoughts,
> And these same thoughts people this little world,
> In humours like the people of this world,
> For no thought is contented . . .

Here we have the philosopher playing with his own thoughts; but
soon the Hamlet-melancholy comes to tune the meditation to sadness,
and Shakespeare speaks to us directly:

> Thus play I in one person many people,
> And none contented: sometimes am I king;
> Then treasons make me wish myself a beggar,
> And so I am: then crushing penury
> Persuades me I was better when a king;
> Then am I king'd again; and by and by
> Think, that I am unking'd by Bolingbroke,
> And straight am nothing; but whate'er I be,
> Nor I nor any man that but man is
> With nothing shall be pleased, till he be eased
> With being nothing.

Later, one hears Kent's lament for Lear in Richard's words:

> How these vain weak nails
> May tear a passage through the flinty ribs
> Of this hard world, my ragged prison walls.

To Richard music is 'sweet music', as it is to all the characters that
are merely Shakespeare's masks, and the scene in which Hamlet asks
Guildenstern to 'play upon the pipe' is prefigured for us in Richard's
self-reproach:

> And here have I the daintiness of ear,
> To check time broke in a disordered string;
> But for the concord of my state and time,
> Had not an ear to hear my true time broke.

In the last three lines of this monologue which I am now about to quote, I can hear Shakespeare speaking as plainly as he spoke in Arthur's appeals; the feminine longing for love is the unmistakable note:

> Yet blessing on his heart that gives it me!
> For 'tis a sign of love; and love to Richard
> Is a strange brooch in this all-hating world.

And at the last, by killing the servant who assaults him, this Richard shows that he has the 'something desperate' in him of which Hamlet boasted.

The murderer's praise that this irresolute-weak and loving Richard is 'as full of valour as of royal blood' is nothing more than an excellent instance of Shakespeare's self-illusion. He comes nearer the fact in *Measure for Measure*, where the Duke, his other self, is shown to be 'an unhurtful opposite' too gentle-kind to remember an injury or punish the offender, and he rings the bell at truth's centre when, in *Julius Caesar*, his mask Brutus admits that he

> . . . carries anger as the flint bears fire
> Who much enforced shows a hasty spark
> And straight is cold again.

If a hasty blow were proof of valour then Walter Scott's Eachin in *The Fair Maid of Perth* would be called brave. But courage to be worth the name must be founded on stubborn resolution, and all Shakespeare's incarnations, and in especial this Richard, are as unstable as water.

The whole play is summed up in York's pathetic description of Richard's entrance into London:

> No man cried, God save him;
> No joyful tongue gave him his welcome home:
> But dust was thrown upon his sacred head;
> Which with such gentle sorrow he shook off –
> His face still combating with tears and smiles,
> The badges of his grief and patience –
> That had not God, for some strong purpose, steel'd

> The hearts of men, they must perforce have melted,
> And barbarism itself have pitied him.

This passage it seems to me both in manner and matter is as truly characteristic of Shakespeare as any that can be found in all his works: his loving pity for the fallen, his passionate sympathy with 'gentle sorrow' were never more perfectly expressed.

Pity, indeed, is the note of the tragedy, as it was in the Arthur-scenes in *King John*, but the knowledge of Shakespeare derived from *King John* is greatly widened by the study of *King Richard II*. In the Arthur of *King John* we found Shakespeare's exquisite pity for weakness, his sympathy with suffering, and, more than all, his girlish-tender love and desire of love. In *Richard II*, the weakness Shakespeare pities is not physical weakness, but mental irresolution and incapacity for action, and these Hamlet-weaknesses are accompanied by a habit of philosophic thought, and are enlivened by a nimble wit and great lyrical power. In Arthur Shakespeare is bent on revealing his qualities of heart, and in *Richard II* his qualities of mind, and that these two are but parts of the same nature is proved by the fact that Arthur shows great quickness of apprehension and felicity of speech, while Richard once or twice at least displays a tenderness of heart and longing for love worthy of Arthur.

It appears then that Shakespeare's nature even in hot, reckless youth was most feminine and affectionate, and that even when dealing with histories and men of action he preferred to picture irresolution and weakness rather than strength, and felt more sympathy with failure than with success.

5

Shakespeare's Men of Action continued: Hotspur, Prince Henry and Henry V

The conclusions we have already reached, will be borne out and strengthened in unexpected ways by the study of Hotspur – Shakespeare's master picture of the man of action. The setting sun of chivalry falling on certain figures threw gigantic shadows across Shakespeare's path, and of these figures no one deserved immortality better than Harry Percy. Though he is not introduced in *The Famous Victories of Henry V*, the old play which gave Shakespeare his roistering Prince and the first faint hint of Falstaff, Harry Percy lived in story and in oral tradition. His nickname itself is sufficient evidence of the impression he had made on the popular fancy. And both Prince Henry when mocking him, and his wife when praising him, bear witness to what were, no doubt, the accepted peculiarities of his character. Hotspur lived in the memory of men, we may be sure, with thick, hasty speech, and hot, impatient temper, and it is easy, I think, even at this late date, to distinguish Shakespeare's touches on the traditional portrait. It is for the reader to say whether Shakespeare blurred the picture, or bettered it.

Hotspur's first words to the King in the first act are admirable; they bring the brusque, passionate soldier vividly before us; but I am sure Shakespeare had the fact from history or tradition.

> My liege, I did deny no prisoners.
> But, I remember, when the fight was done,
> When I was dry with rage and extreme toil,
> Breathless and faint, leaning upon my sword,
> Came there a certain lord, neat, trimly dressed,
> Fresh as a bridegroom.

Hotspur's picture of this 'popinjay' with pouncet-box in hand, and 'perfumed like a milliner', is splendid self-revelation:

> he made me mad,
> To see him shine so brisk and smell so sweet,
> And talk so like a waiting gentlewoman.

But immediately afterwards Hotspur's defence of Mortimer shows the poet Shakespeare rather than the rude soldier who hates nothing more than 'mincing poetry'. The beginning is fairly good:

HOTSPUR   Revolted Mortimer!
> He never did fall off, my sovereign liege,
> But by the chance of war: to prove that true,
> Needs no more but one tongue for all those wounds,
> Those mouthed wounds which valiantly he took,
> When on the gentle Severn's sedgy bank . . .

This 'gentle Severn's sedgy bank' is too poetical for Hotspur; but what shall be said of his description of the river?

> Who then, affrighted with their bloody looks,
> Ran fearfully among the trembling reeds,
> And hid his crisp head in the hollow bank
> Blood-stained with these valiant combatants.

Shakespeare was still too young, too much in love with poetry to confine himself within the nature of Hotspur. But the character of Hotspur was so well known that Shakespeare could not long remain outside it. When the King cuts short the audience with the command to send back the prisoners, we find the passionate Hotspur again:

> And if the devil come and roar for them,
> I will not send them. – I will after straight,
> And tell him so: for I will ease my heart,
> Although it be with hazard of my head.

The last line strikes a false note; such a reflection throws cold water on the heat of passion, and that is not intended, for though reproved by his father Hotspur storms on:

>   Speak of Mortimer!
> 'Zounds! I will speak of him; and let my soul
> Want mercy, if I do not join with him . . .

The next long speech of Hotspur is mere poetic slush; he begins:

> Nay, then, I cannot blame his cousin king,
> That wish'd him on the barren mountains starve . . .

and goes on for thirty lines to reprove the conspirators for having put down 'Richard, that sweet lovely rose', and planted 'this thorn, Boling-broke'. This long speech retards the action, obscures the character of Hotspur, and only shows Shakespeare poetising without a flash of inspiration. Then comes Hotspur's famous speech about honour:

> By heaven, methinks it were an easy leap,
> To pluck bright honour from the pale-faced moon;
> Or dive into the bottom of the deep . . .

And immediately afterwards a speech in which his uncontrollable impatience and the childishness which always lurks in anger, find perfect expression. To soothe him, Worcester says he shall keep his prisoners; Hotspur bursts out:

> Nay, I will: that's flat.
> He said, he would not ransom Mortimer;
> Forbad my tongue to speak of Mortimer;
> But I will find him when he lies asleep,
> And in his ear I'll holla – 'Mortimer!' Nay,
> I'll have a starling shall be taught to speak
> Nothing but 'Mortimer', and give it him,
> To keep his anger still in motion.

No wonder Lord Worcester reproves him, and his father chides him as 'a wasp-stung and impatient fool', who will only talk and not listen. But again Hotspur breaks forth, and again his anger paints him to the life:

> Why, look you, I am whipped and scourged with rods,
> Nettled and stung with pismires, when I hear
> Of this vile politician, Bolingbroke.
> In Richard's time, – what do you call the place? –
> A plague upon 't – it is in Glostershire; –
> 'Twas where the madcap duke his uncle kept, – . . .

The very ecstasy of impatience and of puerile passionate temper has never been better rendered.

His soliloquy, too, in the beginning of scene 3, when he reads the letter which throws the cold light of reason on his enterprise, is excellent, though it repeats qualities we already knew in Hotspur, and does not reveal new ones:

> 'The purpose you undertake is dangerous'; – why, that's certain: 'tis dangerous to take a cold, to sleep, to drink; but I tell you, my lord fool, out of this nettle danger, we pluck this flower safety . . . What a frosty-spirited rogue is this! . . . O, I could divide myself and go to buffets, for moving such a dish of skimmed milk with so honourable an action! Hang him! Let him tell the King: we are prepared. I will set forward tonight.

But the topmost height of self-revealing is reached in the scene with his wife which immediately follows this. Lady Percy enters, and Hotspur greets her:

> How now, Kate? I must leave you within these two hours.

The lady's reply is too long and too poetical. Hotspur interrupts her by calling the servant and giving him orders. Then Lady Percy questions, and Hotspur avoids a direct answer, and little by little Shakespeare works himself into the characters till even Lady Percy lives for us:

> LADY   Come, come, you paraquito, answer me
>   Directly unto this question that I ask.
>   In faith, I'll break thy little finger, Harry,
>   An if thou wilt not tell me true.
>
> HOTSPUR   Away,
>   Away, you trifler! – Love? – I love thee not,
>   I care not for thee, Kate; this is no world
>   To play with mammets and to tilt with lips . . .

It shows a certain immaturity of art that Hotspur should introduce the theme of 'love', and not Lady Percy; but, of course, Lady Percy seizes on the word:

> LADY   Do you not love me? do you not, indeed,
>   Well, do not then; for since you love me not,
>   I will not love myself. Do you not love me?
>   Nay, tell me, if you speak in jest or no?
>
> HOTSPUR   Come, wilt thou see me ride?

> And when I am o' horseback, I will swear
> I love thee infinitely . . .

All this is superb; Hotspur's coarse contempt of love deepens our sense of his soldier-like nature and eagerness for action; but though the qualities are rendered magically the qualities themselves are few: Shakespeare still harps upon Hotspur's impatience; but even a soldier is something more than hasty temper, and disdain of love's dalliance. But the portrait is not finished yet. The first scene in the third act between Hotspur and Glendower is on this same highest level; Hotspur's impatience of Glendower's bragging at length finds an unforgettable phrase:

> GLEND. I can call spirits from the vasty deep.
> HOTSPUR Why, so can I, or so can any man;
> But will they come when you do call for them?

Then Hotspur disputes over the division of England; he wants a larger share than that allotted to him; the trait is typical, excellent; but the next moment Shakespeare effaces it. As soon as Glendower yields, Hotspur cries:

> I do not care; I'll give thrice so much land
> Away to any well-deserving friend;
> But in the way of bargain, mark ye me,
> I'll cavil on the ninth part of a hair . . .

This large generosity is a trait of Shakespeare and not of Hotspur; the poet cannot bear to lend his hero a tinge of meanness, or of avarice, and yet the character needs a heavy shadow or two, and no shadow could be more appropriate than this, for greed of land has always been a characteristic of the soldier-aristocrat.

Shakespeare is perfectly willing to depict Hotspur as scorning the arts. When Glendower praises poetry, Hotspur vows he'd 'rather be a kitten and cry mew . . . than a metre ballad-monger. . . . ' Nothing sets his teeth on edge 'so much as mincing poetry': and a little later he prefers the howling of a dog to music. When he is reproved by Lord Worcester for 'defect of manners, want of government, . . . pride, haughtiness, disdain', his reply is most characteristic:

> Well, I am schooled: good manners be your speed,
> Here come our wives, and let us take our leave.

He is too old to learn, and his self-assurance is not to be shaken; but though he hates schooling he will school his wife:

> Swear me, Kate, like a lady as thou art,
> A good mouth-filling oath; and leave, 'in sooth',
> And such protest of pepper-gingerbread
> To velvet guards and Sunday citizens.

This is merely a repetition of the trait shown in his first speech when he sneered at the popinjay-lord for talking in 'holiday and lady terms'. But not only does Shakespeare repeat well-known traits in Hotspur, he also uses him as a mere mouthpiece again and again, as he used him at the beginning in the poetic description of the Severn. The fourth act opens with a speech of Hotspur to Douglas, which is curiously illustrative of this fault:

> HOTSPUR Well said, my noble Scot, if speaking truth
>   In this fine age were not thought flattery,
>   Such attribution should the Douglas have,
>   As not a soldier of this season's stamp
>   Should go so general current through the world.
>   By God, I cannot flatter; I defy
>   The tongues of soothers; but a braver place
>   In my heart's love hath no man than yourself.
>   Nay, task me to my word; approve me, lord.

In the first five lines of this skimble-skamble stuff I hear Shakespeare speaking in his cheapest way; with the oath, however, he tries to get into the character again, and succeeds indifferently.

Immediately afterwards Hotspur is shocked by the news that his father is sick and has not even sent the promised assistance; struck to the heart by the betrayal, the hot soldier should now reveal his true character; one expects him to curse his father, and rising to the danger, to cry that he is stronger without traitors and faint-heart friends. But Shakespeare the philosopher is chiefly concerned with the effect of such news upon a rebel camp, and again he speaks through Hotspur:

> Sick now! droop now! this sickness doth infect
> The very life-blood of our enterprise;
> 'Tis catching hither, even to our camp.

Then Shakespeare pulls himself up and tries to get into Hotspur's character again by representing to himself the circumstance:

> He writes me here, that inward sickness –
> And that his friends by deputation could not
> So soon be drawn; nor did he think it meet –

and so forth to the question: ' . . . What say you to it?'

> WOR. Your father's sickness is a maim to us.
> HOTSPUR A perilous gash, a very limb lopped off: –

Shakespeare sees that he cannot go on exaggerating the injury – that is not Hotspur's line, is indeed utterly false to Hotspur's nature; and so he tries to stop himself and think of Hotspur:

> And yet, in faith, it's not; his present want
> Seems more than we shall find it: were it good
> To set the exact wealth of all our states
> All at one cast? to set so rich a main
> On the nice hazard of one doubtful hour?
> It were not good; for therein should we read
> The very bottom and the soul of hope,
> The very list, the very utmost bound
> Of all our fortunes.

After the first two lines, which Hotspur might have spoken, we have the sophistry of the thinker poetically expressed, and not one word from the hot, high-couraged soldier. Indeed, in the last four lines from the bookish 'we read' to the end, we have the gentle poet in love with desperate extremities. The passage must be compared with Othello's –

> Here is my journey's end, here is my butt,
> And very sea-mark of my utmost sail.

But at length when Worcester adds fear to danger Hotspur half finds himself:

> HOTSPUR   You strain too far.
> I rather of his absence make this use: –
> It lends a lustre, and more great opinion,
> A larger dare to our great enterprise,
> Than if the earl were here; for men must think,
> If we, without his help can make a head
> To push against the kingdom; with his help

> We shall o'erturn it topsy-turvy down. –
> Yet all goes well, yet all our joints are whole.

And this is all. The scene is designed, the situation constructed to show us Hotspur's courage: here, if anywhere, the hot blood should surprise us and make of danger the springboard of leaping hardihood. But this is the best Shakespeare can reach – this fainting, palefaced 'Yet all goes well, yet all our joints are whole.' The inadequacy, the feebleness of the whole thing is astounding. Milton had not the courage of the soldier, but he had more than this: he found better words for his Satan after defeat than Shakespeare found for Hotspur before the battle:

> What though the field be lost?
> All is not lost; the unconquerable will,
> And study of revenge, immortal hate,
> And courage never to submit or yield,
> And what is else not to be overcome;
> That glory never shall his wrath or might
> Extort from me.

When Shakespeare has to render Hotspur's impatience he does it superbly, when he has to render Hotspur's courage he fails lamentably.

In the third scene of this fourth act we have another striking instance of Shakespeare's shortcoming. Sir Walter Blount meets the rebels 'with gracious offers from the King', whereupon Hotspur abuses the King through forty lines; this is the kind of stuff:

> My father and my uncle and myself
> Did give him that same royalty he wears;
> And when he was not six and twenty strong,
> Sick in the world's regard, wretched and low,
> A poor unminded outlaw sneaking home,
> My father gave him welcome to the shore; . . .

and so on and on, like Hamlet, he unpacks his heart with words, till Blount cries:

> Tut, I came not to hear this.

Hotspur admits the reproof, but immediately starts off again:

> HOTSPUR   Then to the point.
> In short time after he deposed the king;
> Soon after that, deprived him of his life,

and so forth for twenty lines more, till Blount pulls him up again with the shrewd question:

> Shall I return this answer to the king?

Hotspur replies:

> Not so, Sir Walter; we'll withdraw awhile.
> Go to the king . . . .
> And in the morning early shall mine uncle
> Bring him our purposes; and so farewell.

And yet this Hotspur who talks interminably when he would do much better to keep quiet, assures us a little later that he has not well 'the gift of tongue', and again declares he's glad a messenger has cut him short, for 'I profess not talking'.

The truth is the real Hotspur did not talk much, but Shakespeare had the gift of the gab, if ever a man had, and Hotspur was a mouthpiece. It is worth noting that though the dramatist usually works himself into a character gradually, Hotspur is best presented in the earlier scenes: Shakespeare began the work with the Hotspur of history and tradition clear in his mind; but as he wrote he grew interested in Hotspur and identified himself too much with his hero, and so almost spoiled the portrait. This is well seen in Hotspur's end; Prince Henry has said he'd crop his budding honours and make a garland for himself out of them, and this is how the dying Hotspur answers him:

> O Harry, thou hast robbed me of my youth!
> I better brook the loss of brittle life
> Than those proud titles thou hast won of me;
> They wound my thoughts worse than thy sword my flesh: –
> But thought's the slave of life, and life time's fool,
> And time, that takes survey of all the world,
> Must have a stop. O, I could prophesy,
> But that the earthy and cold hand of death
> Lies on my tongue: – no, Percy, thou art dust,
> And food for –

Of course, Prince Henry concludes the phrase, and continues the Hamlet-like philosophic soliloquy:

p. HENRY   For worms, brave Percy: fare thee well, great heart! –
            Ill-weaved ambition, how much art thou shrunk!
            When that this body did contain a spirit,
            A kingdom for it was too small a bound;
            But now two paces of the vilest earth
            Is room enough: . . .

I have tried to do justice to this portrait of Hotspur, for Shakespeare never did a better picture of a man of action, indeed, as we shall soon see, he never did as well again. But take away from Hotspur the qualities given to him by history and tradition, the hasty temper, and thick stuttering speech, and contempt of women, and it will be seen how little Shakespeare added. He makes Hotspur hate 'mincing poetry', and then puts long poetic descriptions in his mouth; he paints the soldier despising 'the gift of tongue' and forces him to talk historic and poetic slush in and out of season; he makes the aristocrat greedy and sets him quarrelling with his associates for more land, and the next moment, when the land is given him, Hotspur abandons it without further thought; he frames an occasion calculated to show off Hotspur's courage, and then allows him to talk faint-heartedly, and finally, when Hotspur should die mutely, or with a bitter curse, biting to the last, Shakespeare's Hotspur loses himself in mistimed philosophic reflection and poetic prediction. Yet such is Shakespeare's magic of expression that when he is revealing the qualities which Hotspur really did possess, he makes him live for us with such intensity of life that no number of false strokes can obliterate the impression. It is only the critic working *sine ira et studio* who will find this portrait blurred by the intrusion of the poet's personality.

It is the companion picture of Prince Henry that shows as in a glass Shakespeare's poverty of conception when he is dealing with the distinctively manly qualities. In order to judge the matter fairly we must remember that Shakespeare did not create Prince Henry any more than he created Hotspur. In the old play entitled *The Famous Victories of Henry V*, and in the popular mouth, Shakespeare found roistering Prince Hal. The madcap Prince, like Harry Percy, was a creature of popular sympathy; his high spirits and extravagances, the vigorous way in which he had sown his wild oats, had taken the English fancy, the historic personage had been warmed to vivid life by the popular emotion. Shakespeare was personally interested in this princely hero. As we have seen, he dims Hotspur's portrait by intrusion of his own peculiarities; and in the case of Harry Percy, this temptation will be stronger.

The subject of the play, a young man of noble gifts led astray by loose companions, was a favourite subject with Shakespeare at this time; he had treated it already in *Richard II*; and he handled it here again with such zest that we are almost forced to believe in the tradition that Shakespeare himself in early youth had sown wild oats in unworthy company. Helped by a superb model, and in full sympathy with his theme, Shakespeare might be expected to paint a magnificent picture. But Prince Henry is anything but a great portrait; he is at first hardly more than a prig, and later a feeble and colourless replica of Hotspur. It is very curious that even in the comedy scenes with Falstaff Shakespeare has never taken the trouble to realise the Prince: he often lends him his own word-wit, and now and then his own high intelligence, but he never for a moment discovers to us the soul of his hero. He does not even tell us what pleasure Henry finds in living and carousing with Falstaff. Did the Prince choose his companions out of vanity, seeking in the Eastcheap tavern a court where he might throne it? Or was it the infinite humour of Falstaff which attracted him? Or did he break bounds merely out of high spirits, when bored by the foolish formalities of the palace? Shakespeare, one would have thought, would have given us the key to the mystery in the very first scene. But this scene, which paints Falstaff to the soul, tells us nothing of the Prince; but rather blurs a figure which everyone imagines he knows at least in outline. Prince Henry's first speech is excellent as description; Falstaff asks him the time of day; he replies:

> Thou art so fat-witted, with drinking of old sack, and unbuttoning thee after supper, and sleeping upon benches after noon, that thou hast forgotten to demand that truly which thou wouldst truly know . . .

This helps to depict Falstaff, but does not show us the Prince, for good-humoured contempt of Falstaff is universal; it has nothing individual and peculiar in it.

Then comes the speech in which the Prince talks of himself in Falstaff's strain as one of 'the moon's men' who 'resolutely snatch a purse of gold on Monday night', and 'most dissolutely spend it on Tuesday morning'. A little later he plays with Falstaff by asking: 'Where shall we take a purse tomorrow, Jack?' It looks as if the Prince were ripe for worse than mischief. But when Falstaff wants to know if he will make one of the band to rob on Gadshill, he cries out, as if indignant and surprised:

P. HENRY   Who, I rob? Ia thief? Not I, by my faith.
FALSTAFF   There's neither honesty, manhood, nor good fellowship in thee, nor thou earnest not of the blood royal, if thou darest not stand for ten shillings.
P. HENRY   Well then, once in my days I'll be a madcap.
FALSTAFF   Why, that's well said.
P. HENRY   Well, come what will, I'll tarry at home.

He is only persuaded at length by Poins's proposal to rob the robbers. It may be said that these changes of the Prince are natural in the situation: but they are too sudden and unmotived; they are like the nodding of the mandarin's head – they have no meaning; and surely, after the Prince talks of himself as one of 'the moon's men', it would be more natural of him, when the direct proposal to rob is made, not to show indignant surprise, which seems forced or feigned; but to talk as if repenting a previous folly. The scene, in so far as the Prince is concerned, is badly conducted. When he yields to Poins and agrees to rob Falstaff, his words are: 'Yea, but I doubt they will be too hard for us', – a phrase which hardly shows wild spirits or high courage, or even the faculty of judging men, and the soliloquy which ends the scene lamely enough is not the Prince's, but Shakespeare's, and unfortunately Shakespeare the poet, and not Shakespeare the dramatist:

P. HENRY   I know you all and will awhile uphold
           The unyoked humour of your idleness.
           Yet herein will I imitate the sun,
           Who doth permit the base contagious clouds
           To smother up his beauty from the world,
           That, when he please again to be himself,
           Being wanted, he may be more wondered at,
           By breaking through the foul and ugly mists
           Of vapours, that did seem to strangle him. . . .

If we could accept this stuff we should take Prince Henry for the prince of prigs; but it is impossible to accept it, and so we shrug our shoulders with the regret that the madcap Prince of history is not illuminated for us by Shakespeare's genius. In this *First Part of Henry*

IV, when the Prince is not calling names with Falstaff, or playing prig, he either shows us a quality of Harry Percy or of Shakespeare himself. Everyone remembers the scene when Falstaff, carrying Percy's corpse, meets the Princes, and tells them he has killed Percy:

P. JOHN   This is the strangest tale that e'er I heard.
P. HENRY This is the strangest fellow, brother John. –
          Come, bring your luggage nobly on your back:
          For my part, if a lie may do thee grace,
          I'll gild it with the happiest terms I have.

Both in manner and in matter these last two lines are pure Shakespeare, and Shakespeare speaks to us, too, when Prince Henry gives up Douglas to his pleasure 'ransomless and free'. But not only does the poet lend the soldier his own sentiments and lilt of phrase, he also presents him to us as a shadowy replica of Hotspur, even during Hotspur's lifetime. We have already noticed Hotspur's admirable answer when Glendower brags that he can call spirits from the vasty deep:

HOTSPUR   Why, so can I, or so can any man;
          But will they come, when you do call for them?

The same love of truth is given to Prince Henry in the previous act:

FALSTAFF Owen, Owen, – the same; – and his son-in-law, Mortimer;
          and old Northumberland; and that sprightly Scot of Scots,
          Douglas, that runs o' horseback up a hill perpendicular, –
P. HENRY He that rides at high speed, and with his pistol kills a
          sparrow flying.
FALSTAFF You have hit it.
P. HENRY So did he never the sparrow.

But this frank contempt of lying is not the only or the chief characteristic possessed by Hotspur and Harry Percy in common. Hotspur disdains the Prince:

HOTSPUR   Where is his son,
          The nimble-footed mad-cap Prince of Wales,
          And his comrades that daffed the world aside
          And bid it pass?

and the Prince mimics and makes fun of Hotspur:

P. HENRY   He that kills me some six or seven dozen of Scots at a
             breakfast, washes his hands and says to his wife, 'Fie upon
             this quiet life! I want work.'

Then Hotspur brags of what he will do when he meets his rival:

HOTSPUR   Once ere night
             I will embrace him with a soldier's arm,
             That he shall shrink under my courtesy.

And in precisely the same strain Prince Henry talks to his father:

P. HENRY   The time will come
             That I shall make this northern youth exchange
             His glorious deeds for my indignities.

It is true that Prince Henry on more than one occasion praises Hotspur,
while Hotspur is content to praise himself, but the differentiation is too
slight to be significant: such as it is, it is well seen when the two heroes
meet.

HOTSPUR My name is Harry Percy.
P. HENRY   Why, then I see
             A very valiant rebel of that name.

but Prince Henry immediately doffs this kingly mood to imitate Hotspur. He goes on:

             I am the Prince of Wales, and think not, Percy,
             To share with me in glory any more;
             Two stars keep not their motion in one sphere,
             Nor can our England brook a double reign
             Of Harry Percy and the Prince of Wales . . .

And so the bombast rolls, and one brags against the other like systole
and diastole which balance each other in the same heart. But the worst
of the matter is, that Prince Henry and Hotspur, as we have already
noticed, have both the same soul and the same inspiring motive in love
of honour. They both avow this again and again, though Hotspur finds
the finer expression for it when he cries that he will 'pluck bright
honour from the pale-faced moon'.

   To the student of the play it really looks as if Shakespeare could not
imagine any other incentive to noble or heroic deeds but this love of

glory: for nearly all the other serious characters in the play sing of honour in the same key. King Henry IV envies Northumberland

> A son who is the theme of honour's tongue,

and declares that Percy hath got 'never-dying honour against renowned Douglas'. The Douglas, too, can find no other word with which to praise Hotspur – 'thou art the king of honour': even Vernon, a mere secondary character, has the same mainspring: he says to Douglas:

> If well-respected honour bid me on,
> I hold as little counsel with weak fear
> As you or any Scot that this day lives.

Falstaff himself declares that nothing 'pricks him on but honour', and bragging Pistol admits that 'honour is cudgelled' from his weary limbs. The French, too, when they are beaten by Henry V all bemoan their shame and loss of honour, and have no word of sorrow for their ruined homesteads and outraged women and children. The Dauphin cries:

> Reproach and everlasting shame
> Sits mocking in our plumes.

And Bourbon echoes him:

> Shame and eternal shame, nothing but shame.

It is curious that Bourbon falls upon the same thought which animated Hotspur. Just before the decisive battle Hotspur cries:

> O, gentlemen! the time of life is short;
> To spend that shortness basely were too long.

And when the battle turns against the French, Bourbon exclaims:

> The devil take order now! I'll to the throng:
> Let life be short; else shame will be too long.

As Jaques in *As You Like It* says of the soldier: they are 'jealous in honour' and all seek 'the bubble reputation, even in the cannon's mouth'.

It is only in Shakespeare that men have no other motive for brave deeds but love of honour, no other fear but that of shame with which to overcome the dread of death. We shall see later that the desire of fame was the inspiring motive of his own youth.

In the *Second Part of King Henry IV* there is very little told us of Prince

Henry; he only appears in the second act, and in the fourth and fifth; and in all he is the mouthpiece of Shakespeare and not the roistering Prince: yet on his first appearance there are traces of characterisation, as when he declares that his 'appetite is not princely', for he remembers 'the poor creature, small beer', whereas in the last act he is merely the poetic prig. Let us give the best scene first:

P. HENRY Shall I tell thee one thing, Poins?
          [. . .]
P. HENRY Marry, I tell thee, – it is not meet that I should be sad, now
          my father is sick: albeit I could tell to thee – as to one it
          pleases me, for fault of a better, to call my friend – I could
          be sad, and sad, indeed, too.
POINS   Very hardly upon such a subject.
P. HENRY By this hand, thou think'st me as far in the devil's book as
          thou and Falstaff for obduracy and persistency: let the end
          try the man. But I tell thee, my heart bleeds inwardly that
          my father is so sick; and keeping such vile company as thou
          art hath in reason taken from me all ostentation of sorrow.
POINS   The reason?
P. HENRY What would'st thou think of me if I should weep?
POINS   I would think thee a most princely hypocrite.
P. HENRY It would be every man's thought; and thou art a blessed
          fellow to think as every man thinks; never a man's thought
          in the world keeps the roadway better than thine: every
          man would think me an hypocrite indeed. And what accites
          your most worshipful thought to think so?
POINS   Why, because you have been so lewd, and so much en-
          graffed to Falstaff.

By far the best thing in this page – the contempt for every man's thought as certain to be mistaken – is, I need hardly say, pure Shakespeare. Exactly the same reflection finds a place in *Hamlet*; the student-thinker tells us of a play which in his opinion, and in the opinion of the best judges, was excellent, but which was only acted once, for it 'pleased not the million; 'twas caviare to the general'. Very early in life Shakespeare made the discovery, which all men of brains make sooner or later, that the thoughts of the million are worthless, and the judgement and taste of the million are execrable.

There is nothing worthy to be called character-drawing in this scene;

but there's just a hint of it in the last remark of Poins. According to his favourite companion the Prince was very 'lewd', and yet Shakespeare never shows us his lewdness in action; does not 'moralise' it as Jaques or Hamlet would have been tempted to do. It is just mentioned and passed over lightly. It is curious, too, that Shakespeare's *alter ego*, Jaques, was also accused of lewdness by the exiled Duke; Vincentio, too, another incarnation of Shakespeare, was charged with lechery by Lucio; but in none of these cases does Shakespeare dwell on the failing. Shakespeare seems to have thought reticence the better part in regard to certain sins of the flesh. But it must be remarked that it is only when his heroes come into question that he practises this restraint: he is content to tell us casually that Prince Henry was a sensualist; but he shows us Falstaff and Doll Tearsheet engaged at lips' length. To put it briefly, Shakespeare attributes lewdness to his impersonations, but will not emphasise the fault by instances. Nor will Shakespeare allow his 'madcap Prince' even to play 'drawer' with hearty goodwill. While consenting to spy on Falstaff in the tavern, the Prince tells Poins that 'from a Prince to a prentice' is 'a low transformation', and scarcely has the fun commenced when he is called to the wars and takes his leave in these terms:

P. HENRY   By Heaven, Poins, I feel me much to blame,
            So idly to profane the precious time
            When tempest of commotion, like the south
            Borne with black vapour, doth begin to melt
            And drop upon our bare, unarmed heads.

The first two lines are priggish, and the last three mere poetic balderdash. But it is in the fourth act, when Prince Henry is watching by the bedside of his dying father, that Shakespeare speaks through him without disguise:

        Why doth the crown lie there upon his pillow
        Being so troublesome a bedfellow?
        O polished perturbation! golden care!
        That keep'st the ports of slumber open wide
        To many a watchful night! – Sleep with it now,
        Yet not so sound and half so deeply sweet
        As he whose brow with homely biggin bound
        Snores out the watch of night.

In the third act we have King Henry talking in precisely the same way:

> O sleep, O gentle sleep,
> Nature's soft nurse, how have I frighted thee? . . .
> [. . .]
> Wilt thou upon the high and giddy mast
> Seal up the ship-boy's eyes, and rock his brains
> In cradle of the rude imperious surge. . . .

The truth is that in both these passages, as in a hundred similar ones, we find Shakespeare himself praising sleep as only those tormented by insomnia can praise it.

When his father reproaches him with 'hunger for his empty chair', this is how Prince Henry answers:

> O pardon me, my liege, but for my tears,
> The moist impediments unto my speech,
> I had forestalled this dear and deep rebuke.
> Ere you with grief had spoke and I had heard
> The course of it so far. . . .

It might be Alfred Austin writing to Lord Salisbury – 'the moist imped-iments', forsooth – and the daredevil young soldier goes on like this for forty lines.

The only memorable thing in the fifth act is the new king's con-temptuous dismissal of Falstaff: I think it appalling at least in matter:

> I know thee not, old man: fall to thy prayers;
> How ill white hairs become a fool and jester!
> I have long dreamed of such a kind of man,
> So surfeit-swelled, so old and so profane;
> But being awake I do despise my dream.
> [. . .]
> Reply not to me with a fool-born jest,
> Presume not that I am the thing I was;
> [. . .]
> Till then, I banish thee on pain of death,
> As I have done the rest of my misleaders,
> Not to come near our person by ten mile.

In the old play, *The Famous Victories*, the sentence of banishment is pronounced; but this bitter contempt for the surfeit-swelled, profane old man is Shakespeare's. It is true that he mitigates the severity of the sentence in characteristic generous fashion: the King says:

> For competence of life I will allow you
> That lack of means enforce you not to evil:
> And as we hear you do reform yourselves,
> We will, according to your strength and qualities,
> Give you advancement.

There is no mention in the old play of this 'competence of life'. But in spite of this generous forethought the sentence is painfully severe, and Shakespeare meant every word of it, for immediately afterwards the Chief Justice orders Falstaff and his company to the Fleet prison; and in *King Henry V* we are told that the King's condemnation broke Falstaff's heart and made the old jester's banishment eternal. To find Shakespeare more severe in judgement than the majority of spectators and readers is so astonishing, so singular a fact, that it cries for explanation. I think there can be no doubt that the tradition which tells us that Shakespeare in his youth played pranks in low company finds further corroboration here. He seems to have resented his own ignominy and the contemptuous estimate put upon him by others somewhat extravagantly.

> Presume not that I am the thing I was;

– is a sentiment put again and again in Prince Henry's mouth; he is perpetually assuring us of the change in himself, and the great results which must ensue from it. It is this distaste for his own loose past and 'his misleaders', which makes Shakespeare so singularly severe towards Falstaff. As we have seen, he was the reverse of severe with Angelo in *Measure for Measure*, though in that case there was better ground for harshness. *Measure for Measure*, it is true, was written six or seven years later than *Henry IV*, and the tragedy of Shakespeare's life separates the two plays. Shakespeare's ethical judgement was more inclined to severity in youth and early manhood than it was later when his own sufferings had deepened his sympathies, and he had been made 'pregnant to good pity', to use his own words, 'by the art of knowing and feeling sorrows'. But he would never have treated old Jack Falstaff as harshly as he did had he not regretted the results, at least, of his own youthful errors. It looks as if Shakespeare, like other weak men, were filled with a desire to throw the blame on his 'misleaders'. He certainly exulted in their punishment.

It is difficult for me to write at length about the character of the King in *Henry V*, and fortunately it is not necessary. I have already pointed out the faults in the painting of Prince Henry with such fullness that I may be absolved from again dwelling on similar weakness where it is even more obvious than it was in the two parts of *Henry IV*. But something I must say, for the critics in both Germany and England are agreed that '*Henry V* must certainly be regarded as Shakespeare's ideal of manhood in the sphere of practical achievement'. Without an exception they have all buttered this drama with extravagant praise as one of Shakespeare's masterpieces, though in reality it is one of the worst pieces of work he ever did, almost as bad as *Titus Andronicus* or *Timon* or *The Taming of the Shrew*. Unfortunately for the would-be judges, Coleridge did not guide their opinions of *Henry V*; he hardly mentioned the play, and so they all write the absurdest nonsense about it, praising because praise of Shakespeare has come to be the fashion, and also no doubt because his bad work is more on the level of their intelligence than his good work.

It can hardly be denied that Shakespeare identified himself as far as he could with Henry V. Before the King appears he is praised extravagantly, as Posthumus was praised, but the eulogy befits the poet better than the soldier. The Archbishop of Canterbury says:

> . . . When he speaks,
> The air, a charter'd libertine, is still,
> And the mute wonder lurketh in men's ears
> To steal his sweet and honey'd sentences.

The Bishop of Ely goes even further in excuse:

> . . . The prince obscured his contemplation
> Under the veil of wildness.

And this is how the soldier-king himself talks:

> My learned lord, we pray you to proceed
> And justly and religiously unfold
> Why the law Salique that they have in France
> Or should, or should not bar us in our claim;
> And God forbid, my dear and faithful lord,
> That you should fashion, wrest, or bow your reading . . .

All this is plainly Shakespeare and Shakespeare at his very worst; and there are hundreds of lines like these, jewelled here and there by an unforgetable phrase, as when the Archbishop calls the bees: 'The singing masons building roofs of gold'. The reply made by the King when the Dauphin sends him the tennis balls has been greatly praised for manliness and modesty; it begins:

> We are glad the Dauphin is so pleasant with us;
> His present and your pains we thank you for:
> When we have match'd our rackets to these balls,
> We will, in France, by God's grace, play a set
> Shall strike his father's crown into the hazard.

The first line is most excellent, but Shakespeare found it in the old play, and the bragging which follows is hardly bettered by the pious imprecation.

Nor does the scene with the conspirators seem to me any better. The soldier-king would not have preached at them for sixty lines before condemning them. Nor would he have sentenced them with this extraordinary mixture of priggishness and pious pity:

K. HENRY God quit you in his mercy. Hear your sentence.
      [. . .]
      Touching our person seek we no revenge;
      But we our kingdom's safety must so tender,
      Whose ruin you have sought, that to her laws
      We do deliver you. Get you therefore hence,
      Poor miserable wretches, to your death,
      The task whereof, God of His mercy give
      You patience to endure, and true repentance
      Of all your dear offences!

This 'poor miserable wretches' would go better with a generous pardon, and such forgiving would be more in Shakespeare's nature. Throughout this play the necessity of speaking through the soldier-king embarrasses the poet, and the infusion of the poet's sympathy and emotion makes the puppet ridiculous. Henry's speech before Harfleur has been praised on all hands; not by the professors and critics merely, but by those who deserve attention. Carlyle finds deathless valour in the saying: 'Ye, good yeomen, whose limbs were made in England', and not deathless valour merely, but 'noble patriotism' as well; 'a true English heart breathes, calm and strong through the whole business . . . this man (Shakespeare) too had a right stroke in him, had it come to that.' I find no valour in it, deathless or otherwise; but the make-believe of valour, the completest proof that valour was absent. Here are the words:

K. HENRY   Once more unto the breach, dear friends, once more;
                        Or close the wall up with our English dead.
                        In peace there's nothing so becomes a man
                        As modest stillness and humility:
                        But when the blast of war blows in our ears,
                        Then imitate the action of the tiger;
                        Stiffen the sinews, summon up the blood,
                        Disguise fair nature with hard-favour'd rage;
                        Then lend the eye a terrible aspect,
                        Let it pry through the portage of the head
                        Like the brass cannon; let the brow o'erwhelm it
                        As fearfully as doth a galled rock
                        O'erhang and jutty his confounded base . . .

And so on for another twenty lines. Now consider this stuff: first comes the reflection, more suitable to the philosopher than the man of action, 'in peace there's nothing so becomes a man . . . '; then the soldier-king wishes his men to 'imitate' the tiger's looks, to 'disguise fair nature', and 'lend the eye a terrible aspect'. But the man who feels the tiger's rage tries to control the aspect of it: he does not put on the frown – that's Pistol's way. The whole thing is mere poetic description of how an angry man looks and not of how a brave man feels, and that it should have deceived Carlyle, surprises me. The truth is that as soon as Shakespeare has to find, I will not say a magical expression for courage, but even an adequate and worthy expression, he fails absolutely. And is the patriotism in 'Ye, good yeomen, whose limbs were made in England' a 'noble patriotism'? or is it the simplest, the crudest, the least justifiable form of patriotism? There is a noble patriotism founded on the high and generous things done by men of one's own blood, just as there is the vain and empty self-glorification of 'limbs made in England', as if English limbs were better than those made in Timbuktu.

In the third scene of the fourth act, just before the battle, Henry talks at his best, or rather Shakespeare's best: and we catch the true accent of courage. Westmoreland wishes

                              . . . That we now had here
                        But one ten thousand of those men in England
                        That do no work today!

but Henry lives on a higher plane:

> No, my fair cousin:
> If we are marked to die, we are enow
> To do our country loss; and if to live,
> The fewer men the greater share of honour.

But this high-couraged sentiment is taken almost word for word from Holinshed. The rest of the speech shows us Shakespeare, as a splendid rhetorician, glorifying glory; now and then the rhetoric is sublimated into poetry:

> We few, we happy few, we band of brothers,
> For he today that sheds his blood with me
> Shall be my brother; be he ne'er so vile,
> This day shall gentle his condition.

Shakespeare's chief ambition about this time was to get a coat of arms for his father, and so gentle his condition. In all the play not one word of praise for the common archers, who won the battle; no mention save of the gentle.

Again and again in *Henry V* the dissonance of character between the poet and his soldier-puppet jars upon the ears, and this dissonance is generally characteristic. For example, in the third act Shakespeare, through King Henry, expressly charges his soldiers that 'there be nothing compelled from the villages, nothing taken but paid for, none of the French upbraided or abused in disdainful language; for when lenity and cruelty play for a kingdom, the gentler gamester is the soonest winner.' Wise words, not yet learned even by statesmen; drops of wisdom's life-blood from the heart of gentle Shakespeare. But an act later, when the battle is over, on the mere news that the French have reinforced their scattered men, Henry V, with tears in his eyes for the Duke of York's death, gives orders to kill the prisoners:

> Then every soldier kill his prisoners;
> Give the word through.

The puppet is not even human: mere wood!

In the fifth act King Henry takes on the voice and nature of buried Hotspur. He woos Katherine exactly as Hotspur talked to his wife: he cannot 'mince' it in love, he tells her, in Hotspur's very words; but is forthright plain; like Hotspur he despises verses and dancing; like

Hotspur he can brag, too; finds it as 'easy' to conquer kingdoms as to speak French; can 'vault into his saddle with his armour on his back'; he is no carpet-soldier; he never 'looks in his glass for love of anything he sees there', and to make the likeness complete he disdains those 'fellows of infinite tongue, that can rhyme themselves into ladies' favours . . . a speaker is but a prater; a rhyme is but a ballad'. But if Shakespeare had had any vital sympathy for soldiers and men of action he would not have degraded Henry V in this fashion, into a feeble replica of the traditional Hotspur. In those narrow London streets by the river he must have rubbed shoulders with great adventurers; he knew Essex; had bowed to Raleigh at the Court; must have heard of Drake: inclination was lacking, not models. He might even have differentiated between Prince Henry and Hotspur without going outside his history-books; but a most curious point is that he preferred to smooth away their differences and accentuate the likeness. As a mere matter of fact Hotspur was very much older than Prince Henry, for he fought at Otterbourne in 1388, the year of the prince's birth; but Shakespeare purposely and explicitly makes them both youths. The King, speaking of Percy to Prince Henry, says:

> And being no more in debt to years than thou. . . .

It would have been wiser, I cannot but think, and more dramatic for Shakespeare to have left the hot-headed Percy as the older man who, in spite of years, is too impatient-quick to look before he leaps, while giving the youthful Prince the calm reflection and impersonal outlook which necessarily belong to a great winner of kingdoms. The dramatist could have further differentiated the rivals by making Percy greedy; he should not only have quarrelled with his associates over the division of the land, but insisted on obtaining the larger share, and even then have grumbled as if aggrieved; the soldier aristocrat has always regarded broad acres as his especial reward. On the other hand, Prince Henry should have been open-handed and carelessly-generous, as the patron of Falstaff was likely to be. Further, Hotspur might have been depicted as inordinately proud of his name and birth; the provincial aristocrat usually is, whereas Henry, the Prince, would surely have been too certain of his own qualities to need adventitious aids to pride. Percy might have been shown to us raging over imaginary slights; Worcester says he was 'governed by a spleen'; while the Prince should have been given that high sense of honour and insatiate love of fame which were the poles of chivalry. Finally, the dramatist might have painted Hotspur, the soldier, as disdainful of women and the arts of music and poetry, while gracing Prince Henry with a wider culture and sympathy.

If I draw attention to such obvious points it is only to show how incredibly careless Shakespeare was in making the conqueror a poor copy of the conquered. He was drawn to Hotspur a little by his quickness and impatience; but he was utterly out of sympathy with the fighter, and never took the trouble even to think of the qualities which a leader of men must possess.

6

Shakespeare's Men of Action concluded:
King Henry VI and Richard III

I think it hardly necessary to extend this review of Shakespeare's historical plays by subjecting the Three Parts of *King Henry VI* and *Richard III* to a detailed and minute criticism. Yet if I passed them over without mention it would probably be assumed that they made against my theory, or at least that I had some more pertinent reason for not considering them than their relative unimportance. In fact, however, they help to buttress my argument, and so at the risk of being tedious I shall deal with them, though as briefly as possible. Coleridge doubted whether Shakespeare had had anything to do with the *First Part of Henry VI*, but his fellow-actors, Heminge and Condell, placed the Three Parts of *King Henry VI* in the first collected edition of Shakespeare's plays, and our latest criticism finds good reasons to justify this contemporary judgement. Mr Swinburne writes: 'The last battle of Talbot seems to me as undeniably the master's work as the scene in the Temple Gardens, or the courtship of Margaret by Suffolk'; and it would be easy to prove that much of what the dying Mortimer says is just as certainly Shakespeare's work as any of the passages referred to by Mr Swinburne. Like most of those who are destined to reach the heights, Shakespeare seems to have grown slowly, and even at twenty-eight or thirty years of age his grasp of character was so uncertain, his style so little formed, so apt to waver from blank verse to rhyme, that it is difficult to determine exactly what he did write. We may take it, I think, as certain that he wrote more than we who have his mature work in mind are inclined to ascribe to him.

The *Second Part of King Henry VI* is a poetic revision of the old play entitled *The First Part of the Contention betwixt the Two Famous Houses of Yorke and Lancaster*, and so forth. It is now generally agreed that Shakespeare's hand can be traced in the old drama, and with especial certainty in the comic scenes wherein Cade and his followers play the chief parts. Notwithstanding this, the revision was most thorough. Half the lines in the *Second Part of Henry VI* are new, and by far the greater number of these are now ascribed to Shakespeare on good grounds. But some of the changes are for the worse, and as my argument does not stand in need of corroboration, I prefer to assume nothing, and shall therefore confine myself to pointing out that whoever revised *The Contention* did it, in the main, as we should have expected our youthful Shakespeare to do it. For example, when Humphrey of Gloster is accused of devising 'strange torments for offenders', he answers in the old play:

> Why, 'tis well known that whilst I was Protector,
> Pitie was all the fault that was in me,

and the gentle reviser adds to this:

> For I should melt at an offender's tears,
> And lowly words were ransom for their fault.

Besides, the reviser adds a great deal to the part of the weak King with the evident object of making his helplessness pathetic. He gives Henry, too, his sweetest phrases, and when he makes him talk of bewailing Gloster's case 'with sad unhelpful tears' we catch the very cadence of Shakespeare's voice. But he does not confine his emendations to the speeches of one personage: the sorrows of the lovers interest him as their affection interested him in the *First Part of Henry VI*, and the farewell words of Queen Margaret to Suffolk are especially characteristic of our gentle poet:

> Oh, go not yet; even thus two friends condemned
> Embrace and kiss and take ten thousand leaves,
> Loather a hundred times to part than die.
> Yet now farewell; and farewell life with thee.

This reminds me almost irresistibly of Juliet's words when parting with Romeo, and of Imogen's words when Posthumus leaves her. Throughout the play Henry is the poet's favourite, and in the gentle King's lament for Gloster's death we find a peculiarity of Shakespeare's art. It was a part of the cunning of his exquisite sensibility to invent a new word whenever he was deeply moved, the intensity of feeling clothing itself aptly in a novel epithet or image. A hundred examples of this might be given, such as 'The multitudinous seas incarnadine'; and so we find here 'paly lips'. The passage is:

> Fain would I go to chafe his paly lips
> With twenty thousand kisses and to drain
> Upon his face an ocean of salt tears,
> To tell my love unto his dumb deaf trunk
> And with my finger feel his hand unfeeling.

It must be noticed, too, that in this *Second Part* the reviser begins to show himself as something more than the sweet lyric poet. He transposes scenes in order to intensify the interest, and where enemies meet, like Clifford and York, instead of making them rant in mere blind hatred, he allows them to show a generous admiration of each other's qualities; in sum, we find here the germs of that dramatic talent which was so soon to bear such marvellous fruit. No better example of Shakespeare's growth in dramatic power and humour could be found than the way he revises the scenes with Cade. It is very probable, as I have said, that the first sketch was his; when one of Cade's followers declares that Cade's 'breath stinks', we are reminded that Coriolanus spoke in the same terms of the Roman rabble. But though it is his own work, Shakespeare evidently takes it up again with the keenest interest, for he adds inimitable touches. For instance, in the first scene, where the two rebels, George Bevis and John Holland, talk of Cade's rising and his intention to set a 'new nap upon the commonwealth', George's remark:

> Oh, miserable age! virtue is not regarded in handicraftsmen –

is an addition, and may be compared with Falstaff's:

> there is no virtue extant.

John answers:

> The nobility think scorn to go in leather aprons,

which is in the first sketch. But George's reply –

> Nay, more; the King's Council are no good workmen –

is only to be found in the revised version. The heightened humour of that 'Oh, miserable age! virtue is not regarded in handicraftsmen', assures us that the reviser was Shakespeare.

What is true of the *Second Part* is true in the main of the *Third Part of King Henry VI*. Shakespeare's revisions are chiefly the revisions of a lyric poet, and he scatters his emendations about without much regard for character. In the Third Part, as in the Second, however, he transposes scenes, gives deeper life to the marionettes, and in various ways quickens the dramatic interest. This Third Part resembles *King John* in some respects and a similar inference can be drawn from it. As in *King John* we have the sharply contrasted figures of the Bastard and Arthur, so in this *Third Part* there are two contrasted characters, Richard Duke of Gloster and King Henry VI, the one a wild beast whose life is action, and who knows neither fear, love, pity, nor touch of any scruple; the other, a saint-like King whose worst fault is gentle weakness. In *The True Tragedie of Richard*, the old play on which this *Third Part* was founded, the character of Richard is powerfully sketched, even though the human outlines are sometimes confused by his devilish malignity. Shakespeare takes this character from the old play, and alters it but very slightly. Indeed, the most splendid piece of character-revealing in his Richard is to be found in the old play:

> I had no father, I am like no father,
> I have no brother, I am like no brother;
> And this word *Love*, which greybeards call divine,
> Be resident in men like one another,
> And not in me: – I am myself alone.

The Satanic energy of this outburst proclaims its author, Marlowe.* Shakespeare copies it word for word, only omitting with admirable art the first line. Indeed, though he alters the speeches of Richard and improves them, he does nothing more; he adds no new quality; his Richard is the Richard of *The True Tragedie*. But King Henry may be regarded as Shakespeare's creation. In the old play the outlines of Henry's character are so feebly, faintly sketched that he is scarcely recognisable, but with two or three touches Shakespeare makes the saint a living man. This King is happier in prison than in his palace; this is how he speaks to his keeper, the Lieutenant of the Tower:

> Nay, be thou sure, I'll well requite thy kindness,
> For that it made my imprisonment a pleasure;

---

* Mr Swinburne was the first, I believe, to attribute this passage to Marlowe; he praises the verses, too, as they deserve; but as I had written the above before reading his work, I let it stand.

> Ay, such a pleasure as encaged birds
> Conceive, when, after many moody thoughts,
> At last by notes of household harmony
> They quite forget their loss of liberty.

Just as the bird runs a little before he springs from the earth and takes flight, so Shakespeare often writes, as in this instance, an awkward weak line or two before his song-wings move with freedom. But the last four lines are peculiarly his; his the thought; his, too, the sweetness of the words 'encaged birds' and 'household harmony'.

Finally, Henry is not only shown to us as gentle and loving, but as a man who prefers quiet and the country to a King's Court and state. Even in eager, mounting youth this was Shakespeare's own choice: Prince Arthur in *King John* longs to be a shepherd: and this crowned saint has the same desire. From boyhood to old age Shakespeare preferred the 'life removed':

> O God, methinks it were a happy life
> To be no better than a homely swain;
> To sit upon a hill, as I do now,
> To carve out dials quaintly point by point,
> Thereby to see the minutes how they run;
> How many make the hour full complete;
> How many hours bring about the day;
> How many days will finish up the year;
> How many years a mortal man may live.
> [. . .]
> So minutes, hours, days, months, and years,
> Passed over to the end they were created,
> Would bring white hairs unto a quiet grave.

All this it seems to me is as finely characteristic of the gentle melancholy of Shakespeare's youth as Jaques' bitter words are of the deeper melancholy of his manhood:

> And so from hour to hour we ripe and ripe,
> And then from hour to hour we rot and rot
> And thereby hangs a tale.

The *Third Part of Henry VI* leads one directly to *Richard III*. It was Coleridge's opinion that Shakespeare 'wrote hardly anything of this play except the character of Richard. He found the piece a stock play and rewrote the parts which developed the hero's character; he certainly did not write the scenes in which Lady Anne yielded to the usurper's solicitations.' In this instance Coleridge's positive opinion deserves to be weighed respectfully. At the time when *Richard III* was written Shakespeare was still rather a lyric than a dramatic poet, and Coleridge was a good judge of the peculiarities of his lyric style. Of course, Professor Dowden, too, is in doubt whether *Richard III* should be ascribed to Shakespeare. He says: 'Its manner of conceiving and presenting character has a certain resemblance, not elsewhere to be found in Shakespeare's writings, to the ideal manner of Marlowe. As in the plays of Marlowe, there is here one dominant figure distinguished by a few strongly marked and inordinately developed qualities.'

This faulty reasoning only shows how dangerous it is for a professor to copy his teacher slavishly: in *Coriolanus*, too, we have the 'one dominant figure', and all the rest of it. The truth seems to be that in the *Third Part of Henry VI* Shakespeare had been working with Marlowe, or, at least, revising Marlowe's work; in either case he was so steeped in Marlowe's spirit that he took, as we have seen, the most splendid piece of Richard's self-revealing directly from the older poet. Moreover, the words of deepest characterisation in Shakespeare's *Richard III*,

> Richard loves Richard – that is, I am I,

are manifestly a weak echo of the tremendous

> I am myself alone

of Marlowe's Richard. At least to this extent, then, Shakespeare used Marlowe in depicting Richard's character. But this trait, important as it was, did not carry him far, and he was soon forced to draw on his own experience of life. Already he seems to have noticed that one characteristic of men of action is a blunt plainness of speech; their courage is shown in their frankness, and, besides, words stand for realities with them, and are, therefore, used with sincerity. Shakespeare's Richard III uses plain speech as a hypocritical mask, but already Shakespeare is a dramatist and in his clever hands Richard's plain speaking is so allied with his incisive intelligence that it appears to be now a mask, now native shamelessness, and thus the characterisation wins in depth and mystery. Every now and then, too, this Richard sees things which no Englishman has been capable of seeing, except Shakespeare himself.

The whole of Plato's *Gorgias* is comprised in the two lines:

> Conscience is but a word that cowards use,
> Devised at first to keep the strong in awe.

The declaration of the second murderer that conscience 'makes a man a coward ... it beggars any man that keeps it; it is turned out of all towns and cities for a dangerous thing; and every man that means to live well endeavours to trust to himself and to live without it', should be regarded as the complement of what Falstaff says of honour; in both the humour of Shakespeare's characteristic irony is not to be mistaken.

The whole play, I think, must be ascribed to Shakespeare; all the memorable words in it are indubitably his, and I cannot believe that any other hand drew for us that marvellous, masterful courtship of Anne which Coleridge, naturally enough, was unwilling to appreciate. The structure of the play, however, shows all the weakness of Marlowe's method: the interest is concentrated on the protagonist; there is not humour enough to relieve the gloomy intensity, and the scenes in which Richard does not figure are unattractive and feeble.

One has only to think of the two characters – Richard II and Richard III – and to recall their handling in order to get a deep impression of Shakespeare's nature. He cannot present the vile Richard II at all; he has no interest in him; but as soon as he thinks of Richard's youth and remembers that he was led astray by others, he begins to identify himself with him, and at once Richard's weakness is made amiable and his sufferings affecting. In measure as Shakespeare lets himself go and paints himself more and more freely, his portraiture becomes astonishing, till at length the imprisoned Richard gives himself up to melancholy philosophic musing, without a tinge of bitterness or envy or hate, and everyone with eyes to see, is forced to recognise in him a younger brother to Hamlet and Posthumus. *Richard III* was produced in a very different way. It was Marlowe's daemonic power and intensity that first interested Shakespeare in this Richard; under the spell of Marlowe's personality Shakespeare conceived the play, and especially the scene between Richard and Anne; but the original impulse exhausted itself quickly, and then Shakespeare fell back on his own experience and made Richard keen of insight and hypocritically blunt of speech – a sort of sketch of Iago. A little later Shakespeare either felt that the action was unsuitable to the development of such a character, or more probably he grew weary of the effort to depict a fiend; in any case, the play becomes less and less interesting, and even the character of Richard begins to waver. There is one astonishing instance of this towards the end of the drama. On the eve of the decisive battle Richard starts awake from his terrifying dreams, and now, if ever, one would expect from him perfect sincerity of utterance. This is what we find:

> There is no creature loves me;
> And if I die no soul shall pity me;
> Nay, wherefore should they, since that I myself
> Find in myself no pity to myself?

The first two lines bespeak a loving, gentle nature, Shakespeare's nature, the nature of a Henry VI or an Arthur, a nature which Richard III would certainly have despised, and the last two lines are merely an objective ethical judgement wholly out of place and very clumsily expressed.

To sum up, then, for this is not the place to consider Shakespeare's share in *Henry VIII*, I find that in the English historical plays the manly characters, Hotspur, Harry V, the great Bastard, and Richard III, are all taken from tradition or from old plays, and Shakespeare did nothing more than copy the traits which were given to him; on the other hand, the weak, irresolute, gentle, melancholy characters are his own, and he shows extraordinary resource in revealing the secret workings of their souls. Even in early manhood, and when handling histories and men of action, Shakespeare cannot conceal his want of sympathy for the practical leaders of men; he neither understands them deeply nor loves them; but in portraying the girlish Arthur and the Hamlet-like Richard II, and in drawing forth the pathos of their weakness, he is already without a rival or second in all literature.

I am anxious not to deform the truth by exaggeration; a caricature of Shakespeare would offend me as a sacrilege, even though the caricature were characteristic, and when I find him even in youth one-sided, a poet and dreamer, I am minded to tell less than the truth rather than more. He was extraordinarily sensitive, I say to myself, and lived in the stress of great deeds; he treated Henry V, a man of action if ever there was one, as an ideal, and lavished on him all his admiration, but it will not do: I cannot shut my eyes to the fact; the effort is worse than useless. He liked Henry V because of his misled youth and his subsequent rise to highest honour, and not because of his practical genius. Where in his portrait gallery is the picture of a Drake, or even of a

Raleigh? The adventurer was the characteristic product of that jostling time; but Shakespeare turned his head away; he was not interested in him. In spite of himself, however, he became passionately interested in the pitiful Richard II and his untimely fate. Notwithstanding the praise of the critics, his King Henry V is a wooden marionette; the intense life of the traditional madcap Prince has died out of him; but Prince Arthur lives deathlessly, and we still hear his childish treble telling Hubert of his love.

Those who disagree with me will have to account for the fact that, even in the historical plays written in early manhood, all his portraits of men of action are mere copies, while his genius shines in the portraits of a gentle saint like Henry VI, of a weakling like Richard II, or of a girlish youth like Arthur – all these favourite studies being alike in pathetic helplessness and tender affection.

It is curious that no one of the commentators has noticed this extraordinary one-sidedness of Shakespeare. In spite of his miraculous faculty of expression, he never found wonderful phrases for the virile virtues or virile vices. For courage, revenge, self-assertion, and ambition we have finer words in English than any that Shakespeare coined. In this field Chapman, Milton, Byron, Carlyle, and even Bunyan are his masters.

Of course, as a man he had the instinct of courage, and an admiration of courage; his intellect, too, gave him some understanding of its range. Dr Brandes declares that Shakespeare has only depicted physical courage, the courage of the swordsman; but that is beside the truth: Dr Brandes has evidently forgotten the passage in *Antony and Cleopatra*, when Caesar contemptuously refuses the duel with Antony and speaks of his antagonist as an 'old ruffian'. Enobarbus, too, sneers at Antony's proposed duel:

> Yes, like enough, high-battled Caesar will
> Unstate his happiness, and be staged to the show
> Against a sworder.

Unhelped by memory, Dr Brandes might have guessed that Shakespeare would exhaust the obvious at first glance. But the soul of courage to Shakespeare is, as we have seen, a love of honour working on quick generous blood – a feminine rather than a masculine view of the matter.

Carlyle has a deeper sense of this aboriginal virtue. With the fanatic's trust in God his Luther will go to Worms 'though it rain devils'; and when in his own person Carlyle spoke of the small, honest minority desperately resolved to maintain their ideas though opposed by a huge hostile majority of fools and the insincere, he found one of the finest expressions for courage in all our literature. The vast host shall be to us, he cried, as 'stubble is to fire'. It may be objected that this is the voice of religious faith rather than of courage pure and simple, and the objection is valid so far as it goes; but this genesis of courage is peculiarly English, and the courage so formed is of the highest. Everyone remembers how Valiant-for-Truth fights in Bunyan's allegory: 'I fought till my sword did cleave to my hand; and when they were joined together, as if a sword grew out of my arm, and when the blood ran through my fingers, then I fought with most courage'. The mere expression gives us an understanding of the desperate resolution of Cromwell's Ironsides.

But if desperate courage is not in Shakespeare, neither are its ancillary qualities – cruelty, hatred, ambition, revenge. Whenever he talks on these themes, he talks from the teeth outwards, as one without experience of their violent delights. His Gloucester rants about ambition without an illuminating or even a convincing word. Hatred and revenge Shakespeare only studied superficially, and cruelty he shudders from like a woman.

It is astounding how ill-endowed Shakespeare was on the side of manliness. His intellect was so fine, his power of expression so magical, the men about him, his models, so brave – founders as they were of the British empire and sea-tyranny – that he is able to use his Hotspurs and Harrys to hide from the general the poverty of his temperament. But the truth will out: Shakespeare was the greatest of poets, a miraculous artist, too, when he liked; but he was not a hero, and manliness was not his *forte*: he was by nature a neuropath and a lover.

He was a master of passion and pity, and it astonishes one to notice how willingly he passed always to that extreme of sympathy where nothing but his exquisite choice of words and images saved him from falling into the silly. For example, in *Titus Andronicus*, with its crude, unmotived horrors, Titus calls Marcus a murderer, and when Marcus replies: 'Alas, my lord, I have but killed a fly', Titus answers:

> But how, if that fly had a father and mother?
> How would he hang his slender gilded wings,
> And buzz lamenting doings in the air?

Poor harmless fly!
That with his pretty buzzing melody,
Came here to make us merry! and thou hast killed him.

Even in his earliest plays in the noontide of lusty youth, when the heat of the blood makes most men cruel, or at least heedless of others' sorrows, Shakespeare was full of sympathy; his gentle soul wept with the stricken deer and suffered through the killing of a fly. Just as Ophelia turned 'thought and affliction, passion, hell itself' to 'favour and to prettiness', so Shakespeare's genius turned the afflictions and passions of man to pathos and to pity.

7

Shakespeare as Lyric Poet: *Twelfth Night*

Shakespeare began the work of life as a lyric poet. It was to be expected therefore that when he took up playwriting he would use the play from time to time as an opportunity for a lyric, and in fact this was his constant habit. From the beginning to the end of his career he was as much a lyric poet as a dramatist. His first comedies are feeble and thin in character-drawing and the lyrical sweetness is everywhere predominant. His apprenticeship period may be said to have closed with his first tragedy, *Romeo and Juliet*. I am usually content to follow Mr Furnival's *Trial Table of the order of Shakspere's Plays*, in which *Richard II*, *Richard III*, and *King John* are all placed later than *Romeo and Juliet*, and yet included in the first period that stretches from 1585 to 1595. But *Romeo and Juliet* seems to me to be far more characteristic of the poet's genius than any of these histories; it is not only a finer work of art than any of them, and therefore of higher promise, but in its lyrical sweetness far more truly representative of Shakespeare's youth than any of the early comedies or historical plays. Whatever their form may be, nearly all Shakespeare's early works are love-songs, *Venus and Adonis*, *Lucrece*, *Love's Labour's Lost*, *The Two Gentlemen of Verona*, and he may be said to have ended his apprenticeship with the imperishable tragedy of first love *Romeo and Juliet*.

In the years from 1585 to 1595 Shakespeare brought the lyric element into something like due subordination and managed to free himself almost completely from his early habit of rhyming. Mr Swinburne has written of Shakespeare's use of rhymed verse with a fullness of knowledge and sympathy that leaves little to be desired. He compares it aptly to the use of the left hand instead of the right, and doubts cogently whether Shakespeare ever attained such mastery of rhyme as Marlowe in *Hero and Leander*. But I like to think that Shakespeare's singing quickly became too sincere in its emotion and too complex in its harmonies to tolerate the definite limits set by rhyme. In any case by 1595 Shakespeare had learned to prefer blank verse to rhyme, at least for playwriting; he thus made the first great step towards a superb knowledge of his instrument.

The period of Shakespeare's maturity defines itself sharply; it stretches from 1595 to 1608 and falls naturally into two parts; the first part includes the trilogy *Henry IV* and *Henry V* and his golden comedies; the second, from 1600 to 1608, is entirely filled with his great tragedies. The characteristic of this period so far as regards the instrument is that Shakespeare has come to understand the proper function of prose. He sees first that it is the only language suited to broad comedy, and goes on to use it in moments of sudden excitement, or when dramatic truth to character seems to him all important. At his best he uses blank verse when some emotion sings itself to him, and prose as the ordinary language of life, the language of surprise, laughter, strife, and of all the commoner feelings. During these twelve or fourteen years the lyric note is not obtrusive; it is usually subordinated to character and suited to action.

His third and last period begins with *Pericles* and ends with *The Tempest*; it is characterised, as we shall see later, by bodily weakness and by a certain contempt for the dramatic fiction. But the knowledge of the instrument once acquired never left Shakespeare. It is true that the lyric note becomes increasingly clear in his late comedies; but prose too is used by him with the same mastery that he showed in his maturity.

In the first period Shakespeare was often unable to give his puppets individual life; in maturity he was interested in the puppets themselves and used them with considerable artistry; in the third period he had grown a little weary of them and in *The Tempest* showed himself inclined, just as Goethe in later life was inclined, to turn his characters into symbols or types.

The place of *Twelfth Night* is as clearly marked in Shakespeare's works as *Romeo and Juliet* or *The Tempest*. It stands on the dividing line between his light, joyous comedies and the great tragedies; it was all done at the topmost height of happy hours, but there are hints in it which we shall have to notice later, which show that when writing it Shakespeare had already looked into the valley of disillusion which he was about to tread. But *Twelfth Night* is written in the spirit of *As You Like It* or *Much Ado*, only it is still more personal-ingenuous and less dramatic than these; it is, indeed, a lyric of love and the joy of living.

There is no intenser delight to a lover of letters than to find Shakespeare singing, with happy unconcern, of the things he loved best –

not the Shakespeare of Hamlet or Macbeth, whose intellect speaks in critical judgements of men and of life, and whose heart we are fain to divine from slight indications; nor Shakespeare the dramatist, who tried now and again to give life to puppets like Coriolanus and Iago, with whom he had little sympathy; but Shakespeare the poet, Shakespeare the lover, Shakespeare whom Ben Jonson called 'the gentle', Shakespeare the sweet-hearted singer, as he lived and suffered and enjoyed. If I were asked to complete the portrait given to us by Shakespeare of himself in Hamlet-Macbeth with one single passage, I should certainly choose the first words of the Duke in *Twelfth Night*. I must transcribe the poem, though it will be in every reader's remembrance; for it contains the completest, the most characteristic, confession of Shakespeare's feelings ever given in a few lines:

> If music be the food of love, play on;
> Give me excess of it, that surfeiting,
> The appetite may sicken, and so die.
> That strain again; – it had a dying fall:
> Oh, it came o'er my ear like the sweet south
> That breathes upon a bank of violets,
> Stealing and giving odour. – Enough! no more;
> 'Tis not so sweet now as it was before.

Everyone will notice that Shakespeare as we know him in Romeo is here depicted again with insistence on a few salient traits; here, too, we have the poet of the Sonnets masquerading as a Duke and the protagonist of yet another play. There is still less art used in characterising this Duke than there is in characterising Macbeth; Shakespeare merely lets himself go and sings his feelings in the most beautiful words. This is his philosophy of music and of love:

> Give me excess of it, that surfeiting,
> The appetite may sicken, and so die;

and then:

> Enough, no more;
> 'Tis not so sweet now as it was before.

– the quick revulsion of the delicate artist-voluptuary who wishes to keep unblunted in memory the most exquisite pang of pleasure.

Speech after speech discovers the same happy freedom and absolute abandonment to the 'sense of beauty'. Curio proposes hunting the hart, and at once the Duke breaks out:

> Why, so I do, the noblest that I have.
> O, when mine eyes did see Olivia first,
> Methought she purged the air of pestilence.
> That instant was I turned into a hart,
> And my desires, like fell and cruel hounds,
> E'er since pursue me.

Valentine then comes to tell him that Olivia is still mourning for her brother, and the Duke seizes the opportunity for another lyric:

> O, she that hath a heart of that fine frame
> To pay this debt of love but to a brother,
> How will she love, when the rich golden shaft
> Hath killed the flock of all affections else
> That live in her; when liver, brain, and heart,
> These sovereign thrones, are all supplied and filled –
> Her sweet perfections – with one self King! –
> Away before me to sweet beds of flowers,
> Love-thoughts lie rich when canopied with bowers.

The last two lines show clearly enough that Shakespeare was not troubled with any thought of reality as he wrote: he was transported by Fancy into that enchanted country of romance where beds of flowers are couches and bowers, canopies of love. But what a sensuality there is in him!

> when liver, brain, and heart,
> These sovereign thrones, are all supplied and filled –
> Her sweet perfections – with one self King! –

Of course, too, this Duke is inconstant, and swings from persistent pursuit of Olivia to love of Viola without any other reason than the discovery of Viola's sex. In the same way Romeo turns from Rosaline to Juliet at first sight. This trait has been praised by Coleridge and others as showing singular knowledge of a young man's character, but I should rather say that inconstancy was a characteristic of sensuality and belonged to Shakespeare himself, for Orsino, like Romeo, has no reason to change his love; and the curious part of the matter is that Shakespeare does not seem to think that the quick change in Orsino requires any explanation at all. Moreover, the love of Duke Orsino for

Olivia is merely the desire of her bodily beauty – the counterpart of the
sensual jealousy of Othello. Speaking from Shakespeare's very heart,
the Duke says:

> Tell her, my love, more noble than the world,
> Prizes not quantity of dirty lands;
> The parts that Fortune hath bestowed upon her,
> Tell her, I hold as giddily as Fortune;
> But 'tis that miracle and queen of gems
> That nature pranks her in attracts my soul.

So the body wins the soul according to this Orsino, who is, I repeat
again, Shakespeare in his most ingenuous and frankest mood; the contempt of wealth – 'dirty lands' – and the sensuality – 'that miracle and
queen of gems' – are alike characteristic. A few more touches and the
portrait of this Duke will be complete; he says to the pretended Cesario
when sending him as ambassador to Olivia:

> Cesario,
> Thou knowest no less but all; I have unclasped
> To thee the book even of my secret soul;
> Therefore, good youth,

and so forth.

It is a matter of course that this Duke should tell everything to his
friend; a matter of course, too, that he should love books and bookish
metaphors. Without being told, one knows that he delights in all
beautiful things – pictures with their faerie false presentment of forms
and life; the flesh-firm outline of marble, the warmth of ivory and the
sea-green patine of bronze – was not the poop of the vessel beaten gold,
the sails purple, the oars silver, and the very water amorous?

This Duke shows us Shakespeare's most intimate traits even when
the action does not suggest the self-revelation. When sending Viola to
woo Olivia for him he adds:

> Some four or five, attend him;
> All if you will; for I myself am best
> When least in company.

Like Vincentio, that other mask of Shakespeare, this Duke too loves
solitude and 'the life removed'; he is 'best when least in company'.

If there is anyone who still doubts the essential identity of Duke

Orsino and Shakespeare, let him consider the likeness in thought and form between the Duke's lyric effusions and the Sonnets, and if that does not convince him I might use a hitherto untried argument. When a dramatist creates a man's character he is apt to make him, as the French say, too much of a piece – too logical. But, in this instance, though Shakespeare has given the Duke only a short part, he has made him contradict himself with the charming ease that belongs peculiarly to self-revealing. The Duke tells us:

> For such as I am all true lovers are, –
> Unstaid and skittish in all motions else,
> Save in the constant image of the creature
> That is beloved.

The next moment he repeats this:

> For, boy, however we do praise ourselves,
> Our fancies are more giddy and unfirm,
> More longing, wavering, sooner lost and won,
> Than women's are.

And the moment after he asserts:

> There is no woman's sides
> Can bide the beating of so strong a passion
> As love doth give my heart; no woman's heart
> So big, to hold so much; they lack retention.
> Alas! their love may be called appetite,
> No motion of the liver, but the palate,
> That suffers surfeit, cloyment, and revolt!

Hamlet contradicts himself, too: at one moment he declares that his soul is immortal, and at the next is full of despair. But Hamlet is so elaborate a portrait, built up of so many minute touches, that self-contradiction is a part, and a necessary part, of his many-sided complexity. But the Duke in *Twelfth Night* reveals himself as it were accidentally; we know little more of him than that he loves music and love, books and flowers, and that he despises wealth and company; accordingly, when he contradicts himself, we may suspect that Shakespeare is letting himself speak freely without much care for the coherence of characterisation. And the result of this frankness is that he has given a more intimate, a more confidential, sketch of himself in Duke Orsino of *Twelfth Night* than he has given us in any play except perhaps *Hamlet* and *Macbeth*.

I hardly need to prove that Shakespeare in his earliest plays, as in his latest, in his Sonnets as in his darkest tragedy, loved flowers and music. In almost every play he speaks of flowers with affection and delight. One only needs to recall the song in *A Midsummer's Night's Dream*, 'I know a bank', or Perdita's exquisite words:

> Daffodils,
> That come before the swallow dares, and take
> The winds of March with beauty; violets dim,
> But sweeter than the lids of Juno's eyes
> Or Cytherea's breath; pale primroses,
> That die unmarried ere they can behold
> Bright Phoebus in his strength, a malady
> Most incident to maids; bold oxlips, and
> The crown-imperial; lilies of all kinds,
> The flower-de-luce being one;

or Arviragus' praise of Imogen:

> Thou shalt not lack
> The flower that's like thy face, pale primrose, nor
> The azured harebell like thy veins; no, nor
> The leaf of eglantine, whom not to slander
> Outsweetened not thy breath.

Shakespeare praises music so frequently and so enthusiastically that we must regard the trait as characteristic of his deepest nature. Take this play which we are handling now. Not only the Duke, but both the heroines, Viola and Olivia, love music. Viola can sing 'in many sorts of music,' and Olivia admits that she would rather hear Viola solicit love than 'music from the spheres'. Romeo almost confounds music with love, as does Duke Orsino:

> How silver-sweet sound lovers' tongues by night,
> Like softest music to attending ears!

And again:

> And let rich music's tongue
> Unfold the imagin'd happiness that both
> Receive in either by this dear encounter.

It is a curious and characteristic fact that Shakespeare gives almost the same words to Ferdinand in the *Tempest* that he gave ten years earlier to the Duke in *Twelfth Night*. In both passages music goes with passion to allay its madness:

> This music crept by me upon the waters,
> Allaying both their fury and my passion
> With its sweet air

and Duke Orsino says:

> That old and antique song we heard last night,
> Methought it did relieve my passion much.

This confession is so peculiar; shows, too, so exquisitely fine a sensibility, that its repetition makes me regard it as Shakespeare's. The most splendid lyric on music is given to Lorenzo in the *Merchant of Venice*, and it may be remarked in passing that Lorenzo is not a character, but, like Claudio, a mere name and a mouthpiece of Shakespeare's feeling. Shakespeare was almost as well content, it appears, to play the lover as to play the Duke. I cannot help transcribing the magical verses, though they must be familiar to every lover of our English tongue:

> How sweet the moonlight sleeps upon this bank!
> Here will we sit, and let the sounds of music
> Creep in our ears; soft stillness and the night
> Become the touches of sweet harmony.
> Sit, Jessica: Look how the floor of heaven
> Is thick inlaid with patines of bright gold.
> There's not the smallest orb which thou behold'st
> But in his motion like an angel sings,
> Still quiring to the young-eyed cherubims.
> Such harmony is in immortal souls;
> But, whilst this muddy vesture of decay
> Doth grossly close it in, we cannot hear it.

The first lines of this poem are conceived in the very spirit of the poems of *Twelfth Night*, and in the last lines Shakespeare puts to use that divine imagination which lifts all his best verse into the higher air of life, and reaches its noblest in Prospero's solemn-sad lyric.

Shakespeare's love of music is so much a part of himself that he condemns those who do not share it; this argument, too, is given to Lorenzo:

> The man that hath no music in himself,
> Nor is not moved with concord of sweet sounds,
> Is fit for treasons, stratagems, and spoils;
> The motions of his spirit are dull as night,
> And his affections dark as Erebus:
> Let no such man be trusted.

That this view was not merely the expression of a passing mood is shown by the fact that Shakespeare lends no music to his villains; but Timon gives welcome to his friends with music, just as Hamlet welcomes the players with music and Portia calls for music while her suitors make their eventful choice. Titania and Oberon both seek the aid of music to help them in their loves, and the war-worn and time-worn Henry IV prays for music to bring some rest to his 'weary spirit'; in much the same mood Prospero desires music when he breaks his wand and resigns his magical powers.

Here, again, in *Twelfth Night* in full manhood Shakespeare shows himself to us as Romeo, in love with flowers and music and passion. True, this Orsino is a little less occupied with verbal quips, a little more frankly sensual, too, than Romeo; but then Romeo would have been more frankly sensual had he lived from twenty-five to thirty-five. As an older man, too, Orsino has naturally more of Hamlet-Shakespeare's peculiar traits than Romeo showed; the contempt of wealth and love of solitude are qualities hardly indicated in Romeo, while in Orsino as in the mature Shakespeare they are salient characteristics. To sum up: Hamlet-Macbeth gives us Shakespeare's mind; but in Romeo-Orsino he has discovered his heart and poetic temperament to us as ingenuously, though not, perhaps, so completely, as he does in the Sonnets.

8

Shakespeare's Humour: Falstaff

Shakespeare's portraits of himself are not to be mistaken; the changes in him caused by age bring into clearer light the indestructible individuality, and no difference of circumstance or position has any effect upon this distinctive character: whether he is the lover, Romeo; the murderer, Macbeth; the courtier, Hamlet; or the warrior, Posthumus; he is always the same – a gentle yet impulsive nature, sensuous at once and meditative; half poet, half philosopher, preferring nature and his own reveries to action and the life of courts; a man physically fastidious to disgust, as is a delicate woman, with dirt and smells and common things; an idealist daintily sensitive to all courtesies, chivalries, and distinctions. The portrait is not yet complete – far from it, indeed; but already it is manifest that Shakespeare's nature was so complex, so tremulously poised between world-wide poles of poetry and philosophy, of what is individual and concrete on the one hand and what is abstract and general on the other, that the task of revealing himself was singularly difficult. It is not easy even to describe him as he painted himself: it may be that, wishing to avoid a mere catalogue of disparate qualities, I have brought into too great prominence the gentle passionate side of Shakespeare's nature; though that would be difficult and in any case no bad fault; for this is the side which has hitherto been neglected or rather overlooked by the critics.

My view of Shakespeare can be made clearer by examples. I began by taking Hamlet the philosopher as Shakespeare's most profound and complex study, and went on to prove that Hamlet is the most complete portrait which Shakespeare has given of himself, other portraits being as it were sides of Hamlet or less successful replicas of him; and finally I tried to complete the Hamlet by uniting him with Duke Orsino, Orsino the poet-lover being, so to speak, Shakespeare's easiest and most natural portrait. In Hamlet, if one may dare to say so, Shakespeare has discovered too much of himself: Hamlet is at one and the same time philosopher and poet, critic and courtier, lover and cynic – the extremes that Shakespeare's intellect could cover – and he fills every part so easily that he might almost be a bookish Admirable Crichton, a type of perfection rather than an individual man, were it not for his feminine gentleness and forgivingness of nature, and particularly for the brooding melancholy and disbelief which darkened Shakespeare's outlook at the time. But though the melancholy scepticism was an abiding characteristic of Shakespeare, to be found in his Richard II as in his Prospero, it did not overshadow all his being as it does Hamlet's. There was a summer-time, too, in Shakespeare's life, and in his nature a capacity for sunny gaiety and a delight in life and love which came to full expression in the golden comedies, *Much Ado*, *As You Like It* and *Twelfth Night*. The complement to Hamlet the sad philosopher-sceptic is the sensuous happy poet-lover Orsino, and when we take these seeming antitheses and unite them we have a good portrait of Shakespeare. But these two, Hamlet and Orsino, are in reality one; every quality of Orsino is to be found or divined in Hamlet, and therefore the easiest and surest way to get at Shakespeare is to take Hamlet and deepen those peculiarities in him which we find in Orsino.

Some critics are sure to say that I have now given a portrait of Coleridge rather than a portrait of Shakespeare. This is not altogether the fact, though I for one see no shame in acknowledging the likeness. Coleridge had a 'smack of Hamlet' in him, as he himself saw; indeed, in his rich endowment as poet and philosopher, and in his gentleness and sweetness of disposition, he was more like Shakespeare than any other Englishman whom I can think of; but in Coleridge the poet soon disappeared, and a little later the philosopher in him faded into the visionary and sophist; he became an upholder of the English Church and found reasons in the immutable constitution of the universe for aprons and shovel-hats. Shakespeare, on the other hand, though similarly endowed, was far more richly endowed: he had stronger passions and greater depth of feeling; the sensuousness of Keats was in him; and this richness of nature not only made him a greater lyric poet than Coleridge and a far saner thinker, but carried him in spite of a constitutional dislike of resolve and action to his astounding achievement.

But even when we thus compare Shakespeare with Coleridge, as we compare trees of the same species, showing that as the roots of the one go deeper and take a firmer hold of earth, so in exact measure the crest rises into higher air, still there is something lacking to our comparison.

Even when we hold Hamlet-Orsino before us as the best likeness of the master-poet, our impression of him is still incomplete.

There remains a host of creations from Launce to Autolycus, and from Dame Quickly to Maria, which proves that Shakespeare was something more than the gentle lover-thinker-poet whom we have shown. It is Shakespeare's humour that differentiates him not only from Coleridge and Keats, but also from the world-poets, Goethe, Dante, and Homer. It is this unique endowment that brings him into vital touch with reality and common life, and hinders us from feeling his all-pervading ideality as disproportioned or one-sided. Strip him of his humour and he would have been seen long ago in his true proportions. His sympathies are not more broad and generous than Balzac's; his nature is too delicate, too sensitive, too sensuous; but his humour blinds us to the truth. Of course his comic characters, like his captains and men of action, are due originally to his faculty of observation; but while his observation of the fighting men is always superficial and at times indifferent, his humorous observation is so intensely interested and sympathetic that its creations are only inferior in artistic value to his portraits of the poet-philosopher-lover.

The intellect in him had little or nothing to go upon in the case of the man of action; he never loved the Captain or watched him at work; it is his mind and second-hand knowledge that made Henry V and Richard III; and how slight and shallow are these portraits in comparison with the portrait of a Parolles or a Sir Toby Belch, or the ever-famous Nurse, where the same intellect has played about the humorous trait and heightened the effect of loving observation. The critics who have ignorantly praised his Hotspur and Bastard as if he had been a man of deeds as well as a man of words have only obscured the truth that Shakespeare the poet-philosopher, the lover *quand même*, only reached a sane balance of nature through his overflowing humour. He whose intellect and sensibilities inspired him with nothing but contempt and loathing for the mass of mankind, the aristocrat who in a dozen plays sneers at the greasy caps and foul breaths of the multitude, fell in love with Dogberry, and Bottom, Quickly and Tearsheet, clod and clown, pimp and prostitute, for the laughter they afforded. His humour is rarely sardonic; it is almost purged of contempt; a product not of hate but of love; full of sympathy; summer-lightning humour, harmless and beautiful.

Sometimes the sympathy fails and the laughter grows grim, and these lapses are characteristic. He hates false friends and timeservers, the whole tribe of the ungrateful, the lords of Timon's acquaintance and his artists; he loathes Shylock, whose god is greed and who battens on others' misfortunes; he laughs at the self-righteous Malvolio and not with him, and takes pleasure in unmasking the pretended ascetic and Puritan Angelo; but for the frailties of the flesh he has an ever-ready forgiveness. Like the greatest of ethical teachers, he can take the publican and the sinner to his heart, but not the hypocrite or the Pharisee or the money-lender.

It does not come within the scope of this essay to attempt a detailed criticism of Shakespeare's comic characters; it will be enough for my purpose to show that even in his masterpiece of humour, the incomparable Falstaff, he betrays himself more than once: more than once we shall find Shakespeare, the poet, or Shakespeare, the thinker, speaking through Falstaff's mouth. Yet to criticise Falstaff is difficult, and if easy, it would still be an offence to those capable of gratitude. I would as soon find fault with Ariel's most exquisite lyric, or the impeccable loveliness of the '*Dove sono*', as weigh the rich words of the Lord of Comedy in small balances of reason. But such considerations must not divert me from my purpose; I have undertaken to discover the very soul of Shakespeare, and I must, therefore, trace him in Falstaff as in Hamlet.

Falstaff enters and asks the Prince the time. The Prince answers that unless 'hours were cups of sack and so forth, he can't understand why Falstaff should care about anything so superfluous as time'. Falstaff replies: 'Indeed you come near me now, Hal; for we that take purses go by the moon and the seven stars and not by Phoebus, he, "that wandering knight so fair"'. Here we have a sort of lyrical strain in Falstaff and then a tag of poetry which gives food for thought; but his next speech is unmistakable:

> Let us be Diana's foresters, gentlemen of the shade, minions of the moon; and let men say we be men of good government, being governed, as the sea is, by our noble and chaste mistress, the moon, under whose countenance we – steal.

This is Shakespeare speaking, and Shakespeare alone: the phrases sing to us in the unmistakable music of the master-poet, though the fall at the last to ' – steal', seems to be an attempt to get into the character of Falstaff. It is, of course, difficult to make the first words of a person sharply characteristic; a writer is apt to work himself into a new character gradually; it is only the sensitive self-consciousness of our time that demands an absolute fidelity in characterisation from the first word to the last. Yet this scene is so excellent and natural, that the uncertainty in the painting of Falstaff strikes me as peculiar. But this first speech is not the only speech of Falstaff in which Shakespeare betrays himself; again and again we catch the very accent of the poet. It is not Falstaff but Shakespeare who says that 'the poor abuses of the time want countenance'; and later in the play, when the character of Falstaff is fully developed, it is Shakespeare, the thinker, who calls Falstaff's ragged regiment 'the cankers of a calm world and a long peace'. In just the same way Hamlet speaks of the expedition of Fortinbras:

> This is the imposthume of much wealth and peace,
> That inward breaks.

But though the belief that Shakespeare sometimes falls out of the character and slips phrases of his own into Falstaff's mouth is well-founded, it should nevertheless be put aside as a heresy, for the true faith is that the white-bearded old footpad who cheered on his fellow-ruffians with

Strike . . . Bacon-fed knaves! they hate us youth: down with them! fleece them!'

and again:

> On, bacons, on! What, ye knaves! young men must live!

is the most splendid piece of humorous portraiture in the world's fiction.

Who but Falstaff would have found his self-justification in his youth? – *splendide mendax*! and yet the excuse is as true to his sack-heated blood when he uses it on Gadshill as it was true also to fact when he first used it forty years before. And who but Falstaff would have had the words of repentance always on his lips and never in his heart? I ascribe these illuminating flashes to Falstaff, and not to Shakespeare, for no imagination in the world has yet accomplished such a miracle; as a miracle of representment Falstaff is astonishing enough, as a miracle of creation he is simply unthinkable. I would almost as soon believe that Falstaff made Shakespeare as that Shakespeare made Falstaff without a living model. All hail to thee, inimitable, incomparable Jack! Never before or since has poet been blessed with such a teacher, as rich and laughterful, as mendacious and corrupting as life itself.

I must not be taken to mean that the living original of Falstaff was as richly humorous, as inexhaustibly diverting as the dramatic counterfeit who is now a citizen and chief personage in that world of literature which outlasts all the fleeting shows of the so-called real world. It seems to me to be possible for a good reader to notice not only Shakespeare's lapses and faults in the drawing of this character, but also to make a very fair guess at his heightening touches, and so arrive at last at the humorous old lewdster who furnished the living model for the inimitable portrait. The first scene in which Falstaff appears talking with Prince Henry will supply examples to illustrate my meaning.

Falstaff's very first speech after he asks Hal the time of day gives us the key; he ends it with:

> And I pr'ythee, sweet wag, when thou art king, – as, God save thy grace – majesty, I should say, for grace thou wilt have none, –

Here he is interrupted and breaks off, but a minute or two later he comes back again to his argument, and curiously enough uses exactly the same words:

> But, I pr'ythee, sweet wag, shall there be gallows standing in England when thou art king? and resolution thus fobbed as it is with the rusty curb of old father Antick, the law?

Now, this question and the hope it expresses that justice would be put to shame in England on Prince Henry's accession to the throne is taken from a speech of the Prince in the old play, *The Famous Victories of Henry the Fifth*. Shakespeare would have done better to leave it out, for Falstaff has far too good brains to imagine that all thieves could ever have his licence and far too much conceit ever to desire so unholy a consummation. And Shakespeare must have felt that the borrowed words were too shallow-common, for he immediately falls back on his own brains for the next phrase and gives us of his hoarded best. The second part of the question, 'resolution thus fobbed', and so forth, is only another statement of the famous couplet in *Richard III*:

> Conscience is but a word that cowards use,
> Devised at first to keep the strong in awe.

These faults show that Shakespeare is at first unsure of his personage; he fumbles a little; yet the vivacity, the roaring life, is certainly a quality of the original Falstaff, for it attends him as constantly as his shadow;

the pun, too, is his, and the phrase 'sweet wag' is probably taken from his mouth, for he repeats it again, 'sweet wag', and again 'mad wag'. The shamelessness, too, and the lechery are marks of him, and the love of witty word-warfare, and, above all, the pretended repentance:

> O, thou hast damnable iteration, and art, indeed, able to corrupt a saint. Thou hast done much harm upon me, Hal, – God forgive thee for it. Before I knew thee, Hal, I knew nothing; and now am I, if a man should speak truly, little better than one of the wicked. I must give over this life, and I will give it over; by the Lord, an I do not, I am a villain; I'll be damned for never a king's son in Christendom.

In this first scene between Falstaff and Prince Henry, Shakespeare is feeling his way, so to speak, blindfold to Falstaff, with gropings of memory and dashes of poetry that lead him past the mark. In this first scene, as we noticed, he puts fine lyric phrases in Falstaff's mouth; but he never repeats the experiment; Falstaff and high poetry are antipodes – all of which merely proves that at first Shakespeare had not got into the skin of his personage. But the real Falstaff had probably tags of verse in memory and lilts of song, for Shakespeare repeats this trait. Here we reach the test: Whenever a feature is accentuated by repetition, we may guess that it belongs to the living model. There was assuredly a strong dash of Puritanism in the real Falstaff, for when Shakespeare comes to render this, he multiplies the brush-strokes with perfect confidence; Falstaff is perpetually repenting.

After the first scene Shakespeare seems to have made up his mind to keep closely to his model and only to permit himself heightening touches.

In order to come closer to the original, I will now take another passage later in the play, when Shakespeare is drawing Falstaff with a sure hand:

FALSTAFF A plague of all cowards, I say, and a vengeance too! marry and amen! – Give me a cup of sack, boy. – Ere I lead this life long, I'll sew netherstocks, and mend them, and foot them, too. A plague of all cowards! – give me a cup of sack, rogue. – Is there no virtue extant? [*drinks*]

Here is surely the true Falstaff; he will not lead this life long; this is the soul of him; but the exquisite heightening phrase, 'Is there no virtue extant?' is pure Shakespeare, Shakespeare generalising as we saw him generalising in just the same way in the scene where Cade is talked of in the *Second Part of King Henry VI*. The form too is Shakespeare's. Who does not remember the magic line in *The Two Noble Kinsmen*?

> She is all the beauty extant.

And the next speech of Falstaff is just as illuminating:

FALSTAFF You rogue, here's lime in this sack, too; there is nothing but roguery to be found in villainous man: yet a coward is worse than a cup of sack with lime in it – a villainous coward. – Go thy ways, old Jack; die when thou wilt, if manhood, good manhood, be not forgot upon the face of the earth, then am I a shotten herring. There live not three good men unhanged in England, and one of them is fat and grows old: God help the while! A bad world I say –

At the beginning the concrete fact, then generalisation, and then merely a repetition of the traits marked in the first scene, with the addition of bragging. Evidently Shakespeare has the model in memory as he writes. I say 'evidently', for Falstaff is the only character in Shakespeare that repeats the same words with damnable iteration, and in whom the same traits are shown again and again and again. When Shakespeare is painting himself in Richard II he depicts irresolution again and again as he depicts it also in Hamlet; but neither Hamlet nor Richard repeats the same words, nor is any trait in either of them accentuated so grossly as are the principal traits of Falstaff's character. The features in Falstaff which are so harped upon, are to me the features of the original model. Shakespeare did not know Falstaff quite as well as he knew himself; so he has to confine himself to certain qualities which he had observed, and stick, besides, to certain tags of speech, which were probably favourites with the living man.

In another important particular, too, Falstaff is unlike any other comic character in Shakespeare: he tells the truth about himself in a magical way. The passage I allude to is the first speech made by Falstaff in the *Second Part of Henry IV*; it shows us Shakespeare getting into the character again – after a certain lapse of time:

FALSTAFF Men of all sorts take a pride to gird at me; the brain of this foolish-compounded clay, man, is not able to invent anything that tends to laughter, more than I invent or is

> invented on me: I am not only witty in myself, but the
> cause that wit is in other men –

Just as in the first act Shakespeare introducing Falstaff makes him talk poetically, so here there is a certain exaltation and lyrical swing which betrays the poet-creator. 'Foolish-compounded', too, shows Shakespeare's hand, but the boast, I feel sure, was a boast often made by the original, and thus brings Shakespeare into intimate union with the character; for after this introduction Falstaff goes on to talk pure Falstaff, unmixed with any slightest dash of poetry.

Who was the original of Falstaff? Is a guess possible? It seems to me it must have been some lover of poetry – perhaps Chettle, the Chettle who years before had published Greene's attack upon Shakespeare and who afterwards made amends for it. In Dekker's tract, *A Knight's Conjuring*, Chettle figures among the poets in Elysium: 'In comes Chettle sweating and blowing by reason of his fatnes; to welcome whom, because hee was of olde acquaintance, all rose up, and fell presentlie on their knees, to drinck a health to all the louers of Hellicon.' Here we have a fat man greeted with laughter and mock reverence by the poets – just such a model as Shakespeare needed, but the guess is mere conjecture: we don't know enough about Chettle to be at all sure. Yet Chettle was by way of being a poet, and Falstaff uses tags of verse – still, as I say, it is all pure guesswork. The only reason I put his name forward is that some have talked of Ben Jonson as Falstaff's original merely because he was fat. I cannot believe that gentle Shakespeare would ever have treated Jonson with such contempt; but Chettle seems to have been a butt by nature.

That Falstaff was taken from one model is to me certain. Shakespeare very seldom tells us what his characters look like; whenever he gives us a photograph, so to speak, of a person, it is always taken from life and extraordinarily significant. We have several portraits of Falstaff: the Prince gives a picture of the 'old fat man, . . . ' that trunk of humours ' . . . that old white-bearded Satan'; the Chief Justice gives us another of his 'moist eye, white beard, increasing belly and double chin'. Falstaff himself has another: 'a goodly portly man, i' faith and a corpulent; of a cheerful look, a pleasing eye, and a most noble carriage'. Such physical portraiture alone would convince me that there was a living model for Falstaff. But there are more obvious arguments: the other humorous characters of Shakespeare are infinitely inferior to

Falstaff, and the best of them are merely sides of Falstaff or poor reflections of him. Autolycus and Parolles have many of his traits, but they are not old, and taken together, they are only a faint replica of the immortal footpad.

Listening with my heart in my ears, I catch a living voice, a round, fat voice with tags of 'pr'ythee', 'wag', and 'marry', and behind the inimitable dramatic counterfeit I see a big man with a white head and round belly who loved wine and women and jovial nights, a Triton among the minnows of boon companions, whose shameless effrontery was backed by cunning, whose wit though common was abundant and effective through long practice – a sort of licensed tavern-king, whose mere entrance into a room set the table in a roar. Shakespeare was attracted by the many-sided racy ruffian, delighted perhaps most by his easy mastery of life and men; he studied him with infinite zest, absorbed him wholly, and afterwards reproduced him with such richness of sympathy, such magic of enlarging invention that he has become, so to speak, the symbol of laughter throughout the world, for men of all races the true Comic Muse.

In any case I may be allowed one last argument. The Falstaff of *The Merry Wives of Windsor* is not the Falstaff of the two parts of *King Henry IV*; it is but a shadow of the great knight that we see, an echo of him that we hear in the later comedy. Falstaff would never have written the same letter to Mrs Ford and Mrs Page; there was too much fancy in him, too much fertility, too much delight in his own mind- and word-wealth ever to show himself so painfully stinted and barren. Nor is it credible that Falstaff would ever have fallen three times running into the same trap; Falstaff made traps; he did not fall into them. We know, too, that Falstaff would not fight 'longer than he saw reason'; his instinct of self-preservation was largely developed; but he could face a sword; he drew on Pistol and chased him from the room; he was not such a pitiful coward as to take Ford's cudgelling. Finally, the Falstaff whom we all know could never have been befooled by the Welshman and his child-fairies. And this objection Shakespeare himself felt, for he meets it by making Falstaff explain how near he came to discovering the fraud, and how wit is made 'a Jack-a-Lent when 'tis upon ill employment'. But the fact that some explanation is necessary is an admission of the fault. Falstaff must indeed have laid his brains in the sun before he could have been taken in by foppery so gross and palpable. This is not the same man who at once recognised the Prince and Poins through their disguise as drawers. Yet there are moments when the Falstaff of *The Merry Wives* resumes his old nature. For example, when he is accused by Pistol of sharing in the proceeds of the theft, he answers with all the old shameless wit:

Reason, you rogue, reason; think'st thou I'll endanger my soul gratis?'

and, again, when he has been cozened and beaten, he speaks almost in the old way:

I never prospered since I forswore myself at primero. Well, if my wind were but long enough to say my prayers, I would repent.

But on the whole the Falstaff of *The Merry Wives* is but a poor thin shadow of the Falstaff of the two parts of *Henry IV*.

Had *The Merry Wives* been produced under ordinary conditions, one would have had to rack one's brains to account for its feebleness. Not only is the genial Lord of Humour degraded in it into a buffoon, but the amusement of it is chiefly in situation; it is almost as much a farce as a comedy. For these and other reasons I believe in the truth of the tradition that Elizabeth was so pleased with the character of Falstaff that she ordered Shakespeare to write another play showing the fat knight in love, and that in obedience to this command Shakespeare wrote *The Merry Wives* in a fortnight. For what does a dramatist do when he is in a hurry to strike while the iron is hot and to catch a Queen's fancy before it changes? Naturally he goes to his memory for his characters, to that vivid memory of youth which makes up by precision of portraiture for what it lacks in depth of comprehension. And this is the distinguishing characteristic of *The Merry Wives*, particularly in the beginning. Even without 'the dozen white luces' in his coat, one would swear that this Justice Shallow, with his pompous pride of birth and his stilted stupidity, is a portrait from life, some Sir Thomas Lucy or other, and Justice Shallow is not so deeply etched in as his cousin, Master Slender – 'a little wee face, with a little yellow beard, – a cane-coloured beard'. Such physical portraiture, as I have said, is very rare and very significant in Shakespeare. This photograph is slightly malevolent, too, as of one whose malice is protected by a Queen's commission. Those who do not believe traditions when thus circumstantially supported would not believe though one rose from the dead to witness to them. *The Merry Wives* is worthful to me as the only piece of Shakespeare's journalism that we possess; here we find him doing task-work, and doing it at utmost speed. Those who wish to measure the difference between the conscious, deliberate work of the artist and the hurried slapdash performance of the journalist, have only to compare the Falstaff of *The Merry Wives* with the Falstaff of the two parts of *Henry IV*. But if we take it for granted that *The Merry Wives* was done in haste and to order, can any inference be fairly drawn from the feebleness of Falstaff and the unreality of his love-making? I think so; it seems to me that, if Falstaff had been a creation, Shakespeare must have reproduced him more effectively. His love-making in the second part of *Henry IV* is real enough. But just because Falstaff was taken from life, and studied from the outside, Shakespeare having painted him once could not paint him again, he had exhausted his model and could only echo him.

The heart of the matter is that, whereas Shakespeare's men of action, when he is not helped by history or tradition, are thinly conceived and poorly painted, his comic characters – Falstaff, Sir Toby Belch, and Dogberry; Maria, Dame Quickly, and the Nurse, creatures of observation though they be, are only inferior as works of art to the portraits of himself which he has given us in Romeo, Hamlet, Macbeth, Orsino, and Posthumus. It is his humour which makes Shakespeare the greatest of dramatists, the most complete of men.

BOOK TWO

I

Shakespeare's Early Attempts to Portray Himself and his Wife: Biron, Adriana, Valentine

In the preceding chapters I have considered those impersonations of Shakespeare which revealed most distinctly the salient features of his character. I now regard this part of my work as finished: the outlines at least of his nature are established beyond dispute, and I may therefore be permitted to return upon my steps, and beginning with the earliest works pass in review most of the other personages who discover him, however feebly or profoundly. Hitherto I have rather challenged contradiction than tried to conciliate or persuade; it was necessary to convince the reader that Shakespeare was indeed Hamlet-Orsino, plus an exquisite sense of humour; and as the proofs of this were almost inexhaustible, and as the stability of the whole structure depended on the firmness of the foundations, I was more than willing to call forth opposition in order once for all to strangle doubt. But now that I have to put in the finer traits of the portrait I have to hope for the goodwill at least of my readers. Even then my task is not easy. The subtler traits of a man's character often elude accurate description, to say nothing of exact proof; the differences in tone between a dramatist's own experiences of life and his observation of the experiences of others are often so slight as to be all but unnoticeable. In the case of some peculiarities I have only a mere suggestion to go upon, in that of others a bare surmise, a hint so fleeting that it may well seem to the judicious as if the meshes of language were too coarse to catch such evanescent indication.

Fortunately in this work I am not called on to limit myself to that which can be proved beyond question, or to the ordinary man. I think my reader will allow me, or indeed expect me, now to throw off constraint and finish my picture as I please.

In this second book then I shall try to correct Shakespeare's portraits of himself by bringing out his concealed faults and vices – the short-comings one's vanity slurs over and omits. Above all I shall try to notice anything that throws light upon his life, for I have to tell here the story of his passion and his soul's wreck. At the crisis of his life he revealed himself almost without affectation; in agony men forget to pose. And this more intimate understanding of the man will enable us to recon-struct, partially at least, the happenings of his life, and so trace not only his development, but the incidents of his life's journey from his school days in 1575 till he crept home to Stratford to die nearly forty years later.

The chief academic critics, such as Professor Dowden and Dr Brandes, take pains to inform us that Biron in *Love's Labour's Lost* is nothing but an impersonation of Shakespeare. This would show much insight on the part of the Professors were it not that Coleridge as usual has been before them, and that Coleridge's statement is to be preferred to theirs. Coleridge was careful to say that the whole play revealed many of Shakespeare's characteristic features, and he added finely, 'as in a por-trait taken of him in his boyhood'. This is far truer than Dowden's more precise statement that 'Berowne is the exponent of Shakespeare's own thought'. For though, of course, Biron is especially the mouth-piece of the poet, yet Shakespeare reveals himself in the first speech of the King as clearly as he does in any speech of Biron:

> Let Fame, that all hunt after in their lives,
> Live registered upon our brazen tombs,
> And then grace us in the disgrace of death;
> When, spite of cormorant devouring Time,
> The endeavour of this present breath may buy
> That honour which shall 'bate his scythe's keen edge,
> And make us heirs of all eternity.

The King's criticism, too, of Armado in the first scene is more finely characteristic of Shakespeare than Biron's criticism of Boyet in the last act. In this, his first drama, Shakespeare can hardly sketch a sympathetic character without putting something of himself into it.

I regard *Love's Labour's Lost* as Shakespeare's earliest comedy, not only because the greater part of it is in rhymed verse, but also because he was unable in it to individualise his serious personages at all; the comic characters, on the other hand, are already carefully observed and distinctly differenced. Biron himself is scarcely more than a charming sketch: he is almost as interested in language as in love, and he plays with words till they revenge themselves by obscuring his wit; he is filled with the high spirits of youth; in fact, he shows us the form and pressure of the Renaissance as clearly as the features of Shakespeare. It is, however, Biron-Shakespeare who understands that the real world is built on broader natural foundations than the King's womanless Academe, and therefore predicts the failure of the ascetic experiment. Another trait in Biron that brings us close to Shakespeare is his contempt for book-learning;

> Small have continual plodders ever won
> Save bare authority from others' books.
> [. . .]
> Too much to know is to know nought but fame;
> And every godfather can give a name.

Again and again he returns to the charge:

> To study now it is too late,
> Climb o'er the house to unlock the little gate.

The summing up is triumphant:

> So, study evermore is overshot.

In fine, Biron ridicules study at such length and with such earnestness and pointed phrase that it is manifest the discussion was intensely interesting to Shakespeare himself. But we should have expected Shakespeare's *alter ego* to be arguing on the other side; for again and again we have had to notice that Shakespeare was a confirmed lover of books; he was always using bookish metaphors, and Hamlet was a student by nature. This attitude on the part of Biron, then, calls for explanation, and it seems to me that the only possible explanation is to be found in Shakespeare's own experience. Those who know England as she was in the days of Elizabeth, or as she is today, will hardly need to be told that when Shakespeare first came to London he was regarded as an unlettered provincial ('with little Latin and less Greek'), and had to bear the mocks and flouts of his beschooled fellows, who esteemed learning and gentility above genius. In his very first independent play he answered the scorners with scorn. But this disdain of study was not Shakespeare's real feeling; and his natural loyalty to the deeper truth forced him to make Biron contradict and excuse his own argument in a way which seems to me altogether charming; but is certainly undramatic:

> – Though I have for barbarism spoke more
> Than for that angel knowledge you can say.

Undramatic the declaration is because it is at war with the length and earnestness with which Biron has maintained his contempt for learning; but here undoubtedly we find the true Shakespeare who as a youth speaks of 'that angel, knowledge', just as in *Cymbeline* twenty years later he calls reverence, 'that angel of the world'.

When we come to his 'Life' we shall see that Shakespeare, who was thrown into the scrimmage of existence as a youth, and had to win his own way in the world, had, naturally enough, a much higher opinion of books and book-learning than Goethe, who was bred a student and knew life only as an amateur:

> Einen Blick in's Buch hinein und zwei in's Leben
> Das muss die rechte Form dem Geiste geben.

Shakespeare would undoubtedly have given 'two glances' to books and one to life, had he been free to choose; but perhaps after all Goethe was right in warning us that life is more valuable to the artist than any transcript of it.

To return to our theme; Biron is not among Shakespeare's successful portraits of himself. As might be expected in a first essay, the drawing is now over-minute, now too loose. When Biron talks of study, he reveals, as we have seen, personal feelings that are merely transient; on the other hand, when he talks about Boyet he talks merely to hear 'the music of his own vain tongue'. He is, however, always nimble-witted and impulsive; 'quick Biron' as the Princess calls him, a gentleman of charming manners, of incomparable fluent, graceful, and witty speech, which qualities afterwards came to blossom in Mercutio and Gratiano. The faults in portraiture are manifestly due to inexperience: Shakespeare was still too youthful-timid to paint his chief features boldly, and it is left for Rosaline to picture Biron for us as Shakespeare doubtless desired to appear:

> A merrier man,
> Within the limits of becoming mirth,
> I never spent an hour's talk withal.

> His eye begets occasion for his wit;
> For every object that the one doth catch,
> The other turns to a mirth-moving jest,
> Which his fair tongue, conceit's expositor,
> Delivers in such apt and gracious words
> That aged ears play truant at his tales,
> And younger hearings are quite ravished,
> So sweet and voluble is his discourse.

Every touch of this self-painted portrait deserves to be studied: it is the first photograph of our poet which we possess – a photograph, too, taken in early manhood. Shakespeare's wit we knew, his mirth too, and that his conversation was voluble and sweet enough to ravish youthful ears and enthrall the aged we might have guessed from Jonson's report. But it is delightful to hear of his mirth-moving words and to know that he regarded himself as the best talker in the world. But just as the play at the end turns from love-making and gay courtesies to thoughts of death and 'world-without-end' pledges, so Biron's merriment is only the effervescence of youth, and love brings out in him Shakespeare's characteristic melancholy:

> By heaven, I do love, and it hath taught me to rhyme, and to be melancholy.

Again and again, as in his apology to Rosaline and his appeal at the end of the play to 'honest plain words', he shows a deep underlying seriousness. The soul of quick talkative mirthful Biron is that he loves beauty whether of women or of words, and though he condemns 'taffeta phrases', he shows his liking for the 'silken terms precise' in the very form of his condemnation.

Of course all careful readers know that the greater seriousness of the last two acts of *Love's Labour's Lost*, and the frequent use of blank verse instead of rhymed verse in them, are due to the fact that Shakespeare revised the play in 1597, some eight or nine years probably after he had first written it. Everyone must have noticed the repetitions in Biron's long speech at the end of the fourth act, which show the original garment and the later, finer embroidery. As I shall have to return to this revision for other reasons, it will be enough here to remark that it is especially the speeches of Biron which Shakespeare improved in the second handling.

Dr Brandes, or rather Coleridge, tells us that in Biron and his Rosaline we have the first hesitating sketch of the masterly Benedick and Beatrice of *Much Ado About Nothing*; but in this I think Coleridge goes too far. Unformed as Biron is, he is Shakespeare in early youth, whereas in Benedick the likeness is not by any means so clear. In fact, Benedick is merely an admirable stage silhouette and needs to be filled out with an actor's personality. Beatrice, on the other hand, is a woman of a very distinct type, whereas Rosaline needs pages of explanation, which Coleridge never dreamed of. A certain similarity rather of situation than of character seems to have misled Coleridge in this instance. Boyet jests with Maria and Rosaline just as Biron does, and just as Benedick jests with Beatrice: all these scenes simply show how intensely young Shakespeare enjoyed a combat of wits, spiced with the suggestiveness that nearly always shows itself when the combatants are of different sexes.

It is almost certain that *Love's Labour's Lost* was wholly conceived and constructed as well as written by Shakespeare; no play or story has yet been found which might, in this case, have served him as a model. For the first and probably the last time he seems to have taken the entire drama from his imagination, and the result from a playwright's point of view is unfortunate; *Love's Labour's Lost* is his slightest and feeblest play. It is scarcely ever seen on the stage – is, indeed, practically unactable. This fact goes to confirm the view already put forth more than once in these pages, that Shakespeare was not a good playwright and took little or no interest in the external incidents of his dramas. The plot and action of the story, so carefully worked out by the ordinary playwright and so highly esteemed by critics and spectators, he always borrows, as if he had recognised the weakness of this first attempt, and when he sets himself to construct a play, it has no action, no plot – is, indeed, merely a succession of fantastic occurrences that give occasion for light love-making and brilliant talk. Even in regard to the grouping of characters the construction of his early plays is puerile, mechanical; in *Love's Labour's Lost* the King with his three courtiers is set against the Princess and her three ladies; in *The Two Gentlemen of Verona* there is the faithful Valentine opposed to the inconstant Proteus, and each of them has a comic servant; and when later his plays from this point of view were not manufactured but grew, and thus assumed the beautiful irregular symmetry of life, the incidents were still neglected. Neither the poet nor the philosopher in Shakespeare felt much of the child's interest in the story; he chose his tales for the sake of the characters and the poetry, and whether they were effective stage-tales or not troubled him but little. There is hardly more plot or action in *Lear* than in *Love's Labour's Lost*.

It is probable that *The Comedy of Errors* followed hard on the heels of *Love's Labour's Lost*. It practically belongs to the same period: it has fewer lines of prose in it than *Love's Labour's Lost*; but, on the other hand, the intrigue-spinning is clever, and the whole play shows a riper knowledge of theatrical conditions. Perhaps because the intrigue is more interesting, the character-drawing is even feebler than that of the earlier comedy: indeed, so far as the men go there is hardly anything worth calling character-drawing at all. Shakespeare speaks through this or that mask as occasion tempts him: and if the women are sharply, crudely differentiated, it is because Shakespeare, as I shall show later, has sketched his wife for us in Adriana, and his view of her character is decided enough if not over kind. Still, any and every peculiarity of character deserves notice, for in these earliest works Shakespeare is compelled to use his personal experience, to tell us of his own life and his own feelings, not having any wider knowledge to draw upon. Every word, therefore, in these first comedies, is important to those who would learn the story of his youth and fathom the idiosyncrasies of his being. When Aegeon, in the opening scenes, tells the Duke about the shipwreck in which he is separated from his wife and child, he declares that he himself 'would gladly have embraced immediate death'. No reason is given for this extraordinary contempt of living. It was the 'incessant weepings' of his wife, the 'piteous plainings of the pretty babes', that forced him, he says, to exert himself. But wives don't weep incessantly in danger, nor are the 'piteous plainings of the pretty babes' a feature of shipwreck; I find here a little picture of Shakespeare's early married life in Stratford – a snapshot of memory. Aegeon concludes his account by saying that his life was prolonged in order

> To tell sad stories of my own mishaps

– which reminds one of similar words used later by Richard II. This personal, melancholy note is here forced and false, for Aegeon surely lives in hope of finding his wife and child and not in order to tell of his misfortunes. Aegeon is evidently a breath of Shakespeare himself, and not more than a breath, because he only appears again when the play is practically finished. Deep-brooding melancholy was the customary habit of Shakespeare even in youth.

Just as in *Love's Labour's Lost* we find Shakespeare speaking first through the King and then more fully through the hero, Biron, so here he first speaks through Aegeon and then at greater length through the protagonist Antipholus of Syracuse. Antipholus is introduced to us as new come to Ephesus, and Shakespeare is evidently thinking of his own first day in London when he puts in his mouth these words:

> Within this hour it will be dinner-time:
> Till that, I'll view the manners of the town,
> Peruse the traders, gaze upon the buildings,
> And then return and sleep within mine inn;
> For with long travel I am stiff and weary.

Though 'stiff and weary' he is too eager-young to rest; he will see everything – even 'peruse the traders' – how the bookish metaphor always comes to Shakespeare's lips! – before he will eat or sleep. The utterly needless last line, with its emphatic description – 'stiff and weary' – corroborates my belief that Shakespeare in this passage is telling us what he himself felt and did on his first arrival in London. In the second scene of the third act Antipholus sends his servant to the port:

> I will not harbour in this town tonight
> If any bark put forth.

From the fact that Shakespeare represented Antipholus to himself as wishing to leave Ephesus by sea, it is probable that he pictured him coming to Ephesus in a ship. But when Shakespeare begins to tell us what he did on reaching London he recalls his own desires and then his own feelings; he was 'stiff and weary' on that first day because he rode, or more probably walked, into London; one does not become 'stiff and weary' on board ship. This is another snapshot at that early life of Shakespeare, and his arrival in London, which one would not willingly miss. And surely it is the country-bred lad from Stratford who, fearing all manner of town-tricks, speaks in this way:

> They say this town is full of cozenage;
> As, nimble jugglers that deceive the eye,
> Dark-working sorcerers that change the mind,
> Soul-killing witches that deform the body,
> Disguised cheaters, prating mountebanks,
> And many suchlike liberties of sin:

[. . .]
I greatly fear my money is not safe.

This Antipholus is most ingenuous-talkative; without being questioned he tells about his servant:

> A trusty villain, sir; that very oft,
> When I am dull with care and melancholy,
> Lightens my humour with his merry jests.

And as if this did not mark his peculiar thoughtful temperament sufficiently, he tells the merchant:

> I will go lose myself,
> And wander up and down to view the city.

And when the merchant leaves him, commending him to his own content, he talks to himself in this strain:

> He that commends me to mine own content,
> Commends me to the thing I cannot get,
> [. . .]
> So I, to find a mother and a brother,
> In quest of them, unhappy, lose myself.

A most curious way, it must be confessed, to seek for anyone; but perfectly natural to the refined, melancholy, meditative, book-loving temperament which was already Shakespeare's. In this 'unhappy' and 'mother' I think I hear an echo of Shakespeare's sorrow at parting from his own mother.

This Antipholus, although very free and open, has a reserve of dignity, as we see in the second scene of the second act, when he talks with his servant, who, as he thinks, has played with him:

> Because that I familiarly sometimes
> Do use you for my fool, and chat with you,
> Your sauciness will jest upon my love,
> And make a common of my serious hours.
> When the sun shines let foolish gnats make sport,
> But creep in crannies when he hides his beams.

The self-esteem seems a little exaggerated here; but, after all, it is only natural; the whole scene is taken from Shakespeare's experience: the man who will chat familiarly with his servant, and jest with him as well, must expect to have to pull him up at times rather sharply. Antipholus proceeds to play with his servant in a fencing match of wit – a practice Shakespeare seems to have delighted in. But it is when Antipholus falls in love with Luciana that he shows us Shakespeare at his most natural as a lover. Luciana has just taken him to task for not loving her sister Adriana, who, she thinks, is his wife. Antipholus answers her thus:

> Sweet mistress, – what your name is else, I know not,
> Nor by what wonder you do hit of mine, –
> Less in your knowledge and your face you show not,
> Than our earth's wonder; more than earth divine,
> Teach me, dear creature, how to think and speak;
> Lay open to my earthy-gross conceit,
> Smother'd in errors, feeble, shallow, weak,
> The folded meaning of your words' deceit . . .

He declares, in fact, that he loves her and not her sister:

> Sing, siren, for thyself and I will dote:
> Spread o'er the silver waves thy golden hairs,
> And as a bed I'll take them and there lie;
> [. . .]
> It is thyself, mine own self's better part,
> Mine eye's clear eye, my dear heart's dearer heart.

And as if this were not enough he goes on:

> My food, my fortune, and my sweet hope's aim,
> My sole earth's heaven, and my heaven's claim.

The word-conceits were a fashion of the time; but in spite of the verbal affectation, the courting shows the cunning of experience, and has, besides, a sort of echo of sincere feeling. How Shakespeare delights in making love! It reminds one of the first flutings of a thrush in early spring; over and over again he tries the notes with delighted iteration till he becomes a master of his music and charms the copses to silence with his song: and so Shakespeare sings of love again and again till at length we get the liquid notes of passion and the trills of joy all perfected in *Romeo and Juliet*; but the voice is the voice we heard before in *Venus and Adonis* and *The Comedy of Errors*.

Antipholus' other appearances are not important. He merely fills his part till in the last scene he assures Luciana that he will make good his earlier protestations of love; but so far as he has any character at all, or distinctive individuality, he is young Shakespeare himself and his experiences are Shakespeare's.

Now a word or two about Adriana. Shakespeare makes her a jealous, nagging, violent scold, who will have her husband arrested for debt, though she will give money to free him. But the comedy of the play would be better brought out if Adriana were pictured as loving and constant, inflicting her inconvenient affection upon the false husband as upon the true. Why did Shakespeare want to paint this unpleasant bitter-tongued wife?

When Adriana appears in the first scene of the second act she is at once sketched in her impatience and jealousy. She wants to know why her husband should have more liberty than she has, and declares that none but asses will be bridled so. Then she will strike her servant. In the first five minutes of this act she is sketched to the life, and Shakespeare does nothing afterwards but repeat and deepen the same strokes: it seems as if he knew nothing about her or would depict nothing of her except her jealousy and nagging, her impatience and violence. We have had occasion to notice more than once that when Shakespeare repeats touches in this way, he is drawing from life, from memory, and not from imagination. Moreover, in this case, he shows us at once that he is telling of his wife, because she defends herself against the accusation of age, which no one brings against her, though everyone knows that Shakespeare's wife was eight years older than himself.

> His company must do his minions grace,
> Whilst I at home starve for a merry look.
> Hath homely age the alluring beauty took
> From my poor cheek? then he hath wasted it
> [. . .]
> My decayed fair
> A sunny look of his would soon repair:
> But, poor unruly deer, he breaks the pale,
> And feeds from home; poor I am but his stale.

The appeal is pathetic; but Luciana will not see it. She cries:

> Self-harming jealousy! fie, beat it hence!

In the second scene of this second act Adriana goes on nagging in almost the same way.

In the second scene of the third act there is a phrase from the hero, Antipholus of Syracuse, about Adriana which I find significant:

> She that doth call me husband, even my soul
> Doth for a wife abhor!

There is no reason in the comedy for such strong words. Most men would be amused or pleased by a woman who makes up to them as Adriana makes up to Antipholus. I hear Shakespeare in this uncalled-for, over-emphatic 'even my soul doth for a wife abhor'.

In the fifth act Adriana is brought before the Abbess, and is proved to be a jealous scold. Shakespeare will not be satisfied till some impartial great person of Adriana's own sex has condemned her. Adriana admits that she has scolded her husband in public and in private, too; the Abbess replies:

> And thereof came it that the man was mad.

And she adds:

> The venom clamours of a jealous woman
> Poisons more deadly than a mad dog's tooth.

Again, a needlessly emphatic condemnation. But Adriana will not accept the reproof: she will have her husband at all costs. The whole scene discovers personal feeling. Adriana is the portrait that Shakespeare wished to give us of his wife.

The learned commentators have seemingly conspired to say as little about *The Two Gentlemen of Verona* as possible. No one of them identifies the protagonist, Valentine, with Shakespeare, though all of them identified Biron with Shakespeare, and yet Valentine, as we shall see, is a far better portrait of the master than Biron. This untimely blindness of the critics is, evidently, due to the fact that Coleridge has hardly mentioned *The Two Gentlemen of Verona*, and they have consequently been unable to parrot his opinions.

The Two Gentlemen of Verona is manifestly a later work than *Love's Labour's Lost*; there is more blank verse and less rhyme in it, and a considerable improvement in character-drawing. Julia, for example, is individualised and lives for us in her affection and jealousy; her talks with her maid Lucetta are taken from life; they are indeed the first sketch of the delightful talks between Portia and Nerissa, and mark an immense advance upon the wordy badinage of the Princess and her ladies in *Love's Labour's Lost*, where there was no attempt at differentiation of character. It seems indubitable to me that *The Two Gentlemen of Verona* is also later than *The Comedy of Errors*, and just as far beyond doubt that it is earlier than *A Midsummer Night's Dream*, in spite of Dr Furnival's *Trial Table*.

The first three comedies, *Love's Labour's Lost*, *The Comedy of Errors*, and *The Two Gentlemen of Verona*, are all noteworthy for the light they throw on Shakespeare's early life.

In *The Two Gentlemen of Verona* Shakespeare makes similar youthful mistakes in portraiture to those we noticed in *Love's Labour's Lost*; mistakes which show that he is thinking of himself and his own circumstances. At the beginning of the play the only difference between Proteus and Valentine is that one is in love, and the other, heart-free, is leaving home to go to Milan. In this first scene Shakespeare speaks frankly through both Proteus and Valentine, just as he spoke through both the King and Biron in the first scene of *Love's Labour's Lost*, and through both Aegeon and Antipholus of Syracuse in *The Comedy of Errors*. But whilst the circumstances in the earliest comedy are imaginary and fantastic, the circumstances in *The Two Gentlemen of Verona* are manifestly, I think, taken from the poet's own experience. In the dialogue between Valentine and Proteus I hear Shakespeare persuading himself that he should leave Stratford. Some readers may regard this assumption as far-fetched, but it will appear the more plausible, I think, the more the dialogue is studied. Valentine begins the argument:

> Home-keeping youth have ever homely wits, –

he will 'see the wonders of the world abroad' rather than live 'dully sluggardis'd at home', wearing out 'youth with shapeless idleness'. But all these reasons are at once superfluous and peculiar. The audience needs no persuasion to believe that a young man is eager to travel and go to Court. Shakespeare's quick mounting spirit is in the lines, and the needlessness of the argument shows that we have here a personal confession. Valentine, then, mocks at love, because it was love that held Shakespeare so long in Stratford, and when Proteus defends it, he replies:

> Even so by Love the young and tender wit
> Is turned to folly; blasting in the bud,
> Losing his verdure even in the prime,
> And all the fair effects of future hopes.

Here is Shakespeare's confession that his marriage had been a failure, not only because of his wife's mad jealousy and violent temper, which we have been forced to realise in *The Comedy of Errors*, but also because love and its home-keeping ways threatened to dull and imprison the eager artist spirit. In the last charming line I find not only the music of Shakespeare's voice, but also one of the reasons – perhaps, indeed, the chief because the highest reason – which drew him from Stratford to London. And what the 'future hope' was, he told us in the very first line of *Love's Labour's Lost*. The King begins the play with

> Let Fame, that all hunt after in their lives.

Now all men don't hunt after fame; it was Shakespeare who felt that Fame pieced out Life's span and made us 'heirs of all eternity'; it was young Shakespeare who desired fame so passionately that he believed all other men must share his immortal longing, the desire in him being a forecast of capacity, as, indeed, it usually is. If anyone is inclined to think that I am here abusing conjecture let him remember that Proteus, too, tells us that Valentine is hunting after honour.

When Proteus defends love we hear Shakespeare just as clearly as when Valentine inveighs against it:

> Yet writers say, as in the sweetest bud
> The eating canker dwells, so eating love
> Inhabits in the finest wits of all.

Shakespeare could not be disloyal to that passion of desire in him which he instinctively felt was, in some way or other, the necessary complement of his splendid intelligence. We must take the summing-up of Proteus when Valentine leaves him as the other half of Shakespeare's personal confession:

> He after honour hunts, I after love:
> He leaves his friends to dignify them more;
> I leave myself, my friends, and all for love.
> Thou, Julia, thou hast metamorphosed me, –
> Made me neglect my studies, lose my time,
> War with good counsel, set the world at naught;
> Made wit with musing weak, heart sick with thought.

Young Shakespeare hunted as much after love as after honour, and these verses show that he has fully understood what a drag on him his foolish marriage has been. That all this is true to Shakespeare appears from the fact that it is false to the character of Proteus. Proteus is supposed to talk like this in the first blush of passion, before he has won Julia, before he even knows that she loves him. Is that natural? Or is it not rather Shakespeare's confession of what two wasted years of married life in Stratford had done for him? It was ambition – desire of fame and new love – that drove the tired and discontented Shakespeare from Anne Hathaway's arms to London.

When his father tells Proteus he must to Court on the morrow, instead of showing indignation or obstinate resolve to outwit tyranny, he generalises in Shakespeare's way, exactly as Romeo and Orsino generalise in poetic numbers:

> O, how this spring of love resembleth
> The uncertain glory of an April day.

Another reason for believing that this play deals with Shakespeare's own experiences is to be found in the curious change that takes place in Valentine. In the first act Valentine disdains love: he prefers to travel and win honour; but as soon as he reaches Milan and sees Silvia, he falls even more desperately in love than Proteus. What was the object, then, in making him talk so earnestly against love in the first act? It may be argued that Shakespeare intended merely to contrast the two characters in the first act; but he contrasts them in the first act on this matter of love, only in the second act to annul the distinction himself created. Moreover, and this is decisive, Valentine rails against love in the first act as one who has experienced love's utmost rage:

> To be
> In love: when scorn is bought with groans; coy looks,
> With heart-sore sighs; one fading moment's mirth,
> With twenty watchful, weary, tedious nights.

The man who speaks like this is not the man who despises love and prefers honour, but one who has already given himself to passion with an absolute abandonment. Such inconsistencies and flaws in workmanship are in themselves trivial, but, from my point of view, significant; for whenever Shakespeare slips in drawing character, in nine cases out of ten he slips through dragging in his own personality or his personal experience, and not through carelessness, much less incompetence; his mistakes, therefore, nearly always throw light on his nature or on his life's story. From the beginning, too, Valentine like Shakespeare is a born lover.

As soon, moreover, as he has gone to the capital and fallen in love he becomes Shakespeare's avowed favourite. He finds Silvia's glove and cries:

> Sweet ornament that decks a thing divine –

the exclamation reminding us of how Romeo talks of Juliet's glove. Like other men, Shakespeare learned life gradually, and in youth poverty of experience forces him to repeat his effects.

Again, when Valentine praises his friend Proteus to the Duke, we find a characteristic touch of Shakespeare. Valentine says:

> His years but young; but his experience old;
> His head unmellowed; but his judgement ripe.

In *The Merchant of Venice* Bellario, the learned doctor of Padua, praises Portia in similar terms:

> I never knew so young a body with so old a head.

But it is when Valentine confesses his love that Shakespeare speaks through him most clearly:

> Ay, Proteus, but that life is altered now,
> I have done penance for contemning love;
> [. . .]
> For in revenge of my contempt of love
> Love hath chased sleep from my enthralled eyes
> And made them watchers of my own heart's sorrow.
> O gentle Proteus, Love's a mighty lord, –

and so on.

Every word in this confession is characteristic of the poet and especially the fact that his insomnia is due to love. Valentine then gives himself to passionate praise of Silvia, and ends with the 'She is alone' that recalls 'She is all the beauty extant' of *The Two Noble Kinsmen*. Valentine the lover reminds us of Romeo as the sketch resembles the finished picture; when banished, he cries:

> And why not death, rather than living torment?
> To die is to be banished from myself;

> And Silvia is myself: banished from her,
> Is self from self; a deadly banishment.
> What light is light, if Silvia be not seen?
> What joy is joy, if Silvia be not by?
> Unless it be to think that she is by
> And feed upon the shadow of perfection.
> Except I be by Silvia in the night
> There is no music in the nightingale,

and so forth. I might compare this with what Romeo says of his banishment, and perhaps infer from this twofold treatment of the theme that Shakespeare left behind in Stratford some dark beauty who may have given Anne Hathaway good cause for jealous rage. It must not be forgotten here that Dryasdust tells us he was betrothed to another girl when Anne Hathaway's relations forced him to marry their kinswoman.

A moment later and this lover Valentine uses the very words that we found so characteristic in the mouth of the lover Orsino in *Twelfth Night*:

> O I have fed upon this woe already,
> And now excess of it will make me surfeit.

Valentine, indeed, shows us traits of nearly all Shakespeare's later lovers, and this seems to me interesting, because of course all the qualities were in the youth, which were later differenced into various characters. His advice to the Duke, who pretends to be in love, is far too ripe, too contemptuous-true, to suit the character of such a votary of fond desire as Valentine was; it is mellow with experience and man-of-the-world wisdom, and the last couplet of it distinctly foreshadows Benedick:

> Flatter and praise, commend, extol their graces;
> Though ne'er so black, say they have angels' faces.
> That man that hath a tongue, I say, is no man
> If with his tongue he cannot win a woman.

But this is only an involuntary *aperçu* of Valentine, as indeed Benedick is only an intellectual mood of Shakespeare. And here Valentine is contrasted with Proteus, who gives somewhat different advice to Thurio, and yet advice which is still more characteristic of Shakespeare than Valentine-Benedick's counsel. Proteus says:

> You must lay lime to tangle her desires

> By wailful sonnets, whose composed rhymes
> Should be full fraught with serviceable vows.

In this way the young poet sought to give expression to different views of life, and so realise the complexity of his own nature.

The other traits of Valentine's character that do not necessarily belong to him as a lover are all characteristic traits of Shakespeare. When he is playing the banished robber-chief far from his love, this is how Valentine consoles himself:

> This shadowy desert, unfrequented woods,
> I better brook than flourishing peopled towns:
> Here can I sit alone unseen of any,
> And to the nightingale's complaining notes
> Tune my distresses and record my woes.

This idyllic love of nature, this marked preference for the country over the city, however peculiar in a highway robber, are characteristics of Shakespeare from youth to age. Not only do his comedies lead us continually from the haunts of men to the forest and stream, but also his tragedies. He turns to nature, indeed, in all times of stress and trouble for its healing unconsciousness, its gentle changes that can be foreseen and reckoned upon, and that yet bring fresh interests and charming surprises; and in times of health and happiness he pictures the pleasant earth and its diviner beauties with a passionate intensity. Again and again we shall have to notice his poet's love for 'unfrequented woods', his thinker's longing for 'the life removed'.

At the end of the drama Valentine displays the gentle forgivingness of disposition which we have already had reason to regard as one of Shakespeare's most marked characteristics. As soon as 'false, fleeting Proteus' confesses his sin Valentine pardons him with words that echo and re-echo through Shakespeare's later dramas:

> Then I am paid,
> And once again I do receive thee honest.
> Who by repentance is not satisfied
> Is nor of heaven nor earth; for these are pleased;
> By patience the Eternal's wrath's appeased.

He even goes further than this, and confounds our knowledge of human nature by adding:

>   And that my love may appear plain and free
>   All that was mine in Silvia I give thee.

And that the meaning may be made more distinct than words can make it, he causes Julia to faint on hearing the proposal. One cannot help recalling the passage in *The Merchant of Venice* when Bassanio and Gratiano both declare they would sacrifice their wives to free Antonio, and a well-known sonnet which seems to prove that Shakespeare thought more of a man's friendship for a man than of a man's love for a woman. But as I shall have to discuss this point at length when I handle the Sonnets, I have, perhaps, said enough for the moment. Nor need I consider the fact here that the whole of this last scene of the last act was manifestly revised or rewritten by Shakespeare *circa* 1598 – years after the rest of the play.

I think everyone will admit now that Shakespeare revealed himself in *The Two Gentlemen of Verona*, and especially in Valentine, much more fully than in Biron and in *Love's Labour's Lost*. The three earliest comedies prove that from the very beginning of his career Shakespeare's chief aim was to reveal and realise himself.

Shakespeare as Antonio, the Merchant

No one, so far as I know, has yet tried to identify Antonio, the Merchant of Venice, with Shakespeare, and yet Antonio is Shakespeare himself, and Shakespeare in what to us, children of an industrial civilisation, is the most interesting attitude possible. Here in Antonio for the first time we discover Shakespeare in direct relations with real life, as real life is understood in the twentieth century. From Antonio we shall learn what Shakespeare thought of business men and business methods – of our modern way of living. Of course we must be on our guard against drawing general conclusions from this solitary example, unless we find from other plays that Antonio's attitude towards practical affairs was indeed Shakespeare's. But if this is the case, if Shakespeare has depicted himself characteristically in Antonio, how interesting it will be to hear his opinion of our money-making civilisation. It will be as if he rose from the dead to tell us what he thinks of our doings. He has been represented by this critic and by that as a master of affairs, a prudent thrifty soul; now we shall see if this monstrous hybrid of tradesman-poet ever had any foundation in fact.

The first point to be settled is: Did Shakespeare reveal himself very ingenuously and completely in Antonio, or was the 'royal merchant' a mere pose of his, a mood or a convention? Let us take Antonio's first words, the words, too, which begin the play:

> In sooth, I know not why I am so sad:
> It wearies me; you say it wearies you;
> But how I caught it, found it, or came by it,
> What stuff 'tis made of, whereof it is born,
> I am to learn;
> And such a want-wit sadness makes of me,
> That I have much ado to know myself.

It is this very sadness that makes it easy for us to know Shakespeare, even when he disguises himself as a Venetian merchant. A little later and Jaques will describe and define the disease as 'humorous melancholy'; but here it is already a settled habit of mind.

Antonio then explains that his sadness has no cause, and incidentally attributes his wealth to fortune and not to his own brains or endeavour. The modern idea of the Captain of Industry who enriches others as well as himself, had evidently never entered into Shakespeare's head. Salarino says Antonio is 'sad to think upon his merchandise'; but Antonio answers:

> Believe me, no: I thank my fortune for it.
> My ventures are not in one bottom trusted,
> Nor to one place: nor is my whole estate
> Upon the fortune of this present year:
> Therefore my merchandise makes me not sad.

This tone of modest gentle sincerity is Shakespeare's habitual tone from about his thirtieth year to the end of his life: it has the accent of unaffected nature. In bidding farewell to Salarino Antonio shows us the exquisite courtesy which Shakespeare used in life. Salarino, seeing Bassanio approaching, says:

> I would have stayed till I had made you merry,
> If worthier friends had not prevented me.

Antonio answers:

> Your worth is very dear in my regard.
> I take it, your own business calls on you,
> And you embrace the occasion to depart.

More characteristic still is the dialogue between Gratiano and Antonio in the same scene. Gratiano, the twin-brother surely of Mercutio, tells Antonio that he thinks too much of the things of this world, and warns him:

> They lose it that do buy it with much care.

Antonio replies:

> I hold the world but as the world, Gratiano;
> A stage, where every man must play a part,
> And mine a sad one.

Everyone who has followed me so far will admit that this is Shakespeare's most usual and most ingenuous attitude towards life; 'I do not esteem worldly possessions', he says; 'life itself is too transient, too unreal to be dearly held'. Gratiano's reflection, too, is Shakespeare's, and puts the truth in a nutshell:

> They lose it that do buy it with much care.

We now come to the most salient peculiarity in this play. When Bassanio, his debtor, asks him for more money, Antonio answers:

> My purse, my person, my extremest means,
> Lie all unlocked to your occasions.

And, though Bassanio tells him his money is to be risked on a romantic and wild adventure, Antonio declares that Bassanio's doubt does him more wrong than if his friend had already wasted all he has, and the act closes by Antonio pressing Bassanio to use his credit 'to the uttermost'. Now, this contempt of money was, no doubt, a pose, if not a habit of the aristocratic society of the time, and Shakespeare may have been aping the tone of his betters in putting to show a most lavish generosity. But even if his social superiors encouraged him in a wasteful extravagance, it must be admitted that Shakespeare betters their teaching. The lord was riotously lavish, no doubt, because he had money, or could get it without much trouble; but, put in Antonio's position, he would not press his last penny on his friend, much less strain his credit 'to the uttermost' for him as Antonio does for Bassanio. Here we have the personal note of Shakespeare: 'Your affection,' says the elder man to the younger, 'is all to me, and money's less than nothing in the balance. Don't let us waste a word on it; a doubt of me were an injury!' But men will do that for affection which they would never do in cool blood, and therefore one cannot help asking whether Shakespeare really felt and practised this extreme contempt of wealth? For the moment, if we leave his actions out of the account, there can be, I think, no doubt about his feelings. His dislike of money makes him disfigure reality. No merchant, it may fairly be said, either of the sixteenth century or the twentieth, ever amassed or kept a fortune with Antonio's principles. In our day of world-wide speculation and immense wealth it is just possible for a man to be a millionaire and generous; but in the sixteenth century, when wealth was made by penurious saving, by slow daily adding of coin to coin, merchants like this Antonio were unheard of, impossible.

Moreover all the amiable characters in this play regard money with unaffected disdain; Portia no sooner hears of Shylock's suit than she cries:

> Pay him six thousand, and deface the bond;
> Double six thousand, and then treble that,
> Before a friend of this description
> Shall lose a hair through Bassanio's fault.

And if we attribute this outburst to her love we must not forget that, when it comes to the test in court, and she holds the Jew in her hand and might save her gold, she again reminds him:

> Shylock, there's thrice thy money offered thee'.

A boundless generosity is the characteristic of Portia, and Bassanio, the penniless fortune-hunter, is just as extravagant; he will pay the Jew's bond twice over, and,

> If that will not suffice,
> I will be bound to pay it ten times o'er,
> On forfeit of my hands, my head, my heart.

It may, of course, be urged that these Christians are all prodigal in order to throw Shylock's avarice and meanness into higher light; but that this disdain of money is not assumed for the sake of any artistic effect will appear from other plays. At the risk of being accused of super-subtlety, I must confess that I find in Shylock himself traces of Shakespeare's contempt of money; Jessica says of him:

> I have heard him swear
> To Tubal and to Chus, his countrymen,
> That he would rather have Antonio's flesh
> Than twenty times the value of the sum
> That he did owe him.

Even Shylock, it appears, hated Antonio more than he valued money, and this hatred, though it may have its root in love of money, half redeems him in our eyes. Shakespeare could not imagine a man who loved money more than anything else; his hated and hateful usurer is more a man of passion than a Jew.

The same prodigality and contempt of money are to be found in nearly all Shakespeare's plays, and, curiously enough, the persons to show this disdain most strongly are usually the masks of Shakespeare himself. A philosophic soliloquy is hardly more characteristic of Shakespeare than a sneer at money. It should be noted, too, that this peculiarity is not a trait of his youth chiefly, as it is with most men who are free-handed. It rather seems, as in the case of Antonio, to be a reasoned attitude towards life, and it undoubtedly becomes more and more marked as Shakespeare grows older. Contempt of wealth is stronger in Brutus than in Antonio; stronger in Lear than in Brutus, and stronger in Timon than in Lear.

But can we be at all certain that Antonio's view of life in this respect was Shakespeare's? It may be that Shakespeare pretended to this generosity in order to loosen the purse-strings of his lordly patrons. Even if his motive for writing in this strain were a worthy motive, who is to assure us that he practised the generosity he preached? When I come to his life I think I shall be able to prove that Shakespeare was excessively careless of money; extravagant, indeed, and generous to a fault. Shakespeare did not win to eminence as a dramatist without exciting the envy and jealousy of many of his colleagues and contemporaries, and if these sharp-eyed critics had found him in drama after drama advocating lavish free-handedness while showing meanness or even ordinary prudence in his own expenditure, we should probably have heard of it as we heard from Greene how he took plays from other playwrights. But the silence of his contemporaries goes to confirm the positive testimony of Ben Jonson, that he was of 'an open and free nature', – openhanded always, and liberal, we may be sure, to a fault. In any case, the burden of proof lies with those who wish us to believe that Shakespeare was 'a careful and prudent man of business', for in a dozen plays the personages who are his heroes and incarnations pour contempt on those who would lock 'rascal counters' from their friends, and, in default of proof to the contrary, we are compelled to assume that he practised the generosity which he so earnestly and sedulously praised. At least it will be advisable for the moment to assume that he pictured himself as generous Antonio, without difficulty or conscious self-deception.

But this Antonio has not only the melancholy, courtesy and boundless generosity of Shakespeare; he has other qualities of the master which need to be thrown into relief.

First of all, Antonio has that submission to misfortune, that resignation in face of defeat and suffering which we have already seen as characteristics of Richard II. The resignation might almost be called saintly, were it not that it seems to spring rather from the natural melancholy and sadness of Shakespeare's disposition; 'the world is a hard, all-hating world', he seems to say, 'and misery is the natural lot of man; defeat comes to all; why should I hope for any better fortune?' At the very beginning of the trial he recognises that he is certain to lose; Bassanio and Gratiano appeal to the Duke for him; but he never speaks in his own defence; he says of his opponent at the outset:

> I do oppose
> My patience to his fury, and am arm'd
> To suffer, with a quietness of spirit,
> The very tyranny and rage of his.

and again he will not contend, but begs the Court,

> . . . with all brief and plain conveniency
> Let me have judgement and the Jew his will.

Even when Bassanio tries to cheer him,

> What, man, courage yet!
> The Jew shall have my flesh, blood, bones and all,
> Ere thou shalt lose for me one drop of blood.

Antonio answers:

> I am a tainted wether of the flock,
> Meetest for death: the weakest kind of fruit
> Drops earliest to the ground: and so let me:
> You cannot better be employed, Bassanio,
> Than to live still and write mine epitaph.

He will not be saved: he gives himself at once to that 'sweet way of despair' which we have found to be the second Richard's way and Shakespeare's way.

Just as we noticed, when speaking of Posthumus in *Cymbeline*, that Shakespeare's hero and *alter ego* is always praised by the other personages of the drama, so this Antonio is praised preposterously by the chief personages of the play, and in the terms of praise we may see how Shakespeare, even in early manhood, liked to be considered. He had no ambition to be counted stalwart, or bold, or resolute like most young males of his race, much less 'a good hater', as Dr Johnson confessed himself: he wanted his gentle qualities recognised, and his intellectual gifts; Hamlet wished to be thought a courtier, scholar, gentleman; and here Salarino says of Antonio:

> A kinder gentleman treads not the earth,

and he goes on to tell how Antonio, when parting from Bassanio, had 'eyes big with tears':

> Turning his face, he put his hand behind him,
> And with affection wondrous sensible
> He wrung Bassanio's hand; and so they parted

This Antonio is as tender-hearted and loving as young Arthur. And Lorenzo speaks of Antonio to Portia just as Salarino spoke of him:

> LORENZO   But if you knew to whom you show this honour,
> How true a gentleman you send relief,
> How dear a lover of my lord your husband,
> I know you would be prouder of the work
> Than customary bounty can enforce you.

And finally Bassanio sums Antonio up in enthusiastic superlatives:

> The dearest friend to me, the kindest man,
> The best-condition'd and unwearied spirit
> In doing courtesies, and one in whom
> The ancient Roman honour more appears
> Than any that draws breath in Italy.

It is as a prince of friends and most courteous gentleman that Antonio acts his part from the beginning to the end of the play with one notable exception to which I shall return in a moment. It is astonishing to find this sadness, this courtesy, this lavish generosity and contempt of money, this love of love and friendship and affection in any man in early manhood; but these qualities were Shakespeare's from youth to old age.

I say that Antonio was most courteous to all with one notable exception, and that exception was Shylock.

It has become the custom on the English stage for the actor to try to turn Shylock into a hero; but that was assuredly not Shakespeare's intention. True, he makes Shylock appeal to the common humanity of both Jew and Christian:

I am a Jew. Hath not a Jew eyes? hath not a Jew hands, organs, dimensions, senses, affections, passions? fed with the same food, hurt with the same weapons, subject to the same diseases, healed by the same means, warmed and cooled by the same winter and summer, as a Christian is? If you prick us, do we not bleed? if you tickle us, do we not laugh? if you poison us, do we not die? and if you wrong us, shall we not revenge?'

But if Shakespeare was far in advance of his age in this intellectual appreciation of the brotherhood of man; yet as an artist and thinker and poet he is particularly contemptuous of the usurer and trader in other men's necessities, and therefore, when Antonio meets Shylock, though he wants a favour from him, he cannot be even decently polite to him. He begins by saying in the third scene of the first act:

> Although I neither lend nor borrow
> By taking nor by giving of excess,
> Yet to supply the ripe wants of my friend,
> I'll break a custom.

The first phrase here reminds me of Polonius: 'neither a borrower nor a lender be'. When Shylock attempts to defend himself by citing the way Jacob cheated Laban, Antonio answers contemptuously 'The devil can cite Scripture for his purpose'. Shylock then goes on:

> Signor Antonio, many a time and oft,
> In the Rialto you have rated me
> About my moneys and my usances:
> Still, I have borne it with a patient shrug,
> For sufferance is the badge of all our tribe.
> You call me mis-believer, cut-throat dog,
> And spit upon my Jewish gaberdine,
> And all for use of that which is mine own.
> Well then, it now appears you need my help:
> Go to, then; you come to me, and you say,
> 'Shylock, we would have moneys': you say so,
> You that did void your rheum upon my beard
> And foot me as you spurn a stranger cur
> Over your threshold: moneys is your suit.
> What should I say to you? Should I not say
> 'Hath a dog money? is it possible
> A cur can lend three thousand ducats?'

Antonio answers this in words which it would be almost impossible to take for Shakespeare's because of their brutal rudeness, were it not, as we shall see later, that Shakespeare loathed the Jew usurer more than any character in all his plays. Here are the words:

ANTONIO I am as like to call thee so again,
To spit on thee again, to spurn thee too.
If thou wilt lend this money, lend it not
As to thy friends; for when did friendship take
A breed for barren metal of his friend?
But lend it rather to thine enemy
Who, if he break, thou mayst with better face
Exact the penalty.

Then Shylock makes peace, and proposes his modest penalty. Bassanio says:

You shall not seal to such a bond for me:
I'll rather dwell in my necessity.

Antonio is perfectly careless and content: he says:

Content, i' faith: I'll seal to such a bond,
And say there is much kindness in the Jew.

Antonio's heedless trust of other men and impatience are qualities most foreign to the merchant; but are shown again and again by Shakespeare's impersonations.

Perhaps it will be well here to prove once for all that Shakespeare did really hate the Jew. In the first place he excites our sympathy again and again for him on the broad grounds of common humanity; but the moment it comes to a particular occasion he represents him as hateful, even where a little thought would have taught him that the Jew must be at his best. It is a peculiarity of humanity which Shakespeare should not have overlooked, that all pariahs and outcasts display intense family affection; those whom the world scouts and hates are generally at their noblest in their own homes. The pressure from the outside, Herbert Spencer would say, tends to bring about cohesion among the members of the despised caste. The family affection of the Jew, his kindness to his kindred, have become proverbial. But Shakespeare admits no such kindness in Shylock: when his daughter leaves Shylock one would think that Shakespeare would picture the father's desolation and misery, his sorrow at losing his only child; but here there is no touch of sympathy in gentle Shakespeare:

> . . . I would my daughter were dead at my foot, and the jewels in her ear! would she were hearsed at my foot, and the ducats in her coffin!

But there is even better proof than this: when Shylock is defeated in his case and leaves the Court penniless and broken, Shakespeare allows him to be insulted by a gentleman. Shylock becomes pathetic in his defeat, for Shakespeare always sympathised with failure, even before he came to grief himself:

> SHYLOCK Nay, take my life and all; pardon not that:
> You take my house when you do take the prop
> That doth sustain my house; you take my life
> When you do take the means whereby I live.
>
> PORTIA What mercy can you render him, Antonio?
>
> GRA. A halter gratis; nothing else for God's sake.

And then Antonio offers to 'quit the fine for one-half his goods'. Utterly broken now, Shylock says:

> I pray you, give me leave to go from hence;
> I am not well: send the deed after me,
> And I will sign it.
>
> DUKE Get thee gone, but do it.
>
> GRA. In christening shalt thou have two godfathers:
> Had I been judge, thou should'st have had ten more,
> To bring thee to the gallows, not the font.

A brutal insult from a gallant gentleman to the broken Jew: it is the only time in all Shakespeare when a beaten and ruined man is so insulted.

Antonio, it must be confessed, is a very charming sketch of Shakespeare when he was about thirty years of age, and it is amusing to reflect that it is just the rich merchant with all his wealth at hazard whom he picks out to embody his utter contempt of riches. The 'royal merchant', as he calls him, trained from youth to barter, is the very last man in the world to back such a venture as Bassanio's – much less would such a man treat money with disdain. But Shakespeare from the beginning of the play put himself quite naively in Antonio's place, and so the astounding antinomy came to expression.

3

The Sonnets – Part One

Ever since Wordsworth wrote that the sonnets were the key to Shakespeare's heart, it has been taken for granted (save by those who regard even the sonnets as mere poetical exercises) that Shakespeare's real nature is discovered in the sonnets more easily and more surely than in the plays. Those readers who have followed me so far in examining his plays will hardly need to be told that I do not agree with this assumption. The author whose personality is rich and complex enough to create and vitalise a dozen characters, reveals himself more fully in his creations than he can in his proper person. It was natural enough that Wordsworth, a great lyric poet, should catch Shakespeare's accent better in his sonnets than in his dramas; but that is owing to Wordsworth's limitations. And if the majority of later English critics have agreed with Wordsworth, it only shows that Englishmen in general are better judges of lyric than of dramatic work. We have the greatest lyrics in the world; but our dramas, with the exception of Shakespeare's, are not remarkable. And in that modern extension of the drama, the novel, we are distinctly inferior to the French and Russians. This inferiority must be ascribed to the newfangled prudery of language and thought which emasculates all our later fiction; but as that prudery is not found in our lyric verse it is evident that here alone the inspiration is full and rich enough to overflow the limits of epicene convention.

Whether the reader agrees with me or not on this point, it may be accepted that Shakespeare revealed himself far more completely in his plays than as a lyric poet. Just as he chose his dramatic subjects with some felicity to reveal his many-sided nature, so he used the sonnets with equal artistry to discover that part of himself which could hardly be rendered objectively. Whatever is masculine in a man can be depicted superbly on the stage, but his feminine qualities – passionate self-abandonment, facile forgivingness, self-pity – do not show well in the dramatic struggle. What sort of a drama would that be in which the hero would have to confess that when in the vale of years he had fallen desperately in love with a girl, and that he had been foolish enough to send a friend, a young noble, to plead his cause, with the result that the girl won the friend and gave herself to him? The protagonist would earn mocking laughter and not sympathy, and this Shakespeare no doubt foresaw. Besides, to Shakespeare, this story, which is in brief the story of the sonnets, was terribly real and intimate, and he felt instinctively that he could not treat it objectively; it was too near him, too exquisitely painful for that.

At some time or other life overpowers the strongest of us, and that defeat we all treat lyrically; when the deepest depth in us is stirred we cannot feign, or depict ourselves from the outside dispassionately; we can only cry our passion, our pain and our despair; this once we use no art, simple truth is all we seek to reach. The crisis of Shakespeare's life, the hour of agony and bloody sweat when his weakness found him out and life's handicap proved too heavy even for his strength – that is the subject of the sonnets.

Now what was Shakespeare's weakness? his besetting temptation? 'Love is my sin', he says; 'Love of love and her soft hours' was his weakness: passion the snare that meshed his soul. No wonder Antony cries:

> Whither hast thou led me, Egypt?

for his gypsy led Shakespeare from shame to shame, to the verge of madness. The sonnets give us the story, the whole terrible, sinful, magical story of Shakespeare's passion.

As might have been expected, Englishmen like Wordsworth, with an intense appreciation of lyric poetry, have done good work in criticism of the sonnets, and one Englishman has read them with extraordinary understanding. Mr Tyler's work on the sonnets ranks higher than that of Coleridge on the plays. I do not mean to say that it is on the same intellectual level with the work of Coleridge, though it shows wide reading, astonishing acuteness, and much skill in the marshalling of argument. But Mr Tyler had the good fortune to be the first to give to the personages of the sonnets a local habitation and a name, and that unique achievement puts him in a place by himself far above the mass of commentators. Before his book appeared in 1890 the sonnets lay in the dim light of guesswork. It is true that Hallam had adopted the hypothesis of Boaden and Bright, and had identified William Herbert, Earl

of Pembroke, with the high-born, handsome youth for whom Shakespeare, in the sonnets, expressed such passionate affection; but still,
there were people who thought that the Earl of Southampton filled the
requirements even better than William Herbert, and as I say, the whole
subject lay in the twilight of surmise and supposition.

Mr Tyler, working on a hint of the Revd W. A. Harrison, identified
Shakespeare's high-born mistress, the 'dark lady' of the sonnets, with
Mistress Mary Fitton, a maid of honour to Queen Elizabeth.

These, then, are the personages of the drama, and the story is very
simple: Shakespeare loved Mistress Fitton and sent his friend, the
young Lord Herbert, to her on some pretext, but with the design that
he should commend Shakespeare to the lady. Mistress Fitton fell in
love with William Herbert, wooed and won him, and Shakespeare had
to mourn the loss of both friend and mistress.

It would be natural to speak of this identification of Mr Tyler's as the
best working hypothesis yet put forward; but it would be unfair to him;
it is more than this. Till his book appeared, even the date of the sonnets
was not fixed; many critics regarded them as an early work, as early
indeed, as 1591 or 1592; he was the first person to prove that the time
they cover extends roughly from 1598 to 1601. Mr Tyler then has not
only given us the names of the actors, but he has put the tragedy in its
proper place in Shakespeare's life, and he deserves all thanks for his
illuminating work.

I bring to this theory fresh corroboration from the plays. Strange to
say, Mr Tyler has hardly used the plays, yet, as regards the story told in
the sonnets, the proof that it is a real and not an imaginary story can be
drawn from the plays. I may have to point out, incidentally, what I
regard as mistakes and oversights in Mr Tyler's work; but in the main it
stands four-square, imposing itself on the reason and satisfying at the
same time instinct and sympathy.

Let us first see how far the story told in the sonnets is borne out by
the plays. For a great many critics, even today, reject the story altogether, and believe that the sonnets were nothing but poetic exercises.

The sonnets fall naturally into two parts: from 1 to 126 they tell how
Shakespeare loved a youth of high rank and great personal beauty;
sonnet 127 is an *envoi*; from 128 to 152 they tell of Shakespeare's love
for a 'dark lady'. What binds the two series together is the story told in
both, or at least told in one and corroborated in the other, that Shakespeare first sent his friend to the lady, most probably to plead his cause,

and that she wooed his friend and gave herself to him. Now this is not a
common or easily invented story. No one would guess that Shakespeare
could be so foolish as to send his friend to plead his love for him. That's
a mistake that no man who knows women would be likely to make: but
the unlikelihood of the story is part of the evidence of its truth – *credo
quia incredibile* has an element of persuasion in it.

No one has yet noticed that the story of the sonnets is treated three
times in Shakespeare's plays. The first time the story appears it is
handled so lightly that it looks to me as if he had not then lived through
the incidents which he narrates. In the *Two Gentlemen of Verona* Proteus
is asked by the Duke to plead Thurio's cause with Silvia, and he
promises to do so; but instead, presses his own suit and is rejected. The
incident is handled so carelessly (Proteus not being Thurio's friend)
that it seems to me to have no importance save as a mere coincidence.
When the scene between Proteus and Silvia was written Shakespeare
had not yet been deceived by his friend. Still in *The Two Gentlemen of
Verona* there is one speech which certainly betrays personal passion. It
is in the last scene of the fifth act, when Valentine surprises Proteus
offering violence to Silvia.

VALENTINE (*coming forward*) Ruffian, let go that rude uncivil touch,
    – Thou friend of an ill fashion!

PROTEUS   Valentine!

VALENTINE *Thou common friend, that's without faith or love, –*
    For such is a friend now; – treacherous man!
    Thou hast beguiled my hopes: nought but mine eye
    Could have persuaded me. Now I dare not say
    I have one friend alive: thou would'st disprove me.
    Who should be trusted when one's own right hand
    Is perjured to the bosom? Proteus,
    I am sorry I must never trust thee more,
    But count the world a stranger for thy sake.
    The private wound is deepest: time most accurst
    'Mongst all foes that a friend should be the worst!

The first lines which I have italicised are too plain to be misread;
when they were written Shakespeare had just been cheated by his friend;
they are his passionate comment on the occurrence – 'For such is a
friend now' – can hardly be otherwise explained. The last couplet, too,
which I have also put in italics, is manifestly a reflection on his betrayal:

it is a twin rendering of the feeling expressed in sonnet 40:

> And yet love knows it is a greater grief
> To bear love's wrong than hate's known injury.

It contrasts 'foe and friend', just as the sonnet contrasts 'love and hate'.

Mr Israel Gollancz declares that 'several critics are inclined to attribute this final scene to another hand', and to his mind 'it bears evident signs of hasty composition'. No guess could be wider from the truth. The scene is most manifestly pure Shakespeare – I take the soliloquy of Valentine, with which the scene opens, as among Shakespeare's most characteristic utterances – but the whole scene is certainly later than the rest of the play. The truth probably is that after his friend had deceived him, *The Two Gentlemen of Verona* was played again, and that Shakespeare rewrote this last scene under the influence of personal feeling. The 170 lines of it are full of phrases which might be taken direct from the sonnets. Here's such a couplet:

> O, 'tis the curse in love, and still approved,
> When women cannot love where they're beloved.

The whole scene tells the story a little more frankly than we find it in the sonnets, as might be expected, seeing that Shakespeare's rival was a great noble and not to be criticised freely. This fact explains to me Valentine's unmotived renunciation of Silvia; explains, too, why he is reconciled to his friend with such unseemly haste. Valentine's last words in the scene are illuminating:

> 'Twere pity two such friends should be long foes.

The way this scene in *The Two Gentlemen of Verona* is told throws more light on Shakespeare's feelings at the moment of his betrayal than the sonnets themselves. Under the cover of fictitious names Shakespeare ventured to show the disgust and contempt he felt for Lord Herbert's betrayal more plainly than he cared, or perhaps dared, to do when speaking in his own person.

There is another play where the same incident is handled in such fashion as to put the truth of the sonnet-story beyond all doubt.

In *Much Ado About Nothing* the incident is dragged in by the ears, and the whole treatment is most remarkable. Everyone will remember how Claudio tells the Prince that he loves Hero, and asks his friend's assistance: 'your highness now may do me good.' There's no reason for

Claudio's shyness: no reason why he should call upon the Prince for help in a case where most men prefer to use their own tongues; but Claudio is young, and so we glide over the inherent improbability of the incident. The Prince at once promises to plead for Claudio with Hero and with her father:

> And thou shalt have her. Was't not to this end
> That thou began'st to twist so fine a story?

Now comes the peculiar handling of the incident. Claudio knows the Prince is wooing Hero for him, therefore when Don John tells him that the Prince 'is enamoured on Hero', he should at once infer that Don John is mistaken through ignorance of this fact; but instead of that he falls suspicious, and questions:

> How know you he loves her?
> DON JOHN   I heard him swear his affection.
>   BOR.   So did I too, and he swore he would marry her tonight.

There is absolutely nothing even in this corroboration by Borachio to shake Claudio's trust in the Prince: neither Don John nor Borachio knows what he knows, that the Prince is wooing for him (Claudio) and at his request. He should therefore smile at the futile attempt to excite his jealousy. But at once he is persuaded of the worst, as a man would be who had already experienced such disloyalty: he cries:

> 'Tis certain so; the prince woos for himself.

And then we should expect to hear him curse the prince as a traitorous friend, and dwell on his own loyal service by way of contrast, and so keep turning the dagger in the wound with the thought that no one but himself was ever so repaid for such honesty of love. But, no! Claudio has no bitterness in him, no reproachings; he speaks of the whole matter as if it had happened months and months before, as indeed it had; for *Much Ado About Nothing* was written about 1599. Reflection had already shown Shakespeare the unreason of revolt, and he puts his own thought in the mouth of Claudio:

> 'Tis certain so; the prince woos for himself.
> Friendship is constant in all other things
> Save in the office and affairs of love:
> Therefore all hearts in love use their own tongues;

> Let every eye negotiate for itself,
> And trust no agent; for beauty is a witch,
> Against whose charms faith melteth into blood.
> *This is an accident of hourly proof,*
> *Which I mistrusted not.* Farewell, therefore, Hero.

The Claudio who spoke like this in the first madness of love lost and friendship cheated would be a monster. Here we have Shakespeare speaking in all calmness of something that happened to himself a considerable time before. The lines I have put in italics admit no other interpretation: they show Shakespeare's philosophic acceptance of things as they are; what has happened to him is not to be assumed as singular but is the common lot of man – 'an accident of hourly proof' – which he blames himself for not foreseeing. In fact, Claudio's temper here is as detached and impartial as Benedick's. Benedick declares that Claudio should be whipped:

DON PEDRO To be whipped! What's his fault?

BENEDICK The flat transgression of a schoolboy, who being overjoyed
          with finding a bird's nest, shows it his companion and he
          steals it.

That is the view of the realist who knows life and men, and plays the game according to the rules accepted. Shakespeare understood this side of life as well as most men. But Don Pedro is a prince – a Shakespearean prince at that – full of all loyalties and ideal sentiments; he answers Benedick from Shakespeare's own heart:

> Wilt thou make a trust a transgression?
> The transgression is in the stealer.

It is curious that Shakespeare doesn't see that Claudio must feel this truth a thousand times more keenly than the Prince. As I have said, Claudio's calm acceptance of the fact is a revelation of Shakespeare's own attitude, an attitude just modified by the moral reprobation put in the mouth of the Prince. The recital itself shows that the incident was a personal experience of Shakespeare, and as one might expect in this case it does not accelerate but retard the action of the drama; it is, indeed, altogether foreign to the drama, an excrescence upon it and not an improvement but a blemish. Moreover, the reflective, disillusioned, slightly pessimistic tone of the narrative is alien and strange to the optimistic temper of the play; finally, this garb of patient sadness does not suit Claudio, who should be all love and eagerness, and diminishes instead of increasing our sympathy with his later actions. Whoever considers these facts will admit that we have here Shakespeare telling us what happened to himself, and what he really thought of his friend's betrayal.

> The transgression is in the stealer.

That is Shakespeare's mature judgement of Lord Herbert's betrayal.

The third mention of this sonnet-story in a play is later still: it is in *Twelfth Night*. The Duke, as we have seen, is an incarnation of Shakespeare himself, and, indeed, the finest incarnation we have of his temperament. In the fourth scene of the first act he sends Viola to plead his cause for him with Olivia, much in the same way, no doubt, as Shakespeare sent Pembroke to Miss Fitton. The whole scene deserves careful reading.

> Cesario,
> Thou know'st no less but all; I have unclasp'd
> To thee the book even of my secret soul:
> Therefore, good youth, address thy gait unto her.
> Be not denied access, stand at her doors,
> And tell them, there thy fixed foot shall grow
> Till thou have audience.

VIOLA   Sure, my noble lord,
> If she be so abandon'd to her sorrow
> As it is spoke, she never will admit me.

DUKE Be clamorous and leap all civil bounds
> Rather than make unprofited return.

VIOLA Say I do speak with her, my lord, what then?

DUKE O, then unfold the passion of my love,
> Surprise her with discourse of my dear faith:
> It shall become thee well to act my woes;
> *She will attend it better in thy youth*
> *Than in a nuncio's of more grave aspect.*

VIOLA I think not so, my lord.

DUKE   Dear lad, believe it;
> For they shall yet belie thy happy years,
> That say thou art a man: Diana's lip

Is not more smooth and rubious; thy small pipe
Is as the maiden's organ, shrill and sound;
And all is semblative a woman's part.
I know thy constellation is right apt
For this affair. Some four or five attend him;
All if you will; for I myself am best
When least in company.

I do not want to find more here than is in the text: the passage simply shows that this idea of sending someone to plead his love was constantly in Shakespeare's mind in these years. The curious part of the matter is that he should pick a youth as ambassador, and a youth who is merely his page. He can discover no reason for choosing such a boy as Viola, and so simply asserts that youth will be better attended to, which is certainly not the fact. Lord Herbert's youth was in his mind: but he could not put the truth in the play that when he chose his ambassador he chose him for his high position and personal beauty and charm, and not because of his youth. The whole incident is treated lightly as something of small import; the bitterness in *Much Ado* has died out: *Twelfth Night* was written about 1601, a year or so later than *Much Ado*.

I do not want to labour the conclusion I have reached; but it must be admitted that I have found in the plays, and especially in *The Two Gentlemen of Verona* and *Much Ado*, the same story which is told in the sonnets; a story lugged into the plays, where, indeed, its introduction is a grave fault in art and its treatment too peculiar to be anything but personal. Here in the plays we have, so to speak, three views of the sonnet-story; the first in *The Two Gentlemen of Verona*, when the betrayal is fresh in Shakespeare's memory and his words are embittered with angry feeling:

Thou common friend that's without faith or love.

The second view is taken in *Much Ado About Nothing* when the pain of the betrayal has been a little salved by time. Shakespeare now moralises the occurrence. He shows us how it would be looked upon by a philosopher (for that is what the lover, Claudio, is in regard to his betrayal) and by a soldier and man of the world, Benedick, and by a Prince. Shakespeare selects the prince to give effect to the view that the fault is in the transgressor and not in the man who trusts. The many-sided treatment of the story shows all the stages through which Shakespeare's mind moved, and the result is to me a more complete confession than is to be found in the sonnets. Finally the story is touched upon in *Twelfth Night*, when the betrayal has faded into oblivion, but the poet lets out the fact that his ambassador was a youth, and the reason he gives for this is plainly insufficient. If after these three recitals anyone can still believe that the sonnet-story is imaginary, he is beyond persuasion by argument.

4

The Sonnets – Part Two

Now that we have found the story of the sonnets repeated three times in the plays, it may be worth our while to see if we can discover in the plays anything that throws light upon the circumstances or personages of this curious triangular drama. At the outset, I must admit that save in these three plays I can find no mention whatever of Shakespeare's betrayer, Lord Herbert. He was 'a false friend', the plays tell us, a 'common friend without faith or love', 'a friend of an ill fashion'; young, too, yet trusted; but beyond this summary superficial characterisation there is silence. *Me judice* Lord Herbert made no deep or peculiar impression on Shakespeare; an opinion calculated to give pause to the scandalmongers. For there can be no doubt whatever that Shakespeare's love, Mistress Fitton, the 'dark lady' of the sonnet-series from 128 to 152 is to be found again and again in play after play, profoundly modifying the poet's outlook upon life and art. Before I take in hand this identification of Miss Fitton and her influence upon Shakespeare, let me beg the reader to bear in mind the fact that Shakespeare was a sensualist by nature, a lover, which is as rare a thing as consummate genius. The story of his idolatrous passion for Mary Fitton is the story of his life. This is what the commentators and critics hitherto have failed to appreciate. Let us now get at the facts and see what light the dramas throw upon the chief personage of the story, Mistress Fitton. The study will probably teach us that Shakespeare was the most impassioned lover and love-poet in all literature.

History tells us that Mary Fitton became a maid of honour to Queen Elizabeth in 1595 at the age of seventeen. From a letter addressed by her father to Sir Robert Cecil on January 29th, 1599, it is fairly certain that she had already been married at the age of sixteen; the union was probably not entirely valid, but the mere fact suggests a certain recklessness of character, or overpowering sensuality, or both, and shows that even as a girl Mistress Fitton was no shrinking, timid, modest maiden. Wrapped in a horseman's cloak she used to leave the Palace at night to meet her lover, Lord William Herbert. Though twice married, she had an illegitimate child by Herbert, and two later by Sir Richard Leveson.

This extraordinary woman is undoubtedly the sort of woman Shakespeare depicted as the 'dark lady' of the sonnets. Nearly every sonnet of the twenty-six devoted to his mistress contains some accusation against her; and all these charges are manifestly directed against one and the same woman. First of all she is described in sonnet 131 as 'tyrannous'; then in sonnet 133 as 'faithless'; in sonnet 137 as 'the bay where all men ride . . . the wide world's commonplace'; in sonnet 138 as 'false'; in 139, she is 'coquettish'; 140, 'proud'; 142, 'false to the bonds of love'; 147, 'black as hell . . . dark as night' – in both looks and character; 'full of foul faults'; 149, 'cruel'; 150, 'unworthy', but of 'powerful' personality; 152, 'unkind – inconstant . . . unfaithful . . . forsworn'.

Now, the first question is: Can we find this 'dark lady' of the sonnets in the plays? The sonnets tell us she was of pale complexion with black eyes and hair; do the plays bear out this description? And if they do bear it out do they throw any new light upon Miss Fitton's character? Did Miss Fitton seem proud and inconstant, tyrannous and wanton, to Shakespeare when he first met her, and before she knew Lord Herbert?

The earliest mention of the poet's mistress in the plays is to be found, I think, in *Romeo and Juliet*. *Romeo and Juliet* is dated by Mr Furnival 1591-1593; it was first mentioned in 1595 by Meres; first published in 1597. I think in its present form it must be taken to date from 1597. Romeo, who as we have already seen, is an incarnation of Shakespeare, is presented to us in the very first scene as in love with one Rosaline. This in itself tells me nothing; but the proof that Shakespeare stands in intimate relation to the girl called Rosaline comes later, and so the first introductory words have a certain significance for me. Romeo himself tells us that 'she hath Dian's wit', one of Shakespeare's favourite comparisons for his love, and speaks of her chastity, or rather of her unapproachableness; he goes on:

> O she is rich in beauty, only poor
> That, when she dies, with beauty dies her store.

which reminds us curiously of the first sonnets.

In the second scene Benvolio invites Romeo to the feast of Capulet, where his love, 'the fair Rosaline', is supping, and adds:

> Compare her face with some that I shall shew,
> And I will make thee think thy swan a crow.

Romeo replies that there is none fairer than his love, and Benvolio retorts:

> Tut! You saw her fair, none else being by.

This bantering is most pointed if we assume that Rosaline was dark rather than fair.

In the second act Mercutio comes upon the scene, and, mocking Romeo's melancholy and passion, cries:

> I conjure thee, by Rosaline's bright eyes,
> By her high forehead and her scarlet lip . . .

This description surprises me. Shakespeare rarely uses such physical portraiture of his personages, and Mercutio is a side of Shakespeare himself; a character all compact of wit and talkativeness, a character wholly invented by the poet.

A little later my suspicion is confirmed. In the fourth scene of the second act Mercutio talks to Benvolio about Romeo; they both wonder where he is, and Mercutio says:

> Ah, that same pale-hearted wench, that Rosaline,
> Torments him so that he will sure run mad.

And again, a moment later, Mercutio laughs at Romeo as already dead, 'stabbed with a white wench's black eye'. Now, here is confirmation of my suspicion. It is most unusual for Shakespeare to give the physical peculiarities of any of his characters; no one knows how Romeo looked, or Juliet or even Hamlet or Ophelia; and here he repeats the description.

The only other examples we have as yet found in Shakespeare of such physical portraiture is the sketching of Falstaff in *Henry IV* and the snapshot of Master Slender in *The Merry Wives of Windsor*, as a 'little wee face, with a little yellow beard, – a cane-coloured beard'. Both these photographs, as we noticed at the time, were very significant, and Slender's extraordinarily significant by reason of its striking and peculiar realism. Though an insignificant character, Slender is photographed for us by Shakespeare's contempt and hatred, just as this Rosaline is photographed by his passionate love, photographed again and again.

Shakespeare's usual way of describing the physical appearance of a man or woman, when he allowed himself to do it at all, which was seldom, was what one might call the ideal or conventional way. A good example is to be found in Hamlet's description of his father; he is speaking to his mother:

> Hyperion's curls, the front of Jove himself,
> An eye like Mars, to threaten and command,
> A station like the herald Mercury
> New-lighted on a heaven-kissing hill.

In the special case I am considering Rosaline is less even than a secondary character; she is not a personage in the play at all. She is merely mentioned casually by Benvolio and then by Mercutio, and even Mercutio is not the protagonist; yet his mention of her is strikingly detailed, astonishingly realistic, in spite of its off-hand brevity. We have a photographic snapshot, so to speak, of this girl: she 'torments' Romeo; she is 'hard-hearted'; a 'white wench' with 'black eyes'; twice in four lines she is called now 'pale', now 'white' – plainly her complexion had no red in it, and was in startling contrast to her black eyes and hair. Manifestly this picture is taken from life, and it is just as manifestly the portrait of the 'dark lady' of the sonnets.

As if to make assurance doubly sure, there is another description of this same Rosaline in another play, so detailed and striking, composed as it is of contrasting and startling peculiarities that I can only wonder that its full significance has not been appreciated ages ago. To have missed its meaning only proves that men do not read Shakespeare with love's fine wit.

The repetition of the portrait is fortunate for another reason: it tells us when the love story took place. The allusion to the 'dark lady' in *Romeo and Juliet* is difficult to date exactly; the next mention of her in a play can be fixed in time with some precision. *Love's Labour's Lost* was revised by Shakespeare for production at Court during the Christmas festivities of 1597. When the quarto was published in 1598 it bore on its title-page the words, 'A pleasant conceited comedy called *Love's Labour's Lost*. As it was presented before Her Highness this last Christmas. Newly corrected and augmented By W. Shakespeare'. It is in the revised part that we find Shakespeare introducing his dark love again, and this time, too, curiously enough, under the name of Rosaline. Evidently he enjoyed the mere music of the word. Biron is an incarnation of Shakespeare himself, as we have already seen, and the meeting of Biron and his love, Rosaline, in the play is extremely interesting for us as Shakespeare in this revised production, one would think, would wish to ingratiate himself with his love, more especially as she would probably be present when the play was produced. Rosaline is made to praise Biron, before he appears, as a merry man and a most excellent talker; but when they meet they simply indulge in a tourney of wit, in which Rosaline more than holds her own, showing indeed astounding self-assurance, spiced with a little contempt of Biron; 'hard-hearted' Mercutio called it. Every word deserves to be weighed:

BIRON	Did not I dance with you in Brabant once?
ROSALINE	Did not I dance with you in Brabant once?
BIRON	I know you did.
ROSALINE	How needless was it, then, to ask the question!
BIRON	You must not be so quick.
ROSALINE	'Tis long of you that spur me with such questions.
BIRON	Your wit's too hot, it speeds too fast, 'twill tire.
ROSALINE	Not till it leave the rider in the mire.
BIRON	What time o' day?
ROSALINE	The hour that fools should ask.
BIRON	Now fair befall your mask!
ROSALINE	Fair fall the face it covers!
BIRON	And send you many lovers!
ROSALINE	Amen, so you be none.
BIRON	Nay, then will I be gone.

Clearly this Rosaline, too, has Dian's wit and is not in love with Biron, any more than the Rosaline of *Romeo and Juliet* was in love with Romeo.

The next allusion is even more characteristic. Biron and Longaville and Boyet are talking; Longaville shows his admiration for one of the Princess's women, 'the one in the white,' he declares, 'is a most sweet lady . . . '

BIRON	What is her name in the cap?
BOYET	Rosaline, by good hap.
BIRON	Is she wedded or no?
BOYET	To her will, sir, or so.
BIRON	You are welcome, sir: adieu.

This, 'To her will, sir, or so', is exactly in the spirit of the sonnets:

everyone will remember the first two lines of sonnet 135:

> Whoever hath her wish, thou hast thy *Will*,
> And *Will* to boot, and *Will* in overplus;

That, 'To her will, sir, or so', I find astonishingly significant, for not only has it nothing to do with the play and is therefore unexpected, but the character-drawing is unexpected, too; maids are not usually wedded to their will in a double sense, and no other of these maids of honour is described at all.

A little later Biron speaks again of Rosaline in a way which shocks expectation. First of all, he rages at himself for being in love at all. 'And I, forsooth in love! I, that have been love's whip!' Here I pause again, it seems to me that Shakespeare is making confession to us, just as when he admitted without reason that Jaques was lewd. Be that as it may, he certainly goes on in words which are astounding, so utterly unforeseen are they, and therefore the more characteristic:

> Nay, to be perjured, which is worst of all;
> And, among three, to love the worst of all;

The first line of this couplet, that he is perjured in loving Rosaline may be taken as applying to the circumstances of the play; but Shakespeare also talks of himself in sonnet 152 as 'perjured', for he only swears in order to misuse his love, or with a side glance at the fact that he is married and therefore perjured when he swears love to one not his wife. It is well to keep this 'perjured' in memory.

But it is the second line which is the more astonishing; there Biron tells us that among the three of the Princess's women he loves 'the worst of all'. Up to this moment we have only been told kindly things of Rosaline and the other ladies; we had no idea that any one of them was bad, much less that Rosaline was 'the worst of all'. The suspicion grows upon us, a suspicion which is confirmed immediately afterwards, that Shakespeare is speaking of himself and of a particular woman; else we should have to admit that his portraiture of Rosaline's character was artistically bad, and bad without excuse, for why should he lavish all this wealth of unpleasant detail on a mere subsidiary character? He goes on, however, to make the fault worse; he next speaks of his love Rosaline as

> A whitely wanton with a velvet brow,
> With two pitch-balls stuck in her face for eyes;

> Ay, and by heaven, one that will do the deed;
> Though Argus were her eunuch and her guard:
> And I to sigh for her! to watch for her!
> To pray for her! Go to! it is a plague.

It is, of course, a blot upon the play for Biron to declare that his love is a wanton of the worst. It is not merely unexpected and uncalled-for; it diminishes our sympathy with Biron and his love, and also with the play. But we have already found the rule trustworthy that whenever Shakespeare makes a mistake in art it is because of some strong personal feeling and not for want of wit, and this rule evidently holds good here. Shakespeare-Biron is picturing the woman he himself loves; for not only does he describe her as a wanton to the detriment of the play; but he pictures her precisely, and this Rosaline is the only person in the play of whom we have any physical description at all. Moreover, he has given such precise and repeated photographs of no other character in any of his plays:

> A whitely wanton with a velvet brow,
> With two pitch-balls stuck in her face for eyes.

This is certainly the same Rosaline we found depicted in *Romeo and Juliet*; but the portraiture here, both physical and moral, is more detailed and peculiar than it was in the earlier play. Shakespeare now knows his Rosaline intimately. The mere facts that here again her physical appearance is set forth with such particularity, and that the 'hard-heartedness' which Mercutio noted in her has now become 'wantonness' is all-important, especially when we remember that Miss Fitton was probably listening to the play. Even at Christmas, 1597, Shakespeare's passion has reached the height of a sex-duel. Miss Fitton has tortured him so that he delights in calling her names to her face in public when the play would have led one to expect ingratiating or complimentary courtesies. It does not weaken this argument to admit that the general audience would not perhaps have understood the allusions.

It is an almost incredible fact that not a single one of his hundreds of commentators has even noticed any peculiarity in this physical portraiture of Rosaline; Shakespeare uses this realism so rarely one would have thought that every critic would have been astounded by it; but no, they all pass over it without a word, Coleridge, Mr Tyler, all of them.

The fourth act of *Love's Labour's Lost* begins with a most characteristic soliloquy of Biron:

> BIRON The king he is hunting the deer; I am coursing myself: they have pitched a toil; I am toiling in a pitch – pitch that defiles: defile! a foul word.

Here Biron is manifestly playing on the 'pitch-balls' his love has for eyes, and also on the 'foul faults' Shakespeare speaks of in the sonnets and in Othello. Biron goes on:

> O, but her eye – by this light, but for her eye, I would not love her; yes, for her two eyes. Well, I do nothing in the world but lie, and lie in my throat. By heaven, I do love: and it hath taught me to rhyme, and to be melancholy; and here is part of my rhyme, and here my melancholy. Well, she hath one o' my sonnets already: the clown bore it, the fool sent it, and the lady hath it: sweet clown, sweeter fool, sweetest lady!

This proves to me that some of Shakespeare's sonnets were written in 1597. True, Mr Tyler would try to bind all the sonnets within the three years from 1598 to 1601, the three years which Shakespeare speaks about in sonnet 104:

> Three winters cold
> Have from the forests shook three summers' pride,
> Three beauteous springs to yellow autumn turn'd
> In process of the seasons have I seen.
> Three April perfumes in three hot Junes burn'd,
> Since first I saw you fresh, which yet are green.

Lord Herbert first came to Court in the spring of 1598, and so sonnet 104 may have represented the fact precisely so far as Herbert was concerned; but I am not minded to take the poet so literally. Instead of beginning in the spring of 1598, some of the sonnets to the lady were probably written in the autumn of 1597, or even earlier, and yet Shakespeare would be quite justified in talking of three years, if the period ended in 1601. A poet is not to be bound to an almanack's exactitude.

In the fourth act of *Love's Labour's Lost*, when Biron confesses his love for 'the heavenly Rosaline', the King banters him in the spirit of the time:

> KING By heaven, thy love is black as ebony.
> BIRON Is ebony like her? O wood divine!
>   A wife of such wood were felicity.
>   O, who can give an oath? Where is a book?
>   That I may swear beauty doth beauty lack,
>   If that she learn not of her eye to look:
>   No face is fair that is not full so black.

Here we have Shakespeare again describing his mistress for us, though he has done it better earlier in the play; he harps upon her dark beauty here to praise it, just as he praised it in sonnet 127; it is passion's trick to sound the extremes of blame and praise alternately.

In the time of Elizabeth it was customary for poets and courtiers to praise red hair and a fair complexion as 'beauty's ensign', and so compliment the Queen. The flunkeyism, which is a characteristic of all the Germanic races, was peculiarly marked in England from the earliest times, and induced men, even in those 'spacious days', not only to overpraise fair hair, but to run down dark hair and eyes as ugly. The King replies:

> O paradox! Black is the badge of hell,
>   The hue of dungeons and the school of night;
> And beauty's crest becomes the heavens well.

Biron answers:

> Devils soonest tempt, resembling spirits of light.
>   O, if in black my lady's brow be deck'd
> It mourns that painting and usurping hair
>   Should ravish doters with a false aspect;
> And therefore is she born to make black fair.
>   Her favour turns the fashion of the days,
> For native blood is counted painting now;
>   And therefore red that would avoid dispraise,
> Paints itself black, to imitate her brow.

Our timid poet is bold enough, when cloaked under a stage-name, to uphold the colour of his love's hair against the Queen's; the mere fact speaks volumes to those who know their Shakespeare.

Sonnet 127 runs in almost the same words; though now the poet speaking in his own person is less bold:

> In the old age black was not counted fair,
>   Or, if it were, it bore not beauty's name;

> But now is black beauty's successive heir,
>   And beauty slandered with a bastard shame:
> For since each hand hath put on nature's power,
>   Fairing the soul with art's false borrow'd face,
> Sweet beauty hath no name, no holy bower,
>   But is profaned, if not lives in disgrace.
> Therefore my mistress' eyes are raven black,
>   Her eyes so suited, and they mourners seem
> At such who, not born fair, no beauty lack,
>   Slandering creation with a false esteem:
> Yet so they mourn, becoming of their woe
>   That every tongue says beauty should look so.

There can be no doubt that in this Rosaline of *Romeo and Juliet* and of *Love's Labour's Lost*, Shakespeare is describing the 'dark lady' of the second sonnet-series, and describing her, against his custom in play-writing, even more exactly than he described her in the lyrics.

There is a line at the end of this act which is very characteristic when considered with what has gone before; it is clearly a confession of Shakespeare himself, and a perfect example of what one might call the conscience that pervades all his mature work:

> Light wenches may prove plagues to men forsworn.

We were right, it seems, in putting some stress on that 'perjured' when we first met it.

In the second scene of the fifth act, which opens with a talk between the Princess and her ladies, our view of Rosaline is confirmed. Katherine calls Rosaline light, and jests upon this in lewd fashion; declares, too, that she is 'a merry, nimble, stirring spirit', in fact, tells her that she is

> A light condition in a beauty dark.

All these needless repetitions prove to me that Shakespeare is describing his mistress as she lived and moved. Those who disagree with me should give another instance in which he has used or abused the same precise portraiture. But there is more in this light badinage of the girls than a description of Rosaline. When Rosaline says that she will torture Biron before she goes, and turn him into her vassal, the Princess adds,

> None are so surely caught when they are catch'd
> As wit turned fool.

Rosaline replies,

> The blood of youth burns not with such excess
> As gravity's revolt to wantonness.

This remark has no pertinence or meaning in Rosaline's mouth. Biron is supposed to be young in the play, and he has never been distinguished for his gravity, but for his wit and humour: the Princess calls him 'quick Biron'. The two lines are clearly Shakespeare's criticism of himself. When he wrote the sonnets he thought himself old, and certainly his years (thirty-four) contrasted badly with those of Mary Fitton who was at this time not more than nineteen.

Late in 1597 then, before William Herbert came upon the scene at all, Shakespeare knew that his mistress was a wanton:

> Ay, and by heaven, one that will do the deed;
> Though Argus were her eunuch and her guard.

Shakespeare has painted his love for us in these plays as a most extraordinary woman: in person she is tall, with pallid complexion and black eyes and black brows, 'a gypsy', he calls her; in nature imperious, lawless, witty, passionate – a 'wanton'; moreover, a person of birth and position. That a girl of the time has been discovered who united all these qualities in herself would bring conviction to almost any mind; but belief passes into certitude when we reflect that this portrait of his mistress is given with greatest particularity in the plays, where in fact it is out of place and a fault in art. When studying the later plays we shall find this gypsy wanton again and again; she made the deepest impression on Shakespeare; was, indeed, the one love of his life. It was her falseness that brought him to self-knowledge and knowledge of life, and turned him from a light-hearted writer of comedies and histories into the author of the greatest tragedies that have ever been conceived. Shakespeare owes the greater part of his renown to Mary Fitton.

5

The Sonnets – Part Three

The most interesting question in the sonnets, the question the vital importance of which dwarfs all others, has never yet been fairly tackled and decided. As soon as English critics noticed, a hundred years or so ago, that the sonnets fell into two series, and that the first, and longer, series was addressed to a young man, they cried, 'shocking! shocking!' and registered judgement with smug haste on evidence that would not hang a cat. Hallam, 'the judicious', held that 'it would have been better for Shakespeare's reputation if the sonnets had never been written', and even Heine, led away by the consensus of opinion, accepted the condemnation, and regretted 'the miserable degradation of humanity' to be found in the sonnets. But before giving ourselves to the novel enjoyment of moral superiority over Shakespeare, it may be worth while to ask, is the fact proved? is his guilt established?

No one, I think, who has followed me so far will need to be told that I take no interest in whitewashing Shakespeare: I am intent on painting him as he lived and loved, and if I found him as vicious as Villon, or as cruel as a stoat, I would set it all down as faithfully as I would give proof of his generosity or his gentleness.

Before the reader can fairly judge of Shakespeare's innocence or guilt, he must hold in mind two salient peculiarities of the man which I have already noted; but which must now be relieved out into due prominence so that one will make instinctive allowance for them at every moment, his sensuality and his snobbishness.

His sensuality is the quality, as we have seen, which unites the creatures of his temperament with those of his intellect, his poets with his thinkers, and proves that Romeo and Jaques, the Duke of *Twelfth Night* and Hamlet, are one and the same person. If the matter is fairly considered it will be found that this all-pervading sensuality is the source, or at least a natural accompaniment of his gentle kindness and his unrivalled sympathy.

Shakespeare painted no portrait of the hero or of the adventurer; found no new word for the virile virtues or virile vices, but he gave immortal expression to desire and its offspring, to love, jealousy, and despair, to every form of pathos, pleading and pity, to all the gentler and more feminine qualities. Desire in especial has inspired him with phrases more magically expressive even than those gasped out by panting Sappho when lust had made her body a lyre of deathless music. Her lyric to the beloved is not so intense as Othello's:

> O, thou weed
> Who art so lovely fair and smell'st so sweet
> That the sense aches at thee;

or as Cleopatra's astonishing:

> There is gold, and here
> My bluest veins to kiss;

– the revelation of a lifetime devoted to vanity and sensuality, sensuality pampered as a god and adored with an Eastern devotion.

I do not think I need labour this point further; as I have already noticed, Orsino, the Duke of *Twelfth Night*, sums up Shakespeare's philosophy of love in the words:

> Give me excess of it, that, surfeiting,
> The appetite may sicken, and so die.

Shakespeare told us the truth about himself when he wrote in sonnet 142, 'Love is my sin'. We can expect from him new words or a new method in the painting of passionate desire.

The second peculiarity of Shakespeare which we must establish firmly in our minds before we attempt to construe the sonnets is his extraordinary snobbishness.

English snobbishness is like a London fog, intenser than can be found in any other country; it is so extravagant, indeed, that it seems different in kind. One instance of this: when Mr Gladstone was being examined once in a case, he was asked by counsel, Was he a friend of a certain lord? Instead of answering simply that he was, he replied that he did not think it right to say he was a friend of so great a noble: 'he had the honour of his acquaintance'. Only in England would the man who could make noblemen at will be found bowing before them with this humility of soul.

In Shakespeare's time English snobbishness was stronger than it is today; it was then supported by law and enforced by penalties. To speak of a lord without his title was regarded as defamation, and was punished as such more than once by the Star Chamber. Shakespeare's position, too, explains how this native snobbishness in him was heightened to flunkeyism. He was an aristocrat born, as we have seen, and felt in himself a kinship for the courtesies, chivalries, and generosities of aristocratic life. This tendency was accentuated by his calling. The middle class, already steeped in Puritanism, looked upon the theatre as scarcely better than the brothel, and showed their contempt for the players in a thousand ways. The groundlings and common people, with their 'greasy caps' and 'stinking breath' were as loathsome to Shakespeare as the crop-headed, gain-loving citizens who condemned him and his like pitilessly. He was thrown back, therefore, upon the young noblemen who had read the classics and loved the arts. His works show how he admires them. He could paint you Bassanio or Benedick or Mercutio to the life. Everybody has noticed the predilection with which he lends such characters his own poetic spirit and charm. His lower orders are all food for comedy or farce: he will not treat them seriously.

His snobbishness carries him to astounding lengths. One instance: every capable critic has been astonished by the extraordinary fidelity to fact he shows in his historical plays; he often takes whole pages of an earlier play or of Plutarch, and merely varying the language uses them in his drama. He is punctiliously careful to set down the fact, whatever it may be, and explain it, even when it troubles the flow of his story; but as soon as the fact comes into conflict with his respect for dignitaries, he loses his nice conscience. He tells us of Agincourt without ever mentioning the fact that the English bowmen won the battle; he had the truth before him; the chronicler from whom he took the story vouched for the fact; but Shakespeare preferred to ascribe the victory to Henry and his lords. Shakespeare loved a lord with a passionate admiration, and when he paints himself it is usually as a duke or prince.

Holding these truths in our mind, Shakespeare's intense sensitiveness and sensuality, and his almost inconceivable snobbishness, we may now take up the sonnets.

The first thing that strikes one in the sonnets is the fact that, though a hundred and twenty-five of them are devoted to a young man, and Shakespeare's affection for him, and only twenty-six to the woman, every one of those to the woman is characterised by a terrible veracity of passion, whereas those addressed to the youth are rather conventional than convincing. He pictures the woman to the life; strong, proud, with dark eyes and hair, pale complexion – a wanton with the rare power of carrying off even a wanton's shame. He finds a method new to literature to describe her. He will have no poetic exaggeration; snow is whiter than her breasts; violets sweeter than her breath:

> And yet, by heaven, I think my love as rare
> As any she belied with false compare.

His passion is so intense that he has no desire to paint her seduction as greater than it was. She has got into his blood, so to speak, and each drop of it under the microscope would show her image. Take any sonnet at haphazard, and you will hear the rage of his desire.

But what is the youth like? – 'the master-mistress' of his passion, to give him the title which seems to have convinced the witless of Shakespeare's guilt. Not one word of description is to be found anywhere; no painting epithet – nothing. Where is the cry of this terrible, shameless, outrageous passion that mastered Shakespeare's conscience and enslaved his will? Hardly a phrase that goes beyond affection – such affection as Shakespeare at thirty-four might well feel for a gifted, handsome aristocrat like Lord Herbert, who had youth, beauty, wealth, wit to recommend him. Herbert was a poet, too: a patron unparagoned! 'If Southampton gave me a thousand pounds', Shakespeare may well have argued, 'perhaps Lord Herbert will get me made Master of the Revels, or even give me a higher place'. An aristocratic society tends to make parasites even of the strong, as Dr Johnson's famous letter to Lord Chesterfield proves. But let us leave supposition and come to the sonnets themselves, which are addressed to the youth. The first sonnet begins:

> From fairest creatures we desire increase,
> That thereby beauty's rose might never die.

This is a very good argument indeed when addressed to a woman; but when addressed to a man by a man it rings strained and false. Yet it is the theme of the first seventeen sonnets. It is precisely the same argument which Shakespeare set forth in *Venus and Adonis* again and again:

> Seeds spring from seeds and beauty breedeth beauty;

> Thou wast begot; to get it is thy duty.   (167–8)

> And so, in spite of death, thou dost survive,
> In that thy likeness still is left alive . . .   (173–4)

> Foul cankering rust the hidden treasure frets,
> But gold that's put to use more gold begets.
>
>   (767–8)

At the end of the third sonnet we find the same argument:

> But if thou live, remember'd not to be,
> Die single, and thine image dies with thee.

Again, in the fourth, sixth, and seventh sonnets the same plea is urged. In the tenth sonnet the poet cries:

> Make thee another self, for love of me,
> That beauty still may live in thine or thee.

And again at the end of the thirteenth sonnet:

> You had a father; let your son say so.

Every one of these sonnets contains simply the argument which is set forth with equal force and far superior pertinence in *Venus and Adonis*.

That is, Shakespeare makes use of the passion he has felt for a woman to give reality to the expression of his affection for the youth. No better proof could be imagined of the fact that he never loved the youth with passion.

In sonnet 18 Shakespeare begins to alter his note. He then tells the youth that he will achieve immortality, not through his children, but through Shakespeare's verses. Sonnet 19 is rounded with the same thought:

> Yet do thy worst, old Time: despite thy wrong,
> My love shall in my verse ever live young.

Sonnet 20 is often referred to as suggesting intimacy:

> A woman's face with Nature's own hand painted,
> Hast thou, the master-mistress of my passion;
> A woman's gentle heart, but not acquainted
> With shifting change, as is false woman's fashion;
> An eye more bright than theirs, less false in rolling

Gilding the object whereupon it gazeth;
A man in hue, all 'hues' in his controlling,
Which steals men's eyes and women's souls amazeth.
And for a woman wert thou first created;
Till Nature, as she wrought thee, fell a-doting,
And by addition me of thee defeated,
By adding one thing to my purpose nothing.
 But since she prick'd thee out for women's pleasure
 Mine be thy love, and thy love's use their treasure.

The sextet of this sonnet absolutely disproves guilty intimacy, and is, I believe, intended to disprove it; Shakespeare had already fathomed the scandal-loving minds of his friends, and wanted to set forth the noble disinterestedness of his affection.

Sonnet 22 is more sincere, though not so passionate; it neither strengthens nor rebuts the argument. Sonnet 23 is the sonnet upon which all those chiefly rely who wish to condemn Shakespeare. Here it is:

As an unperfect actor on the stage,
Who with his fear is put beside his part,
Or some fierce thing replete with too much rage,
Whose strength's abundance weakens his own heart;
So I, for fear of trust, forget to say
The perfect ceremony of love's rite,
And in mine own love's strength seem to decay,
O'ercharged with burthen of mine own love's might.
O, let my looks be then the eloquence
And dumb presagers of my speaking breast;
Who plead for love, and look for recompense,
More than that tongue that more hath more express'd.
 O, learn to read what silent love hath writ:
 To hear with eyes belongs to love's fine wit.

We can interpret the phrases, 'the perfect ceremony of love's rite' and 'look for recompense' as we will; but it must be admitted that even when used to the uttermost they form an astonishingly small base on which to raise so huge and hideous a superstructure.

But we shall be told that the condemnation of Shakespeare is based, not upon any sonnet or any line; but upon the way Shakespeare speaks as soon as he discovers that his mistress has betrayed him in favour of his friend. One is inclined to expect that he will throw the blame on the friend, and, after casting him off, seek to win again the affections of his mistress. Nine men out of ten would act in this way. But the sonnets tell us with iteration and most peculiar emphasis that Shakespeare does not condemn the friend. As soon as he hears of the traitorism he cries (sonnet 33):

> Full many a glorious morning have I seen
> Flatter the mountain-tops with sovereign eye,
> Kissing with golden face the meadows green,
> Gilding pale streams with heavenly alchymy;
> Anon permit the basest clouds to ride
> With ugly rack on his celestial face,
> And from the forlorn world his visage hide,
> Stealing unseen to west with this disgrace:
> Even so my sun one early morn did shine
> With all triumphant splendour on my brow;
> But out! alack! he was but one hour mine,
> The region cloud hath mask'd him from me now.
>   Yet him for this my love no whit disdaineth;
>   Suns of the world may stain, when heaven's sun staineth.

It is the loss of his friend he regrets, rather than the loss of his mistress; she is not mentioned save by comparison with 'basest clouds'. Yet even when read by Gradgrind and his compeers the thirteenth line of this sonnet is utterly inconsistent with passion.

In the next sonnet the friend repents, and weeps the 'strong offence', and Shakespeare accepts the sorrow as salve that 'heals the wound'; his friend's tears are pearls that 'ransom all ill deeds'. The next sonnet begins with the line:

> No more be griev'd at that which thou hast done;

Shakespeare will be an 'accessory' to his friend's 'theft', though he admits that the robbery is still sour. Then come four sonnets in which he is content to forget all about the wrong he has suffered, and simply exhausts himself in praise of his friend. Sonnet 40 begins:

> Take all my loves, my love, yea, take them all;
> What hast thou then more than thou hadst before?

> No love, my love, that thou may'st true love call;
> All mine was thine, before thou hadst this more.

This is surely the very soul of tender affection; but it is significant that even here the word 'true' is emphasised and not 'love'; he goes on:

> I do forgive thy robbery, gentle thief,
> Although thou steal thee all my poverty;
> And yet love knows it is a greater grief
> To bear love's wrong, than hate's known injury.

Never before was a man so gentle-kind; we might be listening to the lament of a broken-hearted woman who smiles through her tears to reassure her lover; yet there is no attempt to disguise the fact that Herbert has done 'wrong'. The next sonnet puts the poet's feeling as strongly as possible.

> Those pretty wrongs that liberty commits,
> When I am sometime absent from thy heart,
> Thy beauty and thy years full well befits,
> For still temptation follows where thou art.
> Gentle thou art, and therefore to be won,
> Beauteous thou art, therefore to be assail'd;
> And when a woman woos, what woman's son
> Will sourly leave her till she have prevail'd?
> Ay me! but yet thou might'st my seat forbear,
> And chide thy beauty and thy straying youth,
> Who lead thee in their riot even there
> Where thou art forced to break a twofold truth;
>   Hers, by thy beauty tempting her to thee,
>   Thine by thy beauty being false to me.

The first lines show that Shakespeare is pretending; he attempts not only to minimise the offence, but to find it charming. A mother who caught her young son kissing a girl would reproach him in this fashion; to her his faults would be the 'pretty wrongs that liberty commits'. But this is not the way passion speaks, and here again the sextet condemns Herbert in the plainest terms. At length we have the summing-up:

> That thou hast her, it is not all my grief,
> And yet it may be said I lov'd her dearly;
> That she hath thee, is of my wailing chief,

> A loss in love that touches me more nearly.
> Loving offenders, thus I will excuse ye:
> Thou dost love her, because thou know'st I love her;
> And for my sake even so doth she abuse me,
> Suffering my friend for my sake to approve her.
> If I lose thee, my loss is my love's gain,
> And losing her, my friend hath found that loss;
> Both find each other, and I lose both twain,
> And both for my sake lay on me this cross:
>   But here's the joy; my friend and I are one;
>   Sweet flattery! then she loves but me alone.

This sonnet, with its affected word-play and wire-drawn consolation, leaves one gaping: Shakespeare's verbal affectations had got into his very blood. To my mind the whole sonnet is too extravagant to be sincere; it is only to be explained by the fact that Shakespeare's liking for Herbert was heightened by snobbishness and by the hope of patronage. None of it rings true except the first couplet. Yet the argument of it is repeated, strange to say, and emphasised in the sonnets addressed to the 'dark lady' whom Shakespeare loved. Sonnet 144 is clear enough:

> Two loves I have of comfort and despair,
> Which like two spirits do suggest me still:
> The better angel is a man, right fair,
> The worser spirit a woman, colour'd ill.
> To win me soon to hell, my female evil
> Tempteth my better angel from my side,
> And would corrupt my saint to be a devil,
> Wooing his purity with her foul pride.
> And whether that my angel be turn'd fiend
> Suspect I may, yet not directly tell;
> But being both from me, both to each friend,
> I guess one angel in another's hell:
>   Yet this shall I ne'er know, but live in doubt,
>   Till my bad angel fire my good one out.

As soon as his mistress comes on the scene Shakespeare's passionate sincerity cannot be questioned. The truth is the intensity of his passion leads him to condemn and spite the woman, while the absence of passion allows him to pretend affection for the friend. Sonnet 133, written to the woman, is decisive:

> Beshrew that heart that makes my heart to groan
> For that deep wound it gives my friend and me!
> Is't not enough to torture me alone,
> But slave to slavery my sweet'st friend must be?
> Me from myself thy cruel eye hath taken,
> And my next self thou harder hast engross'd:
> Of him, myself, and thee, I am forsaken;
> A torment thrice threefold thus to be cross'd.
> Prison my heart in thy steel bosom's ward,
> But then my friend's heart let my poor heart bail;
> Whoe'er keeps me, let my heart be his guard;
> Thou canst not then use rigour in my gaol:
>   And yet thou wilt; for I, being pent in thee,
>   Perforce am thine, and all that is in me.

The last couplet is to me 'perforce' conclusive.

But let us take it that these sonnets prove the contention of the cry of critics that Shakespeare preferred friendship to love, and held his friend dearer than his mistress, and let us see if the plays corroborate the sonnets on this point. We may possibly find that the plays only strengthen the doubt which the sonnets implant in us.

The Merchant of Venice has always seemed to me important as helping to fix the date of the sonnets. Antonio, as I have shown, is an impersonation of Shakespeare himself. It seems to me Shakespeare would have found it impossible to write of Antonio's self-sacrificing love for Bassanio after he himself had been cheated by his friend. This play then must have been written shortly before his betrayal, and should give us Shakespeare's ordinary attitude. Many expressions in the play remind us of the sonnets, and one in especial of sonnet 41. In the sixth scene of the second act, Jessica, when escaping from her father's house, uses Shakespeare's voice to say:

> But love is blind and lovers cannot see
> The pretty follies that themselves commit.

Here we have 'the pretty follies' which is used again as 'pretty wrongs' in sonnet 41. Immediately afterwards Lorenzo, another mask of Shakespeare, praises Jessica as 'wise, fair, and true', just as in sonnet 105

Shakespeare praises his friend as 'kind, fair, and true', using again words which his passion for a woman has taught him.

The fourth act sets forth the same argument we find in the sonnets. When it looks as if Antonio would have to give his life as forfeit to the Jew, Bassanio exclaims:

> Antonio, I am married to a wife
> Which is as dear to me as life itself;
> But life itself, my wife and all the world
> Are not with me esteem'd above thy life.
> I would lose all, ay, sacrifice them all
> Here to this devil to deliver you.

This is the language of passionate exaggeration, one might say. Antonio is suffering in Bassanio's place, paying the penalty, so to speak, for Bassanio's happiness. No wonder Bassanio exaggerates his grief and the sacrifice he would be prepared to make. But Gratiano has no such excuse for extravagant speech, and yet Gratiano follows in the selfsame vein:

> I have a wife whom, I protest, I love:
> I would she were in heaven, so she could
> Entreat some power to change this currish Jew.

The peculiarity of this attitude is heightened by the fact that the two wives, Portia and Nerissa, both take the ordinary view. Portia says:

> Your wife would give you little thanks for that
> If she were by to hear you make the offer.

And Nerissa goes a little further:

> 'Tis well you offer it behind her back,
> The wish would make else an unquiet house.

The blunder is monstrous; not only is the friend prepared to sacrifice all he possesses, including his wife, to save his benefactor, but the friend's friend is content to sacrifice his wife too for the same object. Shakespeare then in early manhood was accustomed to put friendship before love; we must find some explanation of what seems to us so unnatural an attitude.

In the last scene of *The Two Gentlemen of Verona*, which is due to a later revision, the sonnet-case is emphasised. And at this time Shakespeare has suffered Herbert's betrayal. As soon as the false friend Proteus says he is sorry and asks forgiveness, Valentine, another impersonation of Shakespeare, replies:

> Then I am paid;
> And once again I do receive thee honest:
> Who by repentance is not satisfied,
> Is nor of heaven nor earth, for these are pleas'd;
> By penitence the Eternal's wrath's appeased;
> And that my love may appear plain and free,
> All that was mine in Silvia I give thee.

This incarnation of Shakespeare speaks of repentance in Shakespeare's most characteristic fashion, and then coolly surrenders the woman he loves to his friend without a moment's hesitation, and without even considering whether the woman would be satisfied with the transfer. The words admit of no misconstruction; they stand four-square, not to be shaken by any ingenuity of reason, and Shakespeare supplies us with further corroboration of them.

Coriolanus was written fully ten years after *The Merchant of Venice*, and long after the revision of *The Two Gentlemen of Verona*. And yet Shakespeare's attitude at forty-three is, in regard to this matter, just what it was at thirty-three. When Aufidius finds Coriolanus in his house, and learns that he has been banished from Rome and is now prepared to turn his army against his countrymen, he welcomes him as 'more a friend than e'er an enemy', and this is the way he takes to show his joy:

> Know thou first,
> I loved the maid I married: never man
> Sigh'd truer breath; but that I see thee here,
> Thou noble thing! more dances my rapt heart
> Than when I first my wedded mistress saw
> Bestride my threshold.

Here's the same attitude; the same extravagance; the same insistence on the fact that the man loves the maid and yet has more delight in the friend. What does it mean? When we first find it in *The Merchant of Venice* it must give the reader pause; in *The Two Gentlemen of Verona* it surprises us; in the sonnets, accompanied as it is by every flattering expression of tender affection for the friend, it brings us to question; but its repetition in *Coriolanus* must assure us that it is a mere pose. Aufidius was not such a friend of Coriolanus that we can take his protestation seriously. The argument is evidently a stock argument to Shakespeare: a part of the ordinary furniture of his mind: it is like a fashionable dress of the period – the wearer does not notice its peculiarity.

The truth is, Shakespeare found in the literature of his time, and in the minds of his contemporaries, a fantastically high appreciation of friendship, coupled with a corresponding disdain for love as we moderns understand it. In *Wit's Commonwealth*, published in 1598, we find: 'The love of men to women is a thing common and of course, but the friendship of man to man, infinite and immortal'. Passionate devotion to friendship is a sort of mark of the Renaissance, and the words 'love' and 'lover' in Elizabethan English were commonly used for 'friend' and 'friendship'. Moreover, one must not forget that Lyly, whose euphuistic speech affected Shakespeare for years, had handled this same incident in his *Campaspe*, where Alexander gives up his love to his rival, Apelles. Shakespeare, not to be outdone in any loyalty, sets forth the same fantastical devotion in the sonnets and plays. He does this, partly because the spirit of the time infected him, partly out of sincere admiration for Herbert, but oftener, I imagine, out of self-interest. It is pose, flunkeyism and the hope of benefits to come and not passion that inspired the first series of sonnets.

Whoever reads the scene carefully in *Much Ado About Nothing*, cannot avoid seeing that Shakespeare at his best not only does not minimise his friend's offence, but condemns it absolutely:

> The transgression is in the stealer.

And in the sonnets, too, in spite of himself, the same true feeling pierces through the snobbish and affected excuses.

> Ay me! but yet them might'st my seat forbear,
> And chide thy beauty and thy straying youth,
> Who lead thee in their riot even there
> Where thou art forced to break a twofold truth,
> Hers, by thy beauty tempting her to thee,
> Thine, by thy beauty being false to me.

Shakespeare was a sycophant, a flunkey if you will, but nothing worse. Further arguments suggest themselves. Shakespeare lived, as it were, in a glass house with a score of curious eyes watching everything he did and with as many ears pricked for every word he said; but this foul accusation was never even suggested by any of his rivals. In especial Ben Jonson was always girding at Shakespeare, now satirically, now good-humouredly. Is it not manifest that if any such sin had ever been attributed to him, Ben Jonson would have given the suspicion utterance? There is a passage in his *Bartholomew Fair* which I feel sure is meant as a skit upon the relations we find in the Sonnets. In Act V, scene iii, there is a puppet-show setting forth 'the ancient modern history of Hero and Leander, otherwise called the Touchstone of true Love, with as true a trial of Friendship between Damon and Pythias, two faithful friends o' the Bankside'. Hero is a 'wench o' the Bankside', and Leander swims across the Thames to her. Damon and Pythias meet at her lodgings, and abuse each other violently, only to finish as perfect good friends.

DAMON   Whore-master in thy face;

           Thou hast lain with her thyself, I'll prove it in this place.

LEATHER.   They are whore-masters both, sir, that's a plain case.

PYTHIAS   Thou lie like a rogue.

LEATHER.   Do I lie like a rogue?

PYTHIAS   A pimp and a scab.

LEATHER.   A pimp and a scab!

           I say, between you you have both but one drab.

PYTHIAS & DAMON

           Come, now we'll go together to breakfast to Hero.

LEATHER.   Thus, gentles, you perceive without any denial

           'Twixt Damon and Pythias here friendship's true trial.

Rare Ben Jonson would have been delighted to set forth the viler charge if it had ever been whispered.

Then again, it seems to me certain that if Shakespeare had been the sort of man his accusers say he was, he would have betrayed himself in his plays. Consider merely the fact that young boys then played the girls' parts on the stage. Surely if Shakespeare had had any leaning that way, we should have found again and again ambiguous or suggestive expressions given to some of these boys when aping girls; but not one. The temptation was there; the provocation was there, incessant and prolonged for twenty-five years, and yet, to my knowledge, Shakespeare has never used one word that malice could misconstrue. Yet he loved suggestive and lewd speech.

Luckily, however, there is stronger proof of Shakespeare's innocence than even his condemnation of his false friend, proof so strong, that if all the arguments for his guilt were tenfold stronger than they are, this proof would outweigh them all and bring them to nought. Nor should it be supposed, because I have only mentioned the chief arguments for and against, that I do not know all those that can be urged on either side. I have confined myself to the chief ones simply because by merely stating them, their utter weakness must be admitted by everyone who can read Shakespeare, by everyone who understands his impulsive sensitiveness, and the facility with which affectionate expressions came to his lips. Moreover, it must not be forgotten that while the sonnets were being written he was in rivalry with Chapman for this very patron's favour, and this rivalry alone would explain a good deal of the fervour, or, should I say, the affected fervour he put into the first series of sonnets; but now for the decisive and convincing argument for Shakespeare's innocence.

Let us first ask ourselves how it is that real passion betrays itself and proves its force. Surely it is by its continuance; by its effect upon the life later. I have assumed, or inferred, as my readers may decide, that Shakespeare's liking for Herbert was chiefly snobbish, and was deepened by the selfish hope that he would find in him a patron even more powerful and more liberally disposed than Lord Southampton. He probably felt that young Herbert owed him a great deal for his companionship and poetical advice; for Herbert was by way of being a poet himself. If my view is correct, after Shakespeare lost Lord Herbert's affection, we should expect to hear him talking of man's forgetfulness and ingratitude, and that is just what Lord Herbert left in him, bitterness and contempt. Never one word in all his works to show that the loss of this youth's affection touched him more nearly. As we have seen, he cannot keep the incident out of his plays. Again and again he drags it in; but in none of these dramas is there any lingering kindness towards the betrayer. And as soon as the incident was past and done with, as soon as the three or four years' companionship with Lord Herbert was at an end, not one word more do we catch expressive of affection. Again and again Shakespeare rails at man's ingratitude, but nothing more. Think of it. Pembroke, under James, came to great power; was, indeed, made Lord Chamberlain, and set above all the players, so that he could have advanced Shakespeare as he pleased with a word: with a word could have made him Master of the Revels, or given him a higher post. He did not help him in any way. He gave books every Christmas to Ben

Jonson, but we hear of no gift to Shakespeare, though evidently from the dedication to him of the first folio, he remained on terms of careless acquaintance with Shakespeare. Ingratitude is what Shakespeare found in Lord Pembroke; ingratitude is what he complains of in him. What a different effect the loss of Mary Fitton had upon Shakespeare. Just consider what the plays teach us when the sonnet-story is finished. The youth vanishes; no reader can find a trace of him, or even an allusion to him. But the woman comes to be the centre, as we shall see, of tragedy after tragedy. She flames through Shakespeare's life, a fiery symbol, till at length she inspires perhaps his greatest drama, *Antony and Cleopatra*, filling it with the disgrace of him who is 'a strumpet's fool', the shame of him who has become 'the bellows and the fan to cool a harlot's lust'.

The passion for Mary Fitton was the passion of Shakespeare's whole life. The adoration of her, and the insane desire of her, can be seen in every play he wrote from 1597 to 1608. After he lost her, he went back to her; but the wound of her frailty cankered and took on proud flesh in him, and tortured him to nervous breakdown and to madness. When at length he won to peace, after ten years, it was the peace of exhaustion. His love for his 'gypsy-wanton' burned him out, as one is burnt to ashes at the stake, and his passion only ended with his life.

There is no room for doubt in my mind, no faintest suspicion. Hallam and Heine, and all the cry of critics, are mistaken in this matter. Shakespeare admired Lord Herbert's youth and boldness and beauty, hoped great things from his favour and patronage; but after the betrayal, he judged him inexorably as a mean traitor, 'a stealer' who had betrayed 'a twofold trust'; and later, cursed him for his ingratitude, and went about with wild thoughts of bloody revenge, as we shall soon see in *Hamlet* and *Othello*, and then dropped him into oblivion without a pang.

It is bad enough to know that Shakespeare, the sweetest spirit and finest mind in all literature, should have degraded himself to pretend such an affection for the profligate Herbert as has given occasion for misconstruction. It is bad enough, I say, to know that Shakespeare could play flunkey to this extent; but after all, that is the worst that can be urged against him, and it is so much better than men have been led to believe that there may be a certain relief in the knowledge.

6

The First-fruit of the Tree of Knowledge: Brutus

The play of *Julius Caesar* was written about 1600 or 1601. As *Twelfth Night* was the last of the golden comedies, so *Julius Caesar* is the first of the great tragedies, and bears melancholy witness to us that the poet's young-eyed confidence in life and joy in living are dying, if not dead. *Julius Caesar* is the first outcome of disillusion. Before it was written Shakespeare had been deceived by his mistress, betrayed by his friend; his eyes had been opened to the fraud and falsehood of life; but, like one who has just been operated on for cataract, he still sees realities as through a mist, dimly. He meets the shock of traitorous betrayal as we should have expected Valentine or Antonio or Orsino to meet it – with pitying forgiveness. Suffering, instead of steeling his heart and drying up his sympathies, as it does with most men, softened him, induced him to give himself wholly to that 'angel, Pity'. He will not believe that his bitter experience is universal; in spite of Herbert's betrayal, he still has the courage to declare his belief in the existence of the ideal. At the very last his defeated Brutus cries:

> My heart doth joy that yet in all my life
> I found no man but he was true to me.

The pathos of this attempt still to believe in man and man's truth is over the whole play. But the belief was fated to disappear. No man who lives in the world can boast of loyalty as Brutus did; even Jesus had a Judas among the Twelve. But when Shakespeare wrote *Julius Caesar* he still tried to believe, and this gives the play an important place in his life's story.

Before I begin to consider the character of Brutus I should like to draw attention to three passages which place Brutus between the melancholy Jaques of *As You Like It*, whose melancholy is merely temperamental, and the almost despairing Hamlet. Jaques says:

> Invest me in my motley; give me leave
> To speak my mind, and I will through and through
> Cleanse the foul body of the infected world,
> If they will patiently receive my medicine.

This is the view of early manhood which does not doubt its power to cure all the evils which afflict mortality. Then comes the later, more hopeless view, to which Brutus gives expression:

> Till then, my noble friend, chew upon this;
> Brutus had rather be a villager
> Than to repute himself a son of Rome
> Under these hard conditions as this time
> Is like to lay upon us.

And later still, and still more bitter, Hamlet's:

> The time is out of joint; O cursed spite,
> That ever I was born to set it right!

But Shakespeare is a meliorist even in Hamlet, and believes that the ailments of man can all be set right.

The likenesses between Brutus and Hamlet are so marked that even the commentators have noticed them. Professor Dowden exaggerates the similarities. 'Both (dramas),' he writes, 'are tragedies of thought rather than of passion; both present in their chief characters the spectacle of noble natures which fail through some weakness or deficiency rather than through crime; upon Brutus as upon Hamlet a burden is laid which he is not able to bear; neither Brutus nor Hamlet is fitted for action, yet both are called to act in dangerous and difficult affairs.' Much of this is Professor Dowden's view and not Shakespeare's. When Shakespeare wrote *Julius Caesar* he had not reached that stage in self-understanding when he became conscious that he was a man of thought rather than of action, and that the two ideals tend to exclude each other. In the contest at Philippi Brutus and his wing win the day; it is the defeat of Cassius which brings about the ruin; Shakespeare evidently intended to depict Brutus as well 'fitted for action'.

Some critics find it disconcerting that Shakespeare identified himself with Brutus, who failed, rather than with Caesar, who succeeded. But even before he himself came to grief in his love and trust, Shakespeare had always treated the failures with peculiar sympathy. He preferred Arthur to the Bastard, and King Henry VI to Richard III, and Richard II to proud Bolingbroke. And after his agony of disillusion, all his heroes are failures for years and years: Brutus, Hamlet, Macbeth, Lear, Troilus, Antony, and Timon – all fail as he himself had failed.

There is some matter for surprise in the fact that Brutus is an ideal portrait of Shakespeare. Disillusion usually brings a certain bitter sincerity, a measure of realism, into artistic work; but its first effect on Shakespeare was to draw out all the kindliness in him; Brutus is Shakespeare at his sweetest and best. Yet the soul-suffering of the man has assuredly improved his art: Brutus is a better portrait of him than Biron, Valentine, Romeo, or Antonio, a more serious and bolder piece of self-revealing even than Orsino. Shakespeare is not afraid now to depict the deep underlying kindness of his nature, his essential goodness of heart. A little earlier, and occupied chiefly with his own complex growth, he could only paint sides of himself; a little later, and the personal interest absorbed all others, so that his dramas became lyrics of anguish and despair. Brutus belongs to the best time, artistically speaking, to the time when passion and pain had tried the character without benumbing the will or distracting the mind: it is a masterpiece of portraiture, and stands in even closer relation to Hamlet than Romeo stands to Orsino. As Shakespeare appears to us in Brutus at thirty-seven, so he was when they bore him to his grave at fifty-two – the heart does not alter greatly.

Let no one say or think that in all this I am drawing on my imagination; what I have said is justified by all that Brutus says and does from one end of the play to the other. According to his custom, Shakespeare has said it all of himself very plainly, and has put his confession into the mouth of Brutus on his very first appearance (Act 1, sc. 2):

> Cassius,
> Be not deceived: if I have veiled my look
> I turn the trouble of my countenance
> Merely upon myself. Vexed I am
> Of late with passions of some difference,
> Conceptions only proper to myself,
> Which gives some soil, perhaps, to my behaviours,
> But let not therefore my good friends be grieved, –
> Among which number, Cassius, be you one, –
> Nor construe any further in neglect,

> Than that poor Brutus, with himself at war,
> Forgets the shows of love to other men.

What were these 'different passions', complex personal passions, too, which had vexed Brutus and changed his manners even to his friends? There is no hint of them in Plutarch, no word about them in the play. It was not 'poor Brutus', but poor Shakespeare, racked by love and jealousy, tortured by betrayal, who was now 'at war with himself'.

I assume the identity of Brutus with Shakespeare before I have absolutely proved it because it furnishes the solution to the difficulties of the play. As usual, Coleridge has given proof of his insight by seeing and stating the chief difficulty, without, however, being able to explain it, and as usual, also, the later critics have followed him as far as they can, and in this case have elected to pass over the difficulty in silence. Coleridge quotes some of the words of Brutus when he first thinks of killing Caesar, and calls the passage a speech of Brutus, but it is in reality a soliloquy of Brutus, and must be considered in its entirety. Brutus says:

> It must be by his death: and for my part,
> I know no personal cause to spurn at him
> But for the general. He would be crowned: –
> How that might change his nature, there's the question?
> It is the bright day that brings forth the adder,
> And that craves wary walking. Crown him? – that;
> And then, I grant, we put a sting in him
> That at his will he may do danger with.
> The abuse of greatness is, when it disjoins
> Remorse from power: and to speak truth of Caesar,
> I have known his affections swayed
> More than his reason. But 'tis a common proof,
> That lowliness is young ambition's ladder,
> Whereto the climber-upwards turns his face;
> But when he once attains the topmost round,
> He then unto the ladder turns his back,
> Looks in the clouds, scorning the base degrees
> By which he did ascend. So Caesar may:
> Then, lest he may, prevent. And since the quarrel
> Will bear no colour for the thing he is,
> Fashion it thus: that, what he is, augmented,

> Would run to these and these extremities:
> And therefore think him as a serpent's egg,
> Which, hatched, would as his kind grow mischievous;
> And kill him in the shell.

Coleridge's comment on this deserves notice. He wrote: 'This speech is singular; at least, I do not at present see into Shakespeare's motive, his rationale, or in what point of view he meant Brutus' character to appear. For surely . . . nothing can seem more discordant with our historical preconceptions of Brutus, or more lowering to the intellect of the Stoico-Platonic tyrannicide, than the tenets here attributed to him – to him, the stern Roman republican; namely, that he would have no objection to a king, or to Caesar, a monarch in Rome, would Caesar but be as good a monarch as he now seems disposed to be! How, too, could Brutus say that he found no personal cause – none in Caesar's past conduct as a man? Had he not passed the Rubicon? Had he not entered Rome as a conqueror? Had he not placed his Gauls in the Senate? Shakespeare, it may be said, has not brought these things forward. True; – and this is just the ground of my perplexity. What character did Shakespeare mean his Brutus to be?'

All this is sound criticism, and can only be answered by the truth that Shakespeare from the beginning of the play identified himself with Brutus, and paid but little attention to the historic Brutus whom he had met in Plutarch. Let us push criticism a little further, and we shall see that this is the only possible way to read the riddle. We all know why Plutarch's Brutus killed Caesar; but why does Shakespeare's Brutus kill the man he so esteems? Because Caesar may change his nature when king; because like the serpent's egg he may 'grow mischievous'? But when he speaks 'truth' of Caesar he has to admit Caesar's goodness. The 'serpent's egg' reason then is inapplicable. Besides, when speaking of himself on the plains of Philippi, Shakespeare's Brutus explicitly contradicts this false reasoning:

> I know not how
> But I do find it cowardly and vile,
> *For fear of what might fall*, so to prevent
> The term of life.

It would seem, therefore, that Brutus did not kill Caesar, as one crushes a serpent's egg, to prevent evil consequences. It is equally manifest that he did not do it for 'the general', for if ever 'the general' were shown to be despicable and worthless it is in this very play, where the citizens murder Cinna the poet because he has the same name as Cinna the conspirator, and the lower classes are despised as the 'rabblement', 'the common herd', with 'chapped hands', 'sweaty nightcaps', and 'stinking breath'.

It is Dr Brandes' idea and not Shakespeare's that Brutus is a 'man of uncompromising character and principle'. That is the Brutus of Plutarch, who finds in his stern republican love of the common good an ethical motive for killing the ambitious Caesar. But Shakespeare had no understanding of the republican ideal, and no sympathy with the public; accordingly, his Brutus has no adequate reason for contriving Caesar's death. Shakespeare followed Plutarch in freeing Brutus from the suspicion of personal or interested motive, but he didn't see that by doing this he made his Brutus a conspirator without a cause, a murderer without a motive. The truth is our gentle poet could never find a convincing ground for cold-blooded murder. It will be remembered that Macbeth only murders, as the deer murders, out of fear, and the fact that his Brutus can find no justification of any sort for killing Caesar, confirms our view of Shakespeare's gentle kindness. The 'uncompromising character and principle' of the severe republican we find in Plutarch, sit uneasily on Shakespeare's Brutus; it is apparent that the poet had no conception of what we call a fanatic. His difficulties arise from this limitation of insight. He begins to write the play by making Brutus an idealised portrait of himself; he, therefore, dwells on Brutus' perfect nobility, sincerity, and unselfishness, but does not realise that the more perfect he makes Brutus, the more clear and cogent Brutus' motive must be for undertaking Caesar's assassination.

In this confusion Shakespeare's usually fine instinct is at fault, and he blunders from mistake to mistake. His idealising tendency makes him present Brutus as perfect, and at the same time he uses the historical incident of the anonymous letters, which goes to show Brutus as conceited and vain. If these letters influenced Brutus – and they must be taken to have done so, or else why were they introduced? – we have a noble and unselfish man murdering out of paltry vanity. In Plutarch, where Brutus is depicted as an austere republican, the incident of the letters only throws a natural shade of doubt on the rigid principles by which alone he is supposed to be guided. We all feel that rigid principles rest on pride, and may best be led astray through pride. But

Shakespeare's Brutus is pure human sweetness, and the letters are worse than out of place when addressed to him. Shakespeare should never have used this incident; it is a blot on his conception.

All through the first acts of the play Brutus is incredible, for he is in an impossible position. Shakespeare simply could not find any valid reason why his *alter ego*, Brutus, should kill Caesar. But from the moment the murder is committed to the end of the play Brutus-Shakespeare is at peace with himself. And as soon as the dramatist lets himself go and paints Brutus with entire freedom and frankness, he rises to the height of tragic pathos, and we can all recognise the original of the portrait. At first Brutus is merely ideal; his perfect unsuspiciousness – he trusts even Antony; his transparent honesty – he will have no other oath among the conspirators

> Than honesty to honesty engaged;

his hatred of bloodshed – he opposes Cassius, who proposes to murder Antony; all these noble qualities may be contrasted with the subtler shortcomings which make of Hamlet so vital a creation. Hamlet is suspicious even of Ophelia; Hamlet is only 'indifferent honest'; Hamlet makes his friends swear to keep the ghost's appearance a profound secret; Hamlet lives from the beginning, while Brutus at first is a mere bundle of perfections individualised only by that personal intimate confession which I have already quoted, which, however, has nothing to do with the play. But later in the drama Shakespeare begins to lend Brutus his own weaknesses, and forthwith Brutus lives. His insomnia is pure Shakespeare:

> Since Cassius first did whet me against Caesar,
> I have not slept.

The character of Brutus is superbly portrayed in that wonderful scene with Cassius in the fourth act. With all the superiority of conscious genius he treats his confederate as a child or madman, much as Hamlet treats Rosencrantz and Guildenstern:

> Shall I be frighted when a madman stares?

Cassius is mean, too, whereas Brutus is kindly and generous to a degree:

> For I can raise no money by vile means:
> By heaven, I had rather coin my heart,

And drop my blood for drachmas, than to wring
From the hard hands of peasants their vile trash
By any indirection . . .
[. . .]
When Marcus Brutus grows so covetous,
To lock such rascal counters from his friends,
Be ready, gods, with all your thunderbolts,
Dash him to pieces.

And, above all, as soon as Cassius appeals to his affection, Brutus is disarmed:

O Cassius, you are yoked with a lamb
That carries anger, as the flint bears fire;
Who, much enforced, shows a hasty spark,
And straight is cold again.

This is the best expression of Shakespeare's temper; the 'hasty spark' is Hamlet's temper, as we have seen, and Macbeth's, and Romeo's.

And now everything that Brutus does or says is Shakespeare's best. In a bowl of wine he buries 'all unkindness'. His affection for Cassius is not a virtue to one in especial. The scene in the fourth act, in which he begs the pardon of his boy Lucius, should be learned by heart by those who wish to understand our loving and lovable Shakespeare. This scene, be it remarked, is not in Plutarch, but is Shakespeare's own invention. His care for the lad's comfort, at a time when his own life is striking the supreme hour, is exquisitely pathetic. Then come his farewell to Cassius and his lament over Cassius' body; then the second fight and the nobly generous words that hold in them, as flowers their perfume, all Shakespeare's sweetness of nature:

My heart doth joy, that yet in all my life
I found no man, but he was true to me.

And then night hangs upon the weary, sleepless eyes, and we are all ready to echo Antony's marvellous valediction:

This was the noblest Roman of them all;
[. . .]
His life was gentle; and the elements
So mixed in him, that Nature might stand up
And say to all the world, 'This was a man!'

But this Brutus was no murderer, no conspirator, no narrow republican fanatic, but simply gentle Shakespeare discovering to us his own sad heart and the sweetness which suffering had called forth in him.

7

Dramas of Revenge and Jealousy –
Part One: Hamlet

A beautiful, pure and most moral nature, without the strength of
nerve which makes the hero, sinks beneath a burden which it can
neither bear nor throw off; every duty is holy to him, – this too
hard. The impossible is required of him, – not the impossible in
itself, but the impossible to him. How he winds, turns, agonises,
advances and recoils, ever reminded, ever reminding himself,
and at last almost loses his purpose from his thoughts, without
ever again recovering his peace of mind . . .

Hamlet by Goethe

Goethe's criticism of Hamlet is so much finer than any English criticism that I am glad to quote it. It will serve, I think, as a standard to
distinguish the best criticism of the past from what I shall set forth in
the course of this analysis. In this chapter I shall try to show what new
light our knowledge of Shakespeare throws on the play, and conversely
what new light the play throws on its maker.

The first moment of disillusion brought out, as we have seen in
Brutus, all the kindness in Shakespeare's nature. He will believe in men
in spite of experience; but the idealistic pose could not be kept up: sooner
or later Shakespeare had to face the fact that he had been befooled and
scorned by friend and mistress – how did he meet it? Hamlet is the
answer: Shakespeare went about nursing dreams of revenge and murder.
Disillusion had deeper consequences; forced to see other men as they
were, he tried for a moment to see himself as he was. The outcome of
that objective vision was Hamlet – a masterpiece of self-revealing.

Yet, when he wrote *Hamlet*, nothing was clear to him; the significance of the catastrophe had only dawned upon him; he had no notion
how complete his soul-shipwreck was, still less did he dream of painting

himself realistically in all his obsequious flunkeyism and ungovernable sensuality. He saw himself less idealistically than heretofore, and, trying to look at himself fairly, honestly, he could not but accuse himself of irresolution at the very least; he had hung on with Herbert, as the sonnets tell us, hoping to build again the confidence which had been ruined by betrayal, hoping he knew not what of gain or place, to the injury of his own self-respect; while brooding all the time on quite impossible plans of revenge, impossible, for action had been 'sicklied o'er with the pale cast of thought'. Hamlet could not screw his courage to the sticking point, and so became a type for ever of the philosopher or man of letters who, by thinking, has lost the capacity for action.

Putting ourselves in Shakespeare's place for the moment we see at once why he selected this story for treatment at this time. He knew, none better, that no young aristocrat would have submitted patiently to the wrong he had suffered from Lord Herbert; he created Laertes to show how instant and determined such a man would be in taking murderous revenge; but he still felt that what others would regard as faults, his irresolution and shrinking from bloodshed were in themselves nobler, and so, whilst half excusing, half realising himself, he brought forth a masterpiece. This brooding on revenge, which is the heart and explanation of his great play, shows us how little Shakespeare cared for Herbert, how completely he had condemned him. The soliloquy on this point in *Hamlet* is the most characteristic thing in the drama:

> This is most brave,
> That I, the son of a dear father murder'd,,
> Prompted to my revenge by heaven and hell,
> Must, like a whore, unpack my heart with words,
> And fall a-cursing like a very drab.

Shakespeare is thinking of Herbert's betrayal; 'here I am,' he says, 'prompted to revenge by reason and custom, yet instead of acting I fall a-cursing like a drab.' But behind his irresolution is his hatred of bloodshed: he could whip out his sword and on a sudden kill Polonius, mistaking him for the king (Herbert), but he could not, in cold blood, make up his mind to kill and proceed to execution. Like his own Hubert, Shakespeare had to confess:

> Within this bosom never enter'd yet
> The dreadful motion of a murderous thought.

He had none of the direct, passionate, conscienceless resolution of Laertes. He whips himself to anger against the king by thinking of Herbert in the king's place; but lackey-like has to admit that mere regard for position and power gives him pause: Lord Herbert was too far above him:

> There's such divinity doth hedge a king,
> That treason can but peep to what it would.

Shakespeare's personal feeling dominates and inspires the whole play. One crucial instance will prove this. Why did Hamlet hate his mother's lechery? Most men would hardly have condemned it, certainly would not have suffered their thoughts to dwell on it beyond the moment; but to Hamlet his mother's faithlessness was horrible, shameful, degrading, simply because Hamlet-Shakespeare had identified her with Miss Fitton, and it was Miss Fitton's faithlessness, it was her deception he was condemning in the bitterest words he could find. He thus gets into a somewhat unreal tragedy, a passionate intensity which is otherwise wholly inexplicable. This is how he talks to his mother:

> Have you eyes?
> Could you on this fair mountain leave to feed,
> And batten on this moor? Ha! have you eyes
> [. . .]
> What devil was't
> That thus cozen'd you at hoodman-blind?
> Eyes without feeling, feeling without sight,
> Ears without hands or eyes, smelling sans all,
> Or but a sickly part of one true sense
> Could not so mope.
> O, shame! where is thy blush?

If anyone can imagine that this is the way a son thinks of a mother's slip he is past my persuading. In all this Shakespeare is thinking of himself in comparison with Herbert; and his advice to his mother is almost as self-revealing, showing, as it does, what he would wish to say to Miss Fitton:

> Repent what's past; avoid what is to come;
> And do not spread the compost on the weeds
> To make them ranker . . .

> Assume a virtue if you have it not . . .

In his description of the king and queen we get Shakespeare's view of Lord Herbert and Miss Fitton: the king (Herbert) is 'mildew'd' and foul in comparison with his modest poet-rival – 'A satyr to Hyperion'.

Hamlet's view of his mother (Miss Fitton), though bitterer still, is yet the bitterness of disappointed love: he will have her repent, refrain from the adultery, and be pure and good again. When the Queen asks:

> What shall I do?

Hamlet answers:

> Not this, by no means, that I bid you do:
> Let the king tempt you again to bed;
> Pinch wanton on your cheek; call you his mouse;
> And let him, for a pair of reechy kisses,
> Or paddling in your neck with his damned fingers . . .

Maddened with jealousy he sees the act, scourges himself with his own lewd imagining as Posthumus scourges himself. No one ever felt this intensity of jealous rage about a mother or a sister. The mere idea is absurd; it is one's own passion-torture that speaks in such words as I have here quoted.

Hamlet's treatment of Ophelia, too, and his advice to her are all the outcome of Shakespeare's own disappointment:

> Get thee to a nunnery: why wouldst thou be a breeder of sinners?

We all expect from Hamlet some outburst of divine tenderness to Ophelia; but the scenes with the pure and devoted girl whom he is supposed to love are not half realised, are nothing like so intense as the scenes with the guilty mother. It is jealousy that is blazing in Shakespeare at this time, and not love; when Hamlet speaks to the Queen we hear Shakespeare speaking to his own faithless, guilty love. Besides, Ophelia is not even realised; she is submissive affection, an abstraction, and not a character. Shakespeare did not take interest enough in her to give her flesh and blood.

Shakespeare's jealousy and excessive sensuality come to full light in the scene between Hamlet and Ophelia, when they are about to witness the play before the king: he persists in talking smut to her, which she pretends not to understand. The lewdness, we all feel, is out of place in

Hamlet, horribly out of place when Hamlet is talking to Ophelia, but Shakespeare's sensuality has been stung to ecstasy by Miss Fitton's frailty, and he cannot but give it voice. As soon as Ophelia goes out of her mind she, too, becomes coarse – all of which is but a witness to Shakespeare's tortured animality. Yet Goethe can talk of Hamlet's 'pure and most moral nature'. A goat is hardly less pure, though Hamlet was moral enough in the high sense of the word.

There are one or two minor questions still to be considered, and the chief of these is how far, even in this moment of disillusion, did our Shakespeare see himself as he was? Hamlet says:

> I am very proud, revengeful, ambitious; with more offences at my beck than I have thoughts to put them in, imagination to give them shape, or time to act them in. What should such fellows as I do crawling between heaven and earth? We are arrant knaves, all; believe none of us.

All this is mere rhetoric, and full of clever self-excusing. Hamlet is not very revengeful or very ambitious; he is weakly-irresolute, and excessively sensual, with all the faults that accompany these frailties. Even at this moment, when he must know that he is not very revengeful, that forgiveness were easier to him, Shakespeare will pose to himself, and call himself revengeful: he is such an idealist that he absolutely refuses to see himself as he is. In later dramas we shall find that he grows to deeper self-knowledge. Hamlet is but the halfway house to complete understanding.

Fortunately we have each of us an infallible touchstone by which we can judge of our love of truth. Any of us, man or woman, would rather be accused of a mental than a physical shortcoming. Do we see our bodily imperfections as they are? Can we describe ourselves pitilessly with snub nose, or coarse beak, bandy legs or thin shanks, gross paunch or sedgy beard? Shakespeare in Hamlet can hardly bear even to suggest his physical imperfections. Hamlet lets out inadvertently that he was fat, but he will not say so openly. His mother says to Hamlet:

> You are fat and scant of breath.

Many people, especially actors, have been so determined to see Hamlet as slight and student-like, that they have tried to criticise this phrase, and one of them, Mr Beerbohm Tree, even in our day, went so far as to degrade the text to 'faint and scant of breath'. But the fatness is there, and comes to view again in another phrase of Hamlet:

> O, that this too, too solid flesh would melt,
> Thaw, and resolve itself into a dew.

No thin man ever spoke of his flesh in that way. Shakespeare was probably small, too. We know that he used to play Adam in *As You Like it*, and in the play Orlando has to take Adam up and carry him off the stage, a thing no actor would attempt if the Adam had been a big man. Shakespeare was probably of middle height, or below it, and podgy. I always picture him to myself as very like Swinburne. Yet even in Hamlet he would make himself out to be a devil of a fellow: 'valiant Hamlet', a swordsman of the finest, a superb duellist, who can touch Laertes again and again, though lacking practice. At the last push of fate Shakespeare will pose and deceive himself.

It is curiously characteristic of Shakespeare that when Hamlet broods on retaliation he does not brood like a brave man, who gloats on challenging his enemy to a fair fight, and killing him by sheer force or resolution; his passion, his revenge, is almost that of an Italian bravo. Not once does Hamlet think of forcing the king (Herbert) to a duel; he goes about with ideas of assassination, and not of combat.

> Now might I do it pat

he cries as he sees the king praying; and he does not do it because he would thus send the king's soul to Heaven – shrill wordy intensity to excuse want of nerve. Whenever we get under the skin, it is Shakespeare's femininity which startles us.

One cannot leave this great picture of Hamlet-Shakespeare without noticing one curious fact, which throws a flood of light on the relations of literary art to life. Shakespeare, as we have seen, is boiling with jealous passion, brooding continually on murderous revenge, and so becomes conscious of his own irresolution. He dwells on this, and makes this irresolution the chief feature of Hamlet's character, and yet because he is writing about himself he manages to suggest so many other qualities, and such amiable and noble ones, that we are all in love with Hamlet, in spite of his irresolution, erotic mania and bloody thoughts.

In later dramas Shakespeare went on to deal with the deeper and more elemental things in his nature, with jealousy in *Othello*, and passionate desire in *Antony and Cleopatra*; but he never, perhaps, did much better work than in this drama where he chooses to magnify a secondary and ancillary weakness into the chief defect of his whole being. The pathos of the drama is to be found in the fact that Shakespeare realises he is unable to take personal vengeance on Herbert. *Hamlet* is a drama of pathetic weakness, strengthened by a drama of revenge and jealousy. In these last respects it is a preparatory study for *Othello*.

In *Hamlet* Shakespeare let out some of the foul matter which Herbert's mean betrayal had bred in him. Even in *Hamlet*, however, his passion for Mary Fitton, and his jealousy of her, constitute the real theme. We shall soon see how this passion coloured all the rest of his life and art, and at length brought about his ruin.

8

Dramas of Revenge and Jealousy –
Part Two: *Othello*

There is perhaps no single drama which throws such light on Shakespeare and his method of work as *Othello*: it is a long conflict between the artist in him and the man, and, in the struggle, both his artistic ideals and his passionate soul come to clearest view. From it we see that Shakespeare's nature gave itself gradually to jealousy and revenge. The fire of his passion burned more and more fiercely for years; was infinitely hotter in 1604, when *Othello* was written, than it had been when *Julius Caesar* was written in 1600. This proves to me that Shakespeare's connection with Mary Fitton did not come to an end when he first discovered her unfaithfulness. The intimacy continued for a dozen years. In Sonnet 136 he prays her to allow him to be one of her lovers. That she was liberal enough to consent appears clearly from the growth of passion in his plays. It is certain, too, that she went on deceiving him with other lovers, or his jealousy would have waned away, ebbing with fulfilled desire. But his passion increases in intensity from 1597 to 1604, whipped no doubt to ecstasy by continual deception and wild jealousy. Both lust and jealousy swing to madness in *Othello*. But Shakespeare was so great an artist that, when he took the story from Cinthio, he tried to realise it without bringing in his own personality: hence a conflict between his art and his passion.

At first sight *Othello* reminds one of a picture by Titian or Veronese; it is a romantic conception; the personages are all in gala dress; the struggle between Iago and the Moor is melodramatic; the whole picture aglow with a superb richness of colour. It is Shakespeare's finest play, his supreme achievement as a playwright. It is impossible to read *Othello* without admiring the art of it. The beginning is so easy: the introduction of the chief characters so measured and impressive that when the action really begins, it develops and increases in speed as by its own weight to the inevitable end; inevitable – for the end in this case is merely the resultant of the shock of these various personalities. But if the action itself is superbly ordered, the painting of character leaves much to be desired, as we shall see. There is one notable difference between *Othello* and those dramas, *Hamlet*, *Macbeth*, and *Cymbeline*, wherein Shakespeare has depicted himself as the protagonist. In the self-revealing dramas not only does Shakespeare give his hero licence to talk, in and out of season, and thus hinder the development of the story, but he also allows him to occupy the whole stage without a competitor. The explanation is obvious enough. Dramatic art is to be congratulated on the fact that now and then Shakespeare left himself for a little out of the play, for then not only does the construction of the play improve, but the play grows in interest through the encounter of evenly-matched antagonists. The first thing we notice in *Othello* is that Iago is at least as important a character as the hero himself. *Hamlet*, on the other hand, is almost a lyric; there is no counterpoise to the student-prince.

Now let us get to the play itself. Othello's first appearance in converse with Iago in the second scene of the first act does not seem to me to deserve the praise that has been lavished on it. Though Othello knows that 'boasting is (not) an honour', he nevertheless boasts himself of royal blood. We have noticed already Shakespeare's love of good blood, and belief in its wondrous efficacy; it is one of his permanent and most characteristic traits. The passage about royal descent might be left out with advantage; if these three lines are omitted, Othello's pride in his own nature – his 'parts and perfect soul' – is far more strongly felt. But such trivial flaws are forgotten when Brabantio enters and swords are drawn.

> Keep up your bright swords, for the dew will rust them.

is excellent in its contemptuous irony. A little later, however, Othello finds an expression which is intensely characteristic of a great man of action:

> Hold your hands,
> Both you of my inclining, and the rest;
> Were it my cue to fight, I should have known it
> Without a prompter.

This last line and a half is addressed especially to Iago who is bent on provoking a fight, and is, I think, the best piece of character-painting in all *Othello*; the born general knows instinctively the moment to attack just as the trained boxer's hand strikes before he consciously sees the opening. When Othello speaks before the Duke, too, he reveals himself with admirable clearness and truth to nature. His pride is so deep-rooted, his self-respect so great, that he respects all other dignitaries: the Senators are his 'very noble and approved good masters'. Every word weighed and effectual. Admirable, too, is the expression 'round unvarnished tale'.

But pride and respect for others' greatness are not qualities peculiar to the man of action; they belong to all men of ability. As soon as Othello begins to tell how he won Desdemona, he falls out of his character. Feeling certain that he has placed his hero before us in strong outlines, Shakespeare lets himself go, and at once we catch him speaking and not Othello. In 'antres vast and deserts idle' I hear the poet, and when the verse swings to –

> . . . men whose heads
> Do grow beneath their shoulders,

it is plain that Othello, the lord and lover of realities, has deserted the firm ground of fact. But Shakespeare pulls himself in almost before he has yielded to the charm of his own words, and again Othello speaks:

> This to hear
> Would Desdemona seriously incline,
> But still the house-affairs would draw her thence,

and so forth.

The temptation, however, was overpowering, and again Shakespeare yields to it:

> And often did beguile her of her tears
> When I did speak of some distressful stroke
> That my youth suffered.

It is a characteristic of the man of action that he thinks lightly of reverses; he loves hard buffets as a swimmer high waves, and when he tells his life-story he does not talk of his 'distress'. This 'distressful stroke that my youth suffered' is manifestly pure Shakespeare – tender-hearted Shakespeare, who pitied himself and the distressful strokes his youth suffered very profoundly. The characterisation of Othello in the rest of this scene is anything but happy. He talks too much; I miss the short sharp words which would show the man used to command, and not only does he talk too much, but he talks in images like a poet, and exaggerates:

> The tyrant Custom, most grave senators,
> Hath made the flinty and steel couch of war
> My thrice-driven bed of down.

Even the matter here is insincere; this is the poet's explanation of the Captain's preference for a hard bed and hard living: 'he has been accustomed to it', says Shakespeare, not understanding that there are born hunter and soldier natures who absolutely prefer hardships to effeminate luxury. Othello's next speech is just as bad; he talks too much of things particular and private, and the farther he goes, the worse he gets, till we again hear the poet speaking, or rather mouthing:

> No, when light-winged toys
> Of feathered Cupid seel with wanton dullness
> My speculative and officed instruments,
> That my disports corrupt and taint my business,
> Let housewives make a skillet of my helm,
> And all indign and base adversities
> Make head against my estimation.

Again when he says –

> Come, Desdemona: I have but an hour
> Of love, of worldly matters and direction
> To spend with thee; we must obey the time,

I find no sharp impatience to get to work such as Hotspur felt, but a certain reluctance to leave his love – a natural touch which indicates that the poet was thinking of himself and not of his puppet.

The first scene of the second act shows us how Shakespeare, the dramatist, worked. Cassio is plainly Shakespeare the poet; any of his speeches taken at haphazard proves it. When he hears that Iago has arrived he breaks out:

> He has had most favourable and happy speed;
> Tempests themselves, high seas, and howling winds,
> The guttered rocks and congregated sands –
> Traitors ensteeped to clog the guiltless keel –

> As having sense of beauty, do omit
> Their mortal natures, letting go safely by
> The divine Desdemona.

And when Desdemona lands, Cassio's first exclamation is sufficient to establish the fact that he is merely the poet's mask:

> O, behold,
> The riches of the ship is come on shore!

And just as clearly as Cassio is Shakespeare, the lyric poet, so is Iago, at first, the embodiment of Shakespeare's intelligence. Iago has been described as immoral; he does not seem to me to be immoral, but amoral, as the intellect always is. He says to the women:

> Come on, come on; you're pictures out of doors,
> Bells in your parlours, wild cats in your kitchens,
> Saints in your injuries, devils being offended,
> Players in your housewifery, and housewives in your beds.

Iago sees things as they are, fairly and not maliciously; he is 'nothing if not critical', but his criticism has a touch of Shakespeare's erotic mania in it. Think of that 'housewives in your beds'! He will not deceive himself, however; in spite of Cassio's admiration of Desdemona Iago does not imagine that Cassio is in love with her; 'well kissed', he says, 'an excellent courtesy', finding at once the true explanation.*

But having taken up this intellectual attitude in order to create Iago, Shakespeare tries next to make his puppet concrete and individual by giving him revenge for a soul, but in this he does not succeed, for intellect is not maleficent. At moments Iago lives for us; 'drown cats and blind puppies . . . put money in your purse' – his brains delight us; but

---

* At the end of this scene Iago says:

> That Cassio loves her I do well believe it,

but that is merely one of the many inconsistencies in Shakespeare's drawing of Iago. There are others; at one time he talks of Cassio as a mere book soldier, at another equals him with Caesar. Had Coleridge noted these contradictions he would have declared them to be a higher perfection than logical unity, and there is something to be said for the argument, though in these instances I think the contradictions are due to Shakespeare's carelessness rather than to his deeper insight.

when he pursues Desdemona to her end, we revolt; such malignity is inhuman. Shakespeare was so little inclined to evil, knew so little of hate and revenge that his villain is unreal in his cruelty. Again and again the reader asks himself why Iago is so venomous. He hates Othello because Othello has passed him over and preferred Cassio; because he thinks he has had reason to be jealous of Othello, because – but everyone feels that these are reasons supplied by Shakespeare to explain the inexplicable; taken all together they are inadequate, and we are apt to throw them aside with Coleridge as the 'motive hunting of motiveless malignity'. But such a thing as 'motiveless malignity' is not in nature, Iago's villainy is too cruel, too steadfast to be human; perfect pitiless malignity is as impossible to man as perfect innate goodness.

Though Iago and Othello hold the stage for nine-tenths of the play Shakespeare does not realise them so completely as he realises Cassio, an altogether subordinate character. The drinking episode of Cassio was not found by Shakespeare in Cinthio, and is, I think, clearly the confession of Shakespeare himself, for though aptly invented to explain Cassio's dismissal it is unduly prolonged, and thus constitutes perhaps the most important fault in the construction of the play. Consider, too, how the moral is applied by Iago to England in especial, with which country neither Iago nor the story has anything whatever to do.

Othello's appearance stilling the riot, his words to Iago and his dismissal of Cassio are alike honest work. The subsequent talk between Cassio and Iago about 'reputation' is scarcely more than a repetition of what Falstaff said of 'honour'.

Coleridge has made a great deal of the notion that Othello was justified in describing himself as 'not easily jealous'; but poor Coleridge's perverse ingenuity never led him further astray. The exact contrary must, I think, be admitted; Othello was surely very quick to suspect Desdemona; he remembers Iago's first suspicious phrase, ponders it and asks its meaning; he is as quick as Posthumus was to believe the worst of Imogen, as quick as Richard II to suspect his friends Bagot and Green of traitorism, and this proneness to suspicion is the soul of jealousy. And Othello is not only quick to suspect but easy to convince – impulsive at once and credulous. His quick wits jump to the conclusion that Iago, 'this honest creature!' doubtless

> Sees and knows more, much more, than he unfolds.

On hinted imputation he is already half persuaded, and persuaded as

only a sensualist would be that it is lust which has led Desdemona
astray:

> O curse of marriage!
> That we can call these delicate creatures ours,
> And not their appetites.

He is, indeed, so disposed to catch the foul infection that Iago cries:

> Trifles light as air
> Are to the jealous confirmations strong
> As proofs of holy writ.

And well he may, for before he uses the handkerchief or any evidence,
on mere suspicion Othello is already racked with doubt, distraught with
jealousy, maddened with passion; 'his occupation's gone'; he rages
against Iago and demands proof, Iago answers:

> I do not like the office;
> But, sith I am entered in this cause so far
> [. . .]
> I will go on.

This is the same paltry reason Richard III and Macbeth adduced for
adding to the number of their crimes, the truth being that Shakespeare
could find no reason in his own nature for effective hatred.

Othello gives immediate credence to Iago's dream, thinks it 'a shrewd
doubt'; he is a 'credulous fool', as Iago calls him, and it is only our sense
of Iago's devilish cleverness that allows us to excuse Othello's folly. The
strawberry-spotted handkerchief is not needed: the magic in its web is
so strong that the mere mention of it blows his love away and condemns both Cassio and Desdemona to death. If this Othello is not
easily jealous then no man is prone to doubt and quick to turn from love
to loathing.

The truth of the matter is that in the beginning of the play Othello is a
marionette fairly well shaped and exceedingly picturesque; but as soon
as jealousy is touched upon, the mask is thrown aside; Othello, the self-
contained captain, disappears, the poet takes his place and at once shows
himself to be the aptest subject for the green fever. The emotions then
put into Othello's mouth are intensely realised; his jealousy is indeed
Shakespeare's own confession, and it would be impossible to find in all
literature pages of more sincere and terrible self-revealing. Shakespeare

is not more at home in showing us the passion of Romeo and Juliet or the irresolution of Richard II or the scepticism of Hamlet than in depicting the growth and paroxysms of jealousy; his overpowering sensuality, the sensuality of Romeo and of Orsino, has sounded every note of love's mortal sickness:

> OTHELLO I had been happy if the general camp,
> Pioneers and all, had tasted her sweet body,
> So I had nothing known.
> [. . .]
> Damn her, lewd minx! O, damn her!

We have here the proof that the jealousy of Othello was Shakespeare's jealousy; it is all compounded of sensuality. But, and this is the immediate point of my argument, the captain, Othello, is not presented to us as a sensualist to whom such a suspicion would be, of course, the nearest thought. On the contrary, Othello is depicted as sober* and solid, slow to anger, and master of himself and his desires; he expressly tells the lords of Venice that he does not wish Desdemona to accompany him:

> To please the palate of my appetite
> Nor to comply with heat – the young affects,
> In me defunct – and proper satisfaction.

Shakespeare goes out of his way to put this unnecessary explanation in Othello's mouth; he will not have us think of him as passion's fool, but as passion's master; Othello is not to be even suspicious; he tells Iago:

> 'Tis not to make me jealous
> To say – my wife is fair, feeds well, loves company,
> Is free of speech, sings, plays and dances well;
> Where virtue is, these are more virtuous:
> Nor from mine own weak merits will I draw
> The smallest fear or doubt of her revolt;
> For she had eyes and chose me.

---

* Shakespeare makes Lodovico speak of Othello's 'solid virtue' – 'the nature whom passion could not shake'. Even Iago finds Othello's anger ominous because of its rarity:

> There's matter in't, indeed, if he be angry.

It was all this, no doubt, that misled Coleridge. He did not realise that this Othello suddenly changes his nature; the sober lord of himself becomes in an instant very quick to suspect, and being jealous, is nothing if not sensual; he can think of no reason for Desdemona's fall but her appetite; the imagination of the sensual act throws him into a fit; it is this picture which gives life to his hate. The conclusion is not to be avoided; as soon as Othello becomes jealous he is transformed by Shakespeare's own passion. For this is the way Shakespeare conceived jealousy and the only way. The jealousy of Leontes in *The Winter's Tale* is precisely the same; Hermione gives her hand to Polixenes, and at once Leontes suspects and hates, and his rage is all of 'paddling palms* and pinching fingers'. The jealousy of Posthumus, too, is of the same kind:

> Never talk on 't;
> She hath been colted by him.

It is the imagining of the sensual act that drives him to incoherence and the verge of madness, as it drove Othello. In all these characters Shakespeare is only recalling the stages of the passion that desolated his life.

The part that imagination usually plays in tormenting the jealous man with obscene pictures is now played by Iago; the first scene of the fourth act is this erotic self-torture put in Iago's mouth. As Othello's passion rises to madness, as the self-analysis becomes more and more intimate and personal, we have Shakespeare's relived agony clothing itself in his favourite terms of expression:

> O! it comes o'er my memory,
> As doth the raven o'er the infected house,
> Boding to all, – he had my handkerchief.

The interest swings still higher; the scene in which Iago uses Cassio's conceit and laughter to exasperate further the already mad Othello is one of the notable triumphs of dramatic art. But just as the quick growth of his jealousy, and its terrible sensuality, have shown us that Othello is not the self-contained master of his passions that he pretends to be and that Shakespeare wishes us to believe, so this scene, in which the listening Othello rages in savagery, reveals to us an intense femininity

---

* Iago's expression, too; cf. *Othello*, 2, 1, and *Hamlet*, 3, 4.

of nature. For generally the man concentrates his hatred upon the woman who deceives him, and is only disdainful of his rival, whereas the woman for various reasons gives herself to hatred of her rival, and feels only angry contempt for her lover's traitorism. But Othello – or shall we not say Shakespeare? – discovers in the sincerest ecstasy of this passion as much of the woman's nature as of the man's. After seeing his handkerchief in Bianca's hands he asks:

> How shall I murder him, Iago?

Manifestly, Shakespeare is thinking of Herbert and his base betrayal. Othello would have Cassio thrown to the dogs, would have him 'nine years a-killing'; and though he adds that Desdemona shall 'rot and perish and be damned tonight', immediately afterwards we see what an infinite affection for her underlies his anger:

> O, the world hath not a sweeter creature: she might lie by an emperor's side and command him tasks.

And then Shakespeare uses his brains objectively, so to speak, to excuse his persistent tenderness, and at once he reveals himself and proves to us that he is thinking of Mary Fitton, and not of poor Desdemona:

> Hang her! I do but say what she is. – So delicate with her needle! – An admirable musician! O, she will sing the savageness out of a bear. – Of so high and plenteous wit and invention.

Shakespeare himself speaks in this passage. For when has Desdemona shown high and plenteous wit or invention? She is hardly more than a symbol of constancy. It is Mary Fitton who has 'wit and invention', and is 'an admirable musician'.

The feminine tenderness in Shakespeare comes to perfect expression in the next lines; no woman has a more enduring affection:

> IAGO   She's the worse for all this.
> OTHELLO O! a thousand, a thousand times. And, then of so gentle a
>   condition!
> IAGO   Ay, too gentle.
> OTHELLO Nay, that's certain: – but yet the pity of it, Iago! – O, Iago,
>   the pity of it, Iago!'

The tenderness shrills to such exquisite poignancy that it becomes a universal cry, the soul's lament for traitorism: 'The pity of it, Iago! O, Iago, the pity of it!' Othello's jealous passion is at its height in the scene with Desdemona when he gives his accusations precise words, and flings money to Emilia as the guilty confidante. And yet even here, where he delights to soil his love, his tenderness reaches its most passionate expression:

> O thou weed,
> Who art so lovely fair, and smell'st so sweet,
> That the sense aches at thee – would thou hadst ne'er been born!

As soon as jealousy reaches its end, and passes into revenge, Shakespeare tries to get back into Othello the captain again. Othello's first speech in the bedchamber is clear enough in all conscience, but it has been so mangled by unintelligent actors such as Salvini that it cries for explanation. Everyone will remember how Salvini and others playing this part stole into the room like murderers, and then bellowed so that they would have waked the dead. And when the foolish mummers were criticised for thus misreading the character, they answered boldly that Othello was a Moor, that his passion was Southern, and I know not what besides. It is clear that Shakespeare's Othello enters the room quietly as a justicer with a duty to perform: he keeps his resolution to the sticking-point by thinking of the offence; he says solemnly:

> It is the cause, it is the cause, my soul –

and, Englishman-like, finds a moral reason for his intended action:

> Yet she must die, else she'll betray more men.

But the reason fades and the resolution wavers in the passion for her 'body and beauty', and the tenderness of the lover comes to hearing again:

> [*kissing her*] O balmy breath, that dost almost persuade
> Justice to break her sword! – one more, one more. –
> Be thus when thou art dead, and I will kill thee,
> And love thee after. – One more, and this the last.
> So sweet was ne'er so fatal. I must weep,
> But they are cruel tears; this sorrow's heavenly;
> It strikes where it doth love. – She wakes.

So gentle a murderer was never seen save Macbeth, and the 'heavenly sorrow' that strikes where it doth love is one of the best examples in literature of the Englishman's capacity for hypocritical self-deception. The subsequent dialogue shows us in Othello the short, plain phrases of immitigable resolution; in this scene Shakespeare comes nearer to realising strength than anywhere else in all his work. But even here his nature shows itself; Othello has to be misled by Desdemona's weeping, which he takes to be sorrow for Cassio's death, before he can pass to action, and as soon as the murder is accomplished, he regrets:

> O, insupportable! O heavy hour!

His frank avowal, however, is excellently characteristic of the soldier Othello:

> 'Twas I that killed her.

A moment later there is a perfect poetic expression of his love:

> Nay, had she been true
> If Heaven would make me such another world
> Of one entire and perfect chrysolite,
> I'd not have sold her for it.

Then comes a revelation of sensuality and physical fastidiousness so peculiar that by itself it proves much of what I have said of Shakespeare:

> OTHELLO   Ay, 'twas he that told me first;
> An honest man he is, and hates the slime
> That sticks on filthy deeds.

For a breathing-space now before he is convinced of his fatal error, Othello speaks as the soldier, but in spite of the fact that he has fulfilled his revenge, and should be at his sincerest, we have no word of profound self-revealing. But as soon as he realises his mistake, his regret becomes as passionate as a woman's and magical in expression:

> Cold, cold, my girl!
> Even like thy chastity.

Another proof that Shakespeare discards the captain, Othello, in order to give utterance to his own jealousy and love, is to be found in the similarity between this speech of Othello and the corresponding speech of Posthumus in *Cymbeline*. As soon as Posthumus is convinced of his mistake, he calls Iachimo 'Italian fiend' and himself 'most credulous fool', 'egregious murderer', and so forth. He asks for 'some upright justicer' to punish him as he deserves with 'cord or knife or poison', nay, he will have 'torturers ingenious'. He then praises Imogen as 'the temple of virtue', and again shouts curses at himself and finally calls upon his love:

> O Imogen!
> My queen, my life, my wife! O Imogen,
> Imogen, Imogen!

Othello behaves in precisely the same manner; he calls Iago that 'demi-devil', and himself 'an honourable murderer'; and Iago calls him a 'credulous fool'. Othello, too, cries for punishment; instead of 'torturers ingenious', he will have 'devils' to 'whip' him, and 'roast him in sulphur'. He praises Desdemona as chaste, 'ill-starred wench', 'my girl', and so forth; then curses himself lustily and ends his lament with the words:

> O Desdemon! dead, Desdemon! dead! O!

The same changes in mood, the same words even – the likeness is so close that it can only be explained as I have explained it; from beginning to end of *Cymbeline* Posthumus is Shakespeare, and as soon as jealousy, pity, remorse, or any tender emotion seizes Othello he becomes Shakespeare too, and speaks with Shakespeare's voice.

From here on, it is all good work if not great work to Othello's last speech, which merits particular consideration. He begins as the captain, but soon passes into the poet; and then towards the end talks again in quick measure as the man of action. I quote the whole speech,* putting into italics the phrases in which the poet betrays himself:

OTHELLO Soft you; a word or two, before you go.
I have done the State some service, and they know it;
No more of that. – *I pray you in your letters,*
When you shall these unlucky deeds relate,
Speak of me as I am; nothing extenuate,
Nor set down aught in malice; then must you speak
Of one that loved not wisely, but too well;
Of one not easily jealous, but being wrought

---

* This speech is curiously like the long speech of Richard II which I have already noticed; at the beginning Shakespeare speaks as a king for a few lines, then naturally as a poet, and at the end pulls himself up and tries to resume the character.

> *Perplexed in the extreme; of one whose hand,*
> *Like the base Indian, threw a pearl away*
> *Richer than all his tribe; of one whose subdued eyes,*
> *Albeit unused to the melting mood,*
> *Drop tears as fast as the Arabian trees*
> *Their medicinal gum.* Set you down this;
> And say, besides, that in Aleppo once,
> When a malignant and a turban'd Turk
> Beat a Venetian, and traduced the State,
> I took by the throat the circumcised dog
> And smote him – thus.

All the memorable words here are the words of the gentle poet revealing his own nature ingenuously. The relief given by tears is exquisitely expressed, but the relief itself is a feminine experience; men usually find that tears humiliate them, and take refuge from their scalding shame in anger. The deathless phrases of the poet's grief must be contrasted with the braggart mouthings of the captain at the end in order to realise how impossible it was for Shakespeare to depict a man of deeds.

In the first two acts Shakespeare has tried to present Othello with some sincerity and truth to the dramatic fiction. But as soon as jealousy touches Othello, he becomes the transparent vessel of Shakespeare's own emotion, and is filled with it as with his heart's blood. All the magical phrases in the play are phrases of jealousy, passion, and pity. The character of the captain in Othello is never deeply realised. It is a brave sketch, but, after all, only the merest sketch when compared with Hamlet or Macbeth. We know what they thought of life and death, and of all things in the world and over it; but what do we know of Othello's thoughts upon the deepest matters that concern man? Did he believe even in his stories to Desdemona? – in the men whose heads do grow beneath their shoulders? in his magic handkerchief? in what Iago calls his 'fantastical lies'? This, I submit, is another important indication that Shakespeare drew Othello, the captain, from the outside; the jealous, tender heart of him is Shakespeare's, but take that away and we scarcely know more of him than the colour of his skin. What interests us in Othello is not his strength, but his weakness, Shakespeare's weakness – his passion and pity, his torture, rage, jealousy and remorse, the successive stages of his soul's Calvary!

9

Dramas of Lust –
Part One: *Troilus and Cressida*

He probed from hell to hell
Of human passions, but of love deflowered
His wisdom was not . . .

Meredith's Sonnet on Shakespeare

With *Hamlet* and his dreams of an impossible revenge Shakespeare got rid of some of the perilous stuff which his friend's traitorism had bred in him. In *Othello* he gave deathless expression to the madness of his jealous rage and so cleared his soul, to some extent, of that poisonous infection. But passion in Shakespeare survived hatred of the betrayer and jealousy of him; he had quickly finished with Herbert; but Mary Fitton lived still for him and tempted him perpetually – the lust of the flesh, the desire of the eye, insatiable, cruel as the grave. He will now portray his mistress for us dramatically – unveil her very soul, show the gypsy-wanton as she is. He who has always painted in highlights is now going to paint French fashion, in blackest shadows, for with the years his passion and his bitterness have grown in intensity. Mary Fitton is now 'false Cressid'. Pandarus says of her in the first scene of the first act:

An her hair were not somewhat darker than Helen's – well, go to – there were no more comparison between the women.

Mary Fitton's hair, we know, was raven-black, but the evidence connecting Shakespeare's mistress with 'false Cressid' is stronger, as we shall see, than any particular line or expression.

Troilus and Cressida is a wretched, invertebrate play without even a main current of interest. Of course there are fine phrases in it, as in most of the productions of Shakespeare's maturity; but the characterisation is worse than careless, and at first one wonders why Shakespeare wrote the tedious, foolish stuff except to get rid of his own bitterness in the railing of Thersites, and in the depicting of Cressida's shameless wantonness. It is impossible to doubt that 'false Cressid' was meant for Mary Fitton. The moment she appears the play begins to live; personal bitterness turns her portrait into a caricature; every fault is exaggerated and lashed with rage; it is not so much a drama as a scene where Shakespeare insults his mistress.

Let us look at this phase of his passion in perspective. Almost as soon as he became acquainted with Miss Fitton, about Christmas 1597, Shakespeare wrote of her as a wanton; yet so long as she gave herself to him he appears to have been able to take refuge in his tenderness and endure her strayings. But passion in him grew with what it fed on, and after she faulted with Lord Herbert, we find him in a sonnet threatening her that his 'pity-wanting pain' may induce him to write of her as she was. No doubt her pride and scornful strength revolted under this treatment and she drew away from him. Tortured by desire he would then praise her with some astonishing phrases; call her 'the heart's blood of beauty, love's invisible soul', and after some hesitation she would yield again. No sooner was the 'ruined love' rebuilt than she would offend again, and again he would curse and threaten, and so the wretched, half-miserable, half-ecstatic life of passion stormed along, one moment in Heaven, the next in Hell.

All the while Shakespeare was longing, or thought he was longing for truth and constancy, and at length he gave form and name to his desire for winnowed purity of love and perfect constancy, and this consoling but impalpable ideal he called Ophelia, Desdemona, Cordelia. But again and again Miss Fitton reconquered him and at length his accumulated bitterness compelled him to depict his mistress realistically. Cressida is his first attempt, the first dramatic portrait of the mistress who got into Shakespeare's blood and infected the current of his being, and the portrait is spoiled by the poet's hatred and contempt just as the whole drama is spoiled by a passion of bitterness that is surely the sign of intense personal suffering. Cressida is depicted as a vile wanton, a drab by nature; but it is no part even of this conception to make her soulless and devilish. On the contrary, an artist of Shakespeare's imaginative sympathy loves to put in high relief the grain of good in things evil and the taint of evil in things good that give humanity its curious complexity. Shakespeare observed this rule of dramatic presentation more consistently than any of his predecessors or contemporaries – more consistently, more finely far than Homer or Sophocles, whose heroes had only such faults as their creators thought virtues; why then did he forget nature so far as to picture 'false Cressida' without a redeeming quality? He first shows her coquetting with Troilus, and her coquetry even is unattractive, shallow, and obvious; then she gives herself to Troilus out of passionate desire; but Shakespeare omits to tell us why she takes up with Diomedes immediately afterwards. We are to understand merely that she is what Ulysses calls a 'sluttish spoil of opportunity', and 'daughter of the game'. But as passionate desire is not of necessity faithless we are distressed and puzzled by her soulless wantonness. And when she goes on to present Diomedes with the scarf that Troilus gave her, we revolt; the woman is too full of blood to be so entirely heartless. Here is the scene embittered by the fact that Troilus witnesses Cressida's betrayal:

DIOMEDES I had your heart before, this follows it.
  TROILUS [*aside*] I did swear patience.
 CRESSIDA You shall not have it, Diomed, faith you shall not;
          I'll give you something else.
DIOMEDES I will have this: whose was it?
 CRESSIDA   It is no matter.
DIOMEDES Come, tell me whose it was?
 CRESSIDA 'Twas one that loved me better than you will,
          But, now you have it, take it.

The scene is a splendid dramatic scene, a piece torn from life, so realistic that it convinces, and yet we revolt; we feel that we have not got to the heart of the mystery. There is so much evil in Cressida that we want to see the spark of goodness in her, however fleeting and ineffective the spark may be. But Shakespeare makes her attempt at justification a confession of absolute faithlessness:

> Troilus, farewell! one eye yet looks on thee,
> But with my heart the other eye doth see.
> Ah! poor our sex! This fault in us I find,
> The error of our eye directs our mind.

This is plainly Shakespeare's reflection and not Cressida's apology, and if we contrast this speech with the dialogue given above, it becomes plain, I think, that the terrible scene with Diomedes is taken from life, or is at least Shakespeare's vision of the way Mary Fitton behaved. There's a magic in those devilish words of Cressida that outdoes imagination:

> 'Twas one that loved me better than you will,
> But, now you have it, take it.

And then:

> Sweet, honey Greek, tempt me no more to folly:

The very power of the characterisation makes the traitress hateful. If Mary Fitton ever gave any gift of Shakespeare to Lord Herbert, the dramatist should have known that she no longer loved him, had in reality already forgotten him in her new passion; but to paint a woman as remembering a lover, indeed as still loving him, and yet as giving his gift to another, is an offence in art though it may be true to nature. It is a fault in art because it is impossible to motive it in a few lines. The fact of the gift is bad enough; without explanation it is horrible. For this and other reasons I infer that Shakespeare took the fact from his own experience: he had suffered, it seems to me, from some such traitorism on the part of his mistress, or he ascribed to Mary Fitton some traitorism of his own.

In sonnet 122 he finds weighty excuse for having given away the table-book which his friend had given to him. His own confessed shortcoming might have taught him to exercise more lenient judgement towards his frail love.

But when Shakespeare wrote *Troilus and Cressida* a passion of bitterness possessed him; he not only vilified Cressida but all the world, Agamemnon, Nestor, Achilles, Ajax; he seems indeed to have taken more pleasure in the railing of Thersites than in any other part of the work except the scourging of Cressida. He shocks us by the picture of Achilles and his myrmidons murdering Hector when they come upon him unarmed.

One or two incidental difficulties must be settled before we pass to a greater play.

Troilus and Cressida has always been regarded as a sort of enigma. Professor Dowden asks: 'With what intention and in what spirit did Shakespeare write this strange comedy? All the Greek heroes who fought against Troy are pitilessly exposed to ridicule.' And from this fact and the bitterness of *Timon* some German critics have drawn the inference that Shakespeare was incapable of comprehending Greek life, and that indeed he only realised his Romans so perfectly because the Roman was very like the Briton in his mastery of practical affairs,

of the details of administration and of government. This is an excellent instance of German prejudice. No one could have been better
fitted than Shakespeare to understand Greek civilisation and Greek
art with its supreme love of plastic beauty, but his master Plutarch
gave him far better pictures of Roman life than of Greek life, partly
because Plutarch lived in the time of Roman domination and partly
because he was in far closer sympathy with the masters of practical
affairs than with artists in stone like Phidias or artists in thought like
Plato. The true explanation of Shakespeare's caricatures of Greek life,
whether Homeric or Athenian, is to be found in the fact that he was
not only entirely ignorant of it but prejudiced against it. And this
prejudice in him had an obvious root. Chapman had just translated
and published the first books of his *Iliad*, and Chapman was the poet
whom Shakespeare speaks of as his rival in Sonnets 78–86. He cannot
help smiling at the 'strained touches' of Chapman's rhetoric and his
heavy learning. Those who care to remember the first scene of *Love's
Labour's Lost* will recall how Shakespeare in that early work mocked at
learning and derided study. When he first reached London he was no
doubt despised for his ignorance of Greek and Latin; he had had to
bear the sneers and flouts of the many who appraised learning, an
university training and gentility above genius. He took the first opportunity of answering his critics:

> Small have continual plodders ever won,
> Save bare authority from others' books.

But the taunts rankled, and when the bitter days came of disappointment and disillusion he took up that Greek life which his rival had tried
to depict in its fairest colours, and showed what he thought was the
seamy side of it. But had he known anything of Greek life and Greek art
it would have been his pleasure to outdo his rival by giving at once a
truer and a fairer presentation of Greece than Chapman could conceive.
It is the rivalry of Chapman that irritates Shakespeare into pouring
contempt on Greek life in *Troilus and Cressida*. As Chapman was for the
Greeks, Shakespeare took sides with the Trojans.

But why do I assume that *Troilus and Cressida* is earlier than *Antony
and Cleopatra*? Some critics, and among them Dr Brandes, place it later,
and they have some reason for their belief. The bitterness in *Troilus and
Cressida*, they say rightly, is more intense; and as Shakespeare's disappointment with men and things appears to have increased from

Hamlet to *Timon*, or from 1602 to 1607–8, they put the bitterer play later. Cogent as is this reasoning, I cannot believe that Shakespeare could have painted Cressida after having painted Cleopatra. The same model has evidently served for both women; but while Cleopatra is perhaps the most superb portrait of a courtesan in all literature, Cressida is a crude and harsh sketch such as a Dumas or a Pinero might have conceived.

It is more than probable, I think, that *Troilus and Cressida* was planned and the love-story at least written about 1603, while Shakespeare's memory of one of his mistress's betrayals was still vivid and sharp. The play was taken up again four or five years later and the character of Ulysses deepened and strengthened. In this later revision the outlook is so piercing-sad, the phrases of such pregnancy, that the work must belong to Shakespeare's ripest maturity. Moreover, he has grown comparatively careless of characterisation as in all his later work; he gives his wise sayings almost as freely to Achilles as to Ulysses.

Troilus and Cressida is interesting because it establishes the opinion that Chapman was indeed the rival poet whom Shakespeare referred to in the sonnets, and especially because it shows us the poet's mistress painted in a rage of erotic passion so violent that it defeats itself, and the portrait becomes an incredible caricature – that way madness lies. *Troilus and Cressida* points to *Lear* and *Timon*.

10

Dramas of Lust –
Part Two: *Antony and Cleopatra*

We now come to the finest work of Shakespeare's maturity, to the drama in which his passion for Mary Fitton finds supreme expression.

Antony and Cleopatra is an astonishing production not yet fairly appreciated even in England, and perhaps not likely to be appreciated anywhere at its full worth for many a year to come. But when we English have finally left that dark prison of Puritanism and lived for some time in the sunlight where the wayside crosses are hidden under climbing roses, we shall probably couple *Antony and Cleopatra* with *Hamlet* in our love as Shakespeare's supremest works. It was fitting that the same man who wrote *Romeo and Juliet*, the incomparable symphony of first love, should also write *Antony and Cleopatra*, the far more wonderful and more terrible tragedy of mature passion.

Let us begin with the least interesting part of the play, and we shall see that all the difficulties in it resolve themselves as soon as we think of it as Shakespeare's own confession. Wherever he leaves Plutarch, it is to tell his own story.

Some critics have reproached Shakespeare with the sensualism of *Romeo and Juliet*; no one, so far as I can remember, has blamed the Sapphic intensity of *Antony and Cleopatra*, where the lust of the flesh and desire of the eye reign triumphant. Professor Dowden indeed says: 'The spirit of the play, though superficially it appear voluptuous, is essentially severe. That is to say, Shakespeare is faithful to the fact.' Antony and Cleopatra kill themselves, forsooth, and thus conventional virtue is justified by self-murder. So superficial and false a judgement is a quaint example of mid-Victorian taste: it reminds me of the horsehair sofa and the antimacassar. Would Professor Dowden have had Shakespeare alter the historical facts, making Antony conquer Caesar and Cleopatra triumph over death? Would this have been sufficient to prove to the professor that Shakespeare's morals are not his, and that the play is certainly the most voluptuous in modern literature? Well, this is just what Shakespeare has done. Throughout the play Caesar is a subordinate figure while Antony is the protagonist and engages all our sympathies; whenever they meet Antony shows as the larger, richer, more generous nature. In every act he conquers Caesar; leaving on us the gorgeous ineffaceable impression of a great personality whose superb temperament moves everyone to admiration and love; Caesar, on the other hand, affects one as a calculating machine.

But Shakespeare's fidelity to the fact is so extraordinary that he gives Caesar one speech which shows his moral superiority to Antony. When his sister weeps on hearing that Antony has gone back to Cleopatra, Caesar bids her dry her tears,

> But let determined things to destiny
> Hold unbewailed their way . . .

This line alone suffices to show why Antony was defeated; the force of imperial Rome is in the great phrase; but Shakespeare will not admit his favourite's inferiority, and in order to explain Antony's defeat Shakespeare represents luck as being against him, luck or fate, and this is not the only or even the chief proof of the poet's partiality. Pompey, who scarcely notices Caesar when Antony is by, says of Antony:

> his soldiership
> Is twice the other twain.

And, indeed, Antony in the play appears to be able to beat Caesar whenever he chooses or whenever he is not betrayed.

All the personages of the play praise Antony, and when he dies the most magnificent eulogy of him is pronounced by Agrippa, Caesar's friend:

> A rarer spirit never
> Did steer humanity; but you, Gods, will give us
> Some faults to make us men.

Antony is even permitted at the last to console himself; he declares exultantly that in the other world the ghosts shall come to gaze at him and Cleopatra, and:

> Dido and her Aeneas shall want troops.

Shakespeare makes conquering Caesar admit the truth of this boast:

> No grave upon the earth shall clip in it
> A pair so famous.

To win in life universal admiration and love, and in death imperishable renown, is to succeed in spite of failure and suicide, and this is the lesson which Shakespeare read into Plutarch's story. Even Enobarbus is conquered at the last by Antony's noble magnanimity. But why does Shakespeare show this extraordinary, this extravagant liking for him who was 'the bellows and the fan to cool a gypsy's lust', for that Marc Antony who might have been the master of the world, and who threw away empire, life, and honour to be 'a strumpet's fool'? There is only one possible explanation: Shakespeare felt the most intense, the most intimate sympathy with Antony because he, too, was passion's slave, and had himself experienced with his dark mistress, Mary Fitton, the ultimate degradation of lust. For this reason he took Plutarch's portrait of Antony, and, by emphasising the kingly traits, transformed it. In the play, as Dr Brandes sees, Antony takes on something of the 'artist-nature'. It is Antony's greatness and weakness; the spectacle of a high intellect struggling with an overpowering sensuality; of a noble nature at odds with passionate human frailty, that endeared him to Shakespeare. The pomp of Antony's position, too, and his kingly personality pleased our poet. As soon as Shakespeare reached maturity, he began to depict himself as a monarch; from *Twelfth Night* on he assumed royal state in his plays, and surely in this figure of Antony he must for the moment have satisfied his longing for regal magnificence and domination. From the first scene to the last Antony is a king of men by right divine of nature.

It is, however, plain that Antony's pride, his superb mastery of life, the touch of imperious brutality in him, are all traits taken from Plutarch, and are indeed wholly inconsistent with Shakespeare's own character. Had Shakespeare possessed these qualities his portraits of men of action would have been infinitely better than they are, while his portraits of the gentle thinker and lover of the arts, his Hamlets and his Dukes, would have been to seek.

The personal note of every one of his great tragedies is that Shakespeare feels he has failed in life, failed lamentably. His Brutus, we feel, failed of necessity because of his aloofness from practical life; his Coriolanus, too, had to fail, and almost forgoes sympathy by his faults; but this Antony ought not to have failed: we cannot understand why the man leaves the sea-battle to follow Cleopatra's flight, who but an act or two before, with lesser reason, realised his danger and was able to break off from his enchantress. Yet the passion of desire that sways Antony is so splendidly portrayed; is, too, so dominant in all of us, that we accept it at once as explaining the inexplicable.

In measure as Shakespeare ennobled Antony, the historical fact of ultimate defeat and failure allowed him to degrade Cleopatra. And this he did willingly enough, for from the moment he took up the subject he identified the Queen of Egypt with his own faithless mistress, Mary Fitton, whom he had already tried to depict as 'false Cressid'. This identification of himself and his own experience of passion with the persons and passions of the story explains some of the faults of the drama; while being the source, also, of its singular splendour.

In this play we have the finest possible example of the strife between Shakespeare's yielding poetic temperament and the severity of his intellect. He heaps praises on Antony, as we have seen, from all sides; he loved the man as a sort of superb *alter ego*, and yet his intellectual fairness is so extraordinary that it compelled him to create a character who should uphold the truth even against his heart's favourite. Dr Brandes speaks of Enobarbus as a 'sort of chorus'; he is far more than that; he is the intellectual conscience of the play, a weight, so to speak, to redress the balance which Shakespeare used this once and never again. What a confession this is of personal partiality! A single instance will suffice to prove my point: Shakespeare makes Antony cast the blame for the flight at Actium on Cleopatra, and manages almost to hide the unmanly weakness of the plaint by its infinitely pathetic wording:

> Whither hast them led me, Egypt?

A little later Cleopatra asks:

> Is Antony or we in fault for this?

and at once Enobarbus voices the exact truth:

> Antony only, that would make his will
> Lord of his reason. What though you fled
>   . . . why should he follow?

Again and again Antony reproaches Cleopatra, and again and again Enobarbus is used to keep the truth before us. Some of these reproaches, it seems to me, are so extravagant and so ill-founded that they discover the personal passion of the poet. For example, Antony insults Cleopatra:

> You have been a boggler ever.

And the proof forsooth is:

> I found you as a morsel cold upon
> Dead Caesar's trencher.

But to have been Caesar's mistress was Cleopatra's chief title to fame. Shakespeare is here probably reviling Mary Fitton for being deserted by some early lover. Curiously enough, this weakness of Antony increases the complexity of his character, while the naturalistic passion of his words adds enormously to the effect of the play. Again and again in this drama Shakespeare's personal vindictiveness serves an artistic purpose. The story of *Troilus and Cressida* is in itself low and vile, and when loaded with Shakespeare's bitterness outrages probability; but the love of Antony and Cleopatra is so overwhelming that it goes to ruin and suicide and beyond, and when intensified by Shakespeare's personal feeling becomes a world's masterpiece.

We have already seen that the feminine railing Shakespeare puts in the mouth of Antony increases the realistic effect, and just in the same way the low cunning, temper, and mean greed which he attributes to Cleopatra, transform her from a somewhat incomprehensible historical marionette into the most splendid specimen of the courtesan in the world's literature. Heine speaks of her contemptuously as a 'kept woman', but the epithet only shows how Heine in default of knowledge fell back on his racial gift of feminine denigration. Even before she enters we see that Shakespeare has not forgiven his dark scornful mistress; Cleopatra is the finest picture he ever painted of Mary Fitton; but Antony's friends tell us, at the outset, she is a 'lustful gypsy', a 'strumpet', and at first she merely plays on Antony's manliness; she sends for him, and when he comes, departs. A little later she sends again, telling her messenger:

> I did not send you: if you find him sad,
> Say, I am dancing; if in mirth, report
> That I am sudden sick: quick, and return.

And when Charmian, her woman, declares that the way to keep a man is to 'cross him in nothing', she replies scornfully:

Thou teachest, like a fool, the way to lose him.

She uses a dozen taunts to prevent her lover from leaving her; but when she sees him resolved, she wishes him victory and success. And so through a myriad changes of mood and of cunning wiles we discover that love for Antony which is the anchor to her unstable nature.

The scene with the eunuch Mardian is a little gem. She asks:

> Hast thou affections?
> MARDIAN   Yes, gracious madam.
> CLEOPAT.   Indeed?
> MARDIAN   Not in deed, madam; for I can do nothing,
>   But what indeed is honest to be done;
>   Yet have I fierce affections, and think
>   What Venus did with Mars.
> CLEOPAT.   O, Charmian!
>   Where think'st thou he is now? Stands he, or sits he?

She is with her lover again, and recalls his phrase for her, 'my serpent of old Nile', and feeds herself with love's 'delicious poison'.

No sooner does she win our sympathy by her passion for Antony than Shakespeare chills our admiration by showing her as the courtesan:

> CLEOPATRA   Did I, Charmian,
>   Ever love Caesar so?
> CHARMIAN   O, that brave Caesar!
> CLEOPAT.   Be choked with such another emphasis!
>   Say, the brave Antony.
> CHARMIAN   The valiant Caesar!
> CLEOPAT.   By Isis, I will give thee bloody teeth
>   If thou with Caesar paragon again
>   My man of men.
> CHARMIAN   By your most gracious pardon,
>   I sing but after you.
> CLEOPAT.   My salad days,
>   When I was green in judgement: cold in blood,
>   To say as I said then!

Already we see and know her, her wiles, her passion, her quick temper, her chameleon-like changes, her subtle charms of person and of word, and yet we have not reached the end of the first act. Next to

Falstaff and to Hamlet, Cleopatra is the most astonishing piece of portraiture in all Shakespeare. Enobarbus gives the soul of her:

ANTONY   She is cunning past man's thought.
ENOBAR.   Alack, sir, no; her passions are made of nothing but the finest part of pure love . . .
ANTONY   Would I had never seen her!
ENOBAR.   O, sir, you had then left unseen a wonderful piece of work; which not to have been blest withal would have discredited your travel.

Here Shakespeare gives his true opinion of Mary Fitton: then comes the miraculous expression:

> Age cannot wither her, nor custom stale
> Her infinite variety. Other women cloy
> The appetites they feed; but she makes hungry
> Where most she satisfies.

Act by act Shakespeare makes the portrait more complex and more perfect. In the second act she calls for music like the dark lady of the Sonnets:

> Music – moody food of us that trade in love.

and then she'll have no music, but will play billiards, and not billiards either, but will fish and think every fish caught an Antony. And again she flies to memory:

> That time – O times! –
> I laughed him out of patience; and that night
> I laughed him into patience; and next morn,
> Ere the ninth hour, I drunk him to his bed;
> Then put my tires and mantles on him, whilst
> I wore his sword Philippan.

The charm of it all, the deathless charm and the astounding veracity! The messenger enters, and she promises him for good news 'gold and her bluest veins to kiss'. When she hears that Antony is well she pours more gold on him, but when he pauses in his recital she has a mind to strike him. When he tells that Caesar and Antony are friends, it is a fortune she'll give; but when she learns that Antony is betrothed to Octavia she turns to her women with 'I am pale,

Charmian', and when she hears that Antony is married she flies into a fury, strikes the messenger down and hales him up and down the room by his hair. When he runs from her knife she sends for him:

> I will not hurt him.
> These hands do lack nobility, that they strike
> A meaner than myself.

She has the fascination of great pride and the magic of manners. When the messenger returns she is a queen again, most courteous-wise:

> Come hither, sir.
> Though it be honest, it is never good
> To bring bad news.

She wants to know the features of Octavia, her years, her inclination, the colour of her hair, her height – everything.

A most veracious full-length portrait, with the minute finish of a miniature; it shows how Shakespeare had studied every fold and foible of Mary Fitton's soul. In the third act Cleopatra takes up again the theme of Octavia's appearance, only to run down her rival, and so salve her wounded vanity and cheat her heart to hope. The messenger, too, who lends himself to her humour now becomes a proper man. Shakespeare seizes every opportunity to add another touch to the wonderful picture.

Cleopatra appears next in Antony's camp at Actium talking with Enobarbus:

CLEOPAT. I will be even with thee, doubt it not.
ENOBAR. But why, why, why?
CLEOPAT. Thou hast forspoke my being in these wars,
                And say'st it is not fit.

Each phrase of the dialogue reveals her soul, dark fold on fold.

She is the only person who strengthens Antony in his quixotic-foolish resolve to fight at sea.

CLEOPAT. I have sixty sails, Caesar none better.

And then the shameful flight.

I have pursued this bald analysis thus far, not for pleasure merely, but to show the miracle of that portraiture the traits of which can bear examination one by one. So far Cleopatra is, as Enobarbus calls her, 'a wonderful piece of work', a woman of women, inscrutable, cunning, deceitful, prodigal, with a good memory for injuries, yet as quick to forgiveness as to anger, a minion of the moon, fleeting as water yet loving-true withal, a sumptuous bubble, whose perpetual vagaries are but perfect obedience to every breath of passion. But now Shakespeare without reason makes her faithless to Antony and to love. In the second scene of the third act Thyreus comes to her with Caesar's message:

THYREUS He knows that you embrace not Antony
As you did love but as you feared him.

CLEOPAT.   O!

THYREUS The scars upon your honour therefore he
Does pity as constrained blemishes,
Not as deserved.

CLEOPAT.   He is a god, and knows
What is most right. Mine honour was not yielded,
But conquered merely.

ENOBAR. [*aside*]   To be sure of that
I will ask Antony. – Sir, sir, thou'rt so leaky
That we must leave thee to thy sinking, for
Thy dearest quit thee.

And when Thyreus asks her to leave Antony and put herself under Caesar's protection, who 'desires to give', she tells him:

I am prompt
To lay my crown at his feet, and there to kneel.

Thyreus then asks for grace to lay his duty on her hand. She gives it to him with the words:

Your Caesar's father oft,
When he hath mused of taking kingdoms in,
Bestowed his lips on that unworthy place
As it rained kisses.

It is as if Antony were forgotten, clean wiped from her mind. The whole scene is a libel upon Cleopatra and upon womanhood. When betrayed, women are faithless out of anger, pique, desire of revenge; they are faithless out of fear, out of ambition, for fancy's sake – for fifty motives, but not without motive. It would have been easy to justify this scene. All the dramatist had to do was to show us that Cleopatra, a proud woman and scorned queen, could not forget Antony's faith-lessness in leaving her to marry Octavia; but she never mentions Octavia, never seems to remember her after she has got Antony back. This omission, too, implies a slur upon her. Nor does she kiss Caesar's 'conquering hand' out of fear. Thyreus has told her it would please Caesar if she would make of his fortunes a staff to lean upon; she has no fear, and her ambitions are wreathed round Antony: Caesar has nothing to offer that can tempt her, as we shall see later. The scene is a libel upon her. The more one studies it, the clearer it becomes that Shakespeare wrote it out of wounded personal feeling. Cleopatra's prototype, Mary Fitton, had betrayed him again and again, and the faithlessness rankled. Cleopatra, therefore, shall be painted as faith-less, without cause, as Cressid was, from incurable vice of nature. Shakespeare tried to get rid of his bitterness in this way, and if his art suffered, so much the worse for his art. Curiously enough, in this instance, for reasons that will appear later, the artistic effect is deepened.

The conclusion of this scene, where Thyreus is whipped and Cleo-patra overwhelmed with insults by Antony, does not add much to our knowledge of Cleopatra's character: one may notice, however, that it is the reproach of cold-heartedness that she catches up to answer. The scene follows in which she plays squire to Antony and helps to buckle on his armour. But this scene (invented by Shakespeare), which might bring out the sweet woman-weakness in her, and so reconcile us to her again, is used against her remorselessly by the poet. When Antony wakes and cries for his armour she begs him to 'sleep a little'; the touch is natural enough, but coming after her faithlessness to her lover and her acceptance of Caesar it shows more than human frailty. It is plain that, intent upon ennobling Antony, Shakespeare is willing to degrade Cleopatra beyond nature. Then comes Antony's victory, and his passion at length finds perfect lyrical expression:

> O thou day o' the world,
> Chain mine armed neck; leap thou, attire and all,
> Through proof of harness to my heart, and there
> Ride on the pants triumphing.

At once Cleopatra catches fire with that responsive flame of woman-hood which was surely her chiefest charm:

> Lord of lords!
> O infinite virtue! Com'st thou smiling from
> The world's great snare uncaught?

What magic in the utterance, what a revelation of Cleopatra's character and of Shakespeare's! To Cleopatra's feminine weakness the world seems one huge snare which only cunning may escape.

Another day, and final irremediable defeat drives her in fear to the monument and to that pretended suicide which is the immediate cause of Antony's despair:

> Unarm, Eros: the long day's task is done,
> And we must sleep.

When Antony leaves the stage, Shakespeare's idealising vision turns to Cleopatra. About this point, too, the historical fact fetters Shakespeare and forces him to realise the other side of Cleopatra. After Antony's death Cleopatra did kill herself. One can only motive and explain this suicide by self-immolating love. It is natural that at first Shakespeare will have it that Cleopatra's nobility of nature is merely a reflection, a light borrowed from Antony. She will not open the monument to let the dying man enter, but her sincerity and love enable us to forgive this:

> I dare not, dear, –
> Dear my lord, pardon, – I dare not,
> Lest I be taken . . .

Here occurs a fault of taste which I find inexplicable. While Cleopatra and her women are drawing Antony up, he cries;

> O quick, or I am gone.

And Cleopatra answers:

> Here's sport, indeed! – How heavy weighs my lord!
> Our strength has all gone into heaviness,
> That makes the weight.

The 'Here's sport, indeed'! seems to me a terrible fault, an inexcusable lapse of taste. I should like to think it a misprint or misreading, but it is unfortunately like Shakespeare in a certain mood, possible to him, at least, here as elsewhere.

Cleopatra's lament over Antony's dead body is a piece of Shake-speare's self-revealing made lyrical by beauty of word and image. The allusion to his boy-rival, Pembroke, is unmistakable; for women are not contemptuous of youth:

> Young boys and girls
> Are level now with men; the odds is gone,
> And there is nothing left remarkable
> Beneath the visiting moon.

When Cleopatra comes to herself after swooning, her anger is char-acteristic because wholly unexpected; it is one sign more that Shake-speare had a living model in his mind:

> It were for me
> To throw my sceptre at the injurious gods;
> To tell them that this world did equal theirs
> Till they had stolen our jewel. All's but naught.

Her resolve to kill herself is borrowed:

> We'll bury him; and then, what's brave, what's noble,
> Let's do it after the high Roman fashion,
> And make death proud to take us.

But the resolution holds:

> It is great
> To do that thing that ends all other deeds,
> Which shackles accidents and bolts up change.

It is this greatness of soul in Cleopatra which Shakespeare has now to portray. Caesar's messenger, Proculeius, whom Antony has told her to trust, promises her everything in return for her 'sweet dependency'. On being surprised she tries to kill herself, and when disarmed shows again that characteristic petulant anger:

> Sir, I will eat no meat, I'll not drink, sir;
>   . . . This mortal house I'll ruin,
> Do Caesar what he can.

And her reasons are all of pride and hatred of disgrace. She'll not be 'chastised with the sober eye of dull Octavia', nor shown 'to the shouting varletry of censuring Rome'. Her imagination is at work now, that quick forecast of the mind that steels her desperate resolve:

> Rather on Nilus' mud
> Lay me stark nak'd, and let the water-flies
> Blow me into abhorring.

The heroic mood passes. She tries to deceive Caesar as to her wealth, and is shamed by her treasurer Seleucus. The scene is appalling; poor human nature stripped to the skin – all imperfections exposed; Cleopatra cheating, lying, raging like a drab; her words to Seleucus are merciless while self-revealing:

> O slave, of no more trust
> Than love that's hired.

This scene deepens and darkens the impression made by her unmotived faithlessness to Antony. It is, however, splendidly characteristic and I think needful; but it renders that previous avowal of faithlessness to Antony altogether superfluous, the sole fault in an almost perfect portrait. For, as I have said already, Shakespeare's mistakes in characterisation nearly always spring from his desire to idealise; but here his personal vindictiveness comes to help his art. The historical fact compels him now to give his harlot, Cleopatra, heroic attributes; in spite of Caesar's threats to treat her sons severely if she dares to take her own life and thus deprive his triumph of its glory, she outwits him and dies a queen, a worthy descendant, as Charmian says, of 'many royal kings'. Nothing but personal bitterness could have prevented Shakespeare from idealising such a woman out of likeness to humanity. But in this solitary and singular case his personal suffering bound him to realism though the history justified idealisation. The highlights were for once balanced by the depths of shadow, and a masterpiece was the result.

Shakespeare leaves out Caesar's threats to put Cleopatra's sons to death; had he used these menaces he would have made Caesar more natural in my opinion, given a touch of characteristic brutality to the calculating intellect; but he omitted them probably because he felt that Cleopatra's pedestal was high enough without that addition.

The end is very characteristic of Shakespeare's temper. Caesar becomes nobly generous; he approves Cleopatra's wisdom in swearing falsehoods about her treasure; he will not reckon with her like 'a merchant', and Cleopatra herself puts on the royal robes, and she who has played wanton before us so long becomes a queen of queens. And yet her character is wonderfully maintained; no cunning can cheat this mistress of duplicity:

> He words me, girls, he words me that I should not
> Be noble to myself.

She holds to her heroic resolve; she will never be degraded before the base Roman public; she will not see

> Some squeaking Cleopatra boy my greatness.

It is, perhaps, worth noting here that Shakespeare lends Cleopatra, as he afterwards lent Coriolanus, his own delicate senses and neuropathic loathing for mechanic slaves with 'greasy aprons' and 'thick breaths rank of gross diet'; it is Shakespeare too and not Cleopatra who speaks of death as bringing 'liberty'. In *Cymbeline*, Shakespeare's mask Posthumus dwells on the same idea. But these lapses are momentary; the superb declaration that follows is worthy of the queen:

> My resolution's placed, and I have nothing
> Of woman in me: now from head to foot
> I am marble-constant; now the fleeting moon
> No planet is of mine.

The scene with the clown who brings the 'pretty worm' is the solid ground of reality on which Cleopatra rests for a breathing space before rising into the blue:

CLEOPATRA   Give me my robe, put on my crown; I have
> Immortal longings in me. Now no more
> The juice of Egypt's grape shall moist this lip. –
> Yare, yare, good Iras! quick. – Methinks I hear
> Antony call; I see him rouse himself
> To praise my noble act; I hear him mock
> The luck of Caesar, which the gods give men
> To excuse their after-wrath. Husband, I come,
> Now to that name my courage prove my title!
> I am fire and air; my other elements
> I give to baser life.

The whole speech is miraculous in speed of mounting emotion, and

when Iras dies first, this Cleopatra finds again the perfect word in which
truth and beauty meet:

> This proves me base:
> If she first meet the curled Antony
> He'll make demand of her, and spend that kiss
> Which is my heaven to have. Come, thou mortal wretch,
> > [*to the asp, which she applies to her breast*]
> With thy sharp teeth this knot intrinsicate
> Of life at once untie: poor venomous fool,
> Be angry, and despatch. O, could'st thou speak,
> That I might hear thee call great Caesar, ass
> Unpolicied!

The characteristic high temper of Mary Fitton breaking out again –
'ass unpolicied' – and then the end:

> Peace, peace!
> Dost thou not see my baby at my breast,
> That sucks the nurse asleep?

The final touch is of soft pleasure:

> As sweet a balm, as soft as air, as gentle, –
> O, Antony! – Nay, I will take thee too.
> > [*applying another asp to her arm*]
> What should I stay –

For ever fortunate in her self-inflicted death Cleopatra thereby
frees herself from the ignominy of certain of her actions: she is woman
at once and queen, and if she cringes lower than other women, she
rises, too, to higher levels than other women know. The historical fact
of her self-inflicted death forced the poet to make false Cressid a
Cleopatra – and his wanton gypsy-mistress was at length redeemed by
a passion of heroic resolve. The majority of critics are still debating
whether indeed Cleopatra is the 'dark lady' of the sonnets or not.
Professor Dowden puts forward the theory as a daring conjecture; but
the identity of the two cannot be doubted. It is impossible not to
notice that Shakespeare makes Cleopatra, who was a fair Greek,
gypsy-dark like his sonnet-heroine. He says, too, of the 'dark lady' of
the sonnets:

> Whence hast thou this becoming of things ill,
> That in the very refuse of thy deeds
> There is such strength and warrantise of skill,
> That, in my mind, thy worst all best exceeds?

Enobarbus praises Cleopatra in precisely the same words:

> Vilest things,
> Become themselves in her.

Antony, too, uses the same expression:

> Fie, wrangling queen!
> Whom everything becomes – to chide, to laugh,
> To weep; whose every passion fully strives
> To make itself, in thee, fair and admired.

These professors have no distinct mental image of the 'dark lady' or of Cleopatra, or they would never talk of 'daring conjecture' in regard to this simple identification. The points of likeness are numberless. Ninety-nine poets and dramatists out of a hundred would have followed Plutarch and made Cleopatra's love for Antony the mainspring of her being, the *causa causans* of her self-murder. Shakespeare does not do this; he allows the love of Antony to count with her, but it is imperious pride and hatred of degradation that compel his Cleopatra to embrace the Arch-fear. And just this same quality of pride is attributed to the 'dark lady'. Sonnet 131 begins:

> Thou art as tyrannous, so as thou art,
> As those whose beauties proudly make them cruel.

Both are women of infinite cunning and small regard for faith or truth; hearts steeled with an insane pride, and violent tempers suited with scolding slanderous tongues. Prolonged analysis is not needed. A point of seeming difference between them establishes their identity. Cleopatra is beautiful, 'a lass unparalleled', as Charmian calls her, and accordingly we can believe that all emotions became her, and that when hopping on the street or pretending to die she was alike bewitching; beauty has this magic. But how can all things become a woman who is not beautiful, whose face some say 'hath not the power to make love groan', who cannot even blind the senses with desire? And yet the 'dark lady' of the sonnets who is thus described, has the 'powerful might' of personality in as full measure as Egypt's queen. The point of seeming unlikeness is as convincing as any likeness could be; the peculiarities of both women are the same and spring from the same dominant quality. Cleopatra is cunning, wily, faithless, passionately unrestrained in speech and proud as Lucifer, and so is the sonnet-heroine. We may be sure that the faithlessness, scolding, and mad vanity of his mistress were defects in Shakespeare's eyes as in ours; these, indeed, were 'the things ill' which nevertheless became her. What Shakespeare loved in her was what he himself lacked or possessed in lesser degree – that daemonic power of personality which he makes Enobarbus praise in Cleopatra and which he praises directly in the sonnet-heroine. Enobarbus says of Cleopatra:

> I saw her once
> Hop forty paces through the public street,
> And, having lost her breath, she spoke and panted,
> That she did make defect perfection,
> And, breathless, power breathe forth.

One would be willing to wager that Shakespeare is here recalling a performance of his mistress; but it is enough for my purpose now to draw attention to the unexpectedness of the attribute 'power'. The sonnet fastens on the same word:

> O, from what power hast thou this powerful might
> With insufficiency my heart to sway?

In the same sonnet he again dwells upon her 'strength': she was bold, too, to unreason, and of unbridled tongue, for, 'twice forsworn herself', she had yet urged his 'amiss', though guilty of the same fault. What he admired most in her was force of character. Perhaps the old saying held in her case: *ex forti dulcedo*; perhaps her confident strength had abandonments more flattering and complete than those of weaker women; perhaps in those moments her forceful dark face took on a soulful beauty that entranced his exquisite susceptibility; perhaps – but the suppositions are infinite.

Though a lover and possessed by his mistress Shakespeare was still an artist. In the sonnets he brings out her overbearing will, boldness, pride – the elemental force of her nature; in the play, on the other hand, while just mentioning her 'power', he lays the chief stress upon the cunning wiles and faithlessness of her whose trade was love. But just as Cleopatra has power, so there can be no doubt of the wily cunning – 'the warrantise of skill' – of the sonnet-heroine, and no doubt her faithlessness was that 'just cause of hate' which Shakespeare bemoaned.

It is worth while here to notice his perfect comprehension of the powers and limits of the different forms of his art. Just as he has used the sonnets in order to portray certain intimate weaknesses and maladies of his own nature that he could not present dramatically without making his hero ridiculously effeminate, so also he used the sonnets to convey to us the domineering will and strength of his mistress – qualities which if presented dramatically would have seemed masculine-monstrous.

By taking the sonnets and the play together we get an excellent portrait of Shakespeare's mistress. In person she was probably tall and vain of her height, as Cleopatra is vain of her superiority in this respect to Octavia, with dark complexion, black eyebrows and hair, and pitch-black eyes that mirrored emotion as the lakelet mirrors the ever-changing skies; her cheeks are 'damask'd white'; her breath fragrant with health, her voice melodious, her movements full of dignity – a superb gypsy to whom beauty may be denied but not distinction.

If we have a very good idea of her person we have a still better idea of her mind and soul. I must begin by stating that I do not accept implicitly Shakespeare's angry declarations that his mistress was a mere strumpet. A nature of great strength and pride is seldom merely wanton; but the fact stands that Shakespeare makes a definite charge of faithlessness against his mistress; she is, he tells us, 'the bay where all men ride'; no 'several plot', but 'the wide world's common place'. The accusation is most explicit. But if it were well founded why should he devote two sonnets (135 and 136) to imploring her to be as liberal as the sea and to receive his love-offering as well as the tributes of others?

> Among a number one is reckon'd none;
> Then in the number let me pass untold.

It is plain that Mistress Fitton drew away from Shakespeare after she had given herself to his friend, and this fact throws some doubt upon his accusations of utter wantonness. A true 'daughter of the game', as he says *Troilus and Cressida*, is nothing but 'a sluttish spoil of opportunity' who falls to Troilus or to Diomedes in turn, knowing no reserve. It must be reckoned to the credit of Mary Fitton, or to her pride, that she appears to have been faithful to her lover for the time being, and able to resist even the solicitings of Shakespeare. But her desires seem to have been her sole restraint, and therefore we must add an extraordinary lewdness to that strength, pride, and passionate temper which Shakespeare again and again attributes to her. Her boldness is so reckless that she shows her love for his friend even before Shakespeare's face; she knows no pity in her passion, and always defends herself by attacking her accuser. But she is cunning in love's ways and dulls Shakespeare's resentment with 'I don't hate you'. Unwilling perhaps to lose her empire over him and to forego the sweetness of his honeyed flatteries, she blinded him to her faults by occasional caresses. Yet this creature, with the soul of a strumpet, the tongue of a fishwife and the 'proud heart' of a queen, was the crown and flower of womanhood to Shakespeare, his counterpart and ideal. Hamlet in love with Cleopatra, the poet lost in desire of the wanton – that is the tragedy of Shakespeare's life.

In this wonderful world of ours great dramatic writers are sure to have dramatic lives. Again and again in his disgrace Antony cries:

> Whither hast thou led me, Egypt?

Shakespeare's passion for Mary Fitton led him to shame and madness and despair; his strength broke down under the strain and he never won back again to health. He paid the price of passion with his very blood. It is Shakespeare and not Antony who groans:

> O this false soul of Egypt! this grave charm, –
> [. . .]
> Like a right gypsy, hath, at fast and loose,
> Beguil'd me to the very heart of loss.

Shakespeare's love for Mary Fitton is to me one of the typical tragedies of life – a symbol for ever. In its progress through the world genius is inevitably scourged and crowned with thorns and done to death; inevitably, I say, for the vast majority of men hate and despise what is superior to them: Don Quixote, too, was trodden into the mire by the swine. But the worst of it is that genius suffers also through its own excess; is bound, so to speak, to the stake of its own passionate sensibilities, and consumed, as with fire.

11

The Drama of Madness: *Lear*

Ever since Lessing and Goethe it has been the fashion to praise Shakespeare as a demigod; whatever he wrote is taken to be the rose of perfection. This senseless hero-worship, which reached idolatry in the superlatives of the *Encyclopaedia Britannica* and elsewhere in England, was certain to provoke reaction, and the reaction has come to vigorous expression in Tolstoy, who finds nothing to praise in any of Shakespeare's works, and everything to blame in most of them, especially in *Lear*. Lamb and Coleridge, on the other hand, have praised *Lear* as a world's masterpiece. Lamb says of it:

> While we read it, we see not Lear; but we are Lear, – we are in his mind, we are sustained by a grandeur which baffles the malice of daughters and storms; in the aberrations of his reason we discover a mighty irregular power of reasoning, immethodised from the ordinary purposes of life, but exerting its powers, as the wind bloweth where it listeth, at will upon the corruptions and abuses of mankind'.

Coleridge calls *Lear*, 'the open and ample playground of Nature's passions'.

These dithyrambs show rather the lyrical power of the writers than the thing described.

Tolstoy, on the other hand, keeps his eyes on the object, and sets himself to describe the story of *Lear* 'as impartially as possible'. He says of the first scene:

> Not to mention the pompous, characterless language of King Lear, the same in which all Shakespeare's kings speak, the reader or spectator cannot conceive that a king, however old and stupid he may be, could believe the words of the vicious daughters with whom he had passed his whole life, and not believe his favourite daughter, but curse and banish her; and therefore, the spectator or reader

cannot share the feelings of the persons participating in this unnatural scene.

He goes on to condemn the scene between Gloucester and his sons in the same way. The second act he describes as 'absurdly foolish'. The third act is 'spoiled, by the characteristic Shakespearean language'. The fourth act is 'marred in the making', and of the fifth act, he says: 'Again begin Lear's awful ravings, at which one feels ashamed, as at unsuccessful jokes'. He sums up in these words:

Such is this celebrated drama. However absurd it may appear in my rendering (which I have endeavoured to make as impartial as possible), I may confidently say that in the original it is yet more absurd. For any man of our time – if he were not under the hypnotic suggestion that this drama is the height of perfection – it would be enough to read it to its end (were he to have sufficient patience for this) in order to be convinced that, far from being the height of perfection, it is a very bad, carelessly-composed production, which, if it could have been of interest to a certain public at a certain time, cannot evoke amongst us anything but aversion and weariness. Every reader of our time who is free from the influence of suggestion will also receive exactly the same impression from all the other extolled dramas of Shakespeare, not to mention the senseless dramatised tales, *Pericles*, *Twelfth Night*, *The Tempest*, *Cymbeline*, and *Troilus and Cressida*.

Everyone must admit, I think, that what Tolstoy has said of the hypothesis of the play is justified. Shakespeare, as I have shown, was nearly always an indifferent playwright, careless of the architectural construction of his pieces, contemptuous of stagecraft. So much had already been said in England, if not with the authority of Tolstoy.

It may be conceded, too, that the language which Shakespeare puts into Lear's mouth in the first act is 'characterless and pompous', even silly; but Tolstoy should have noticed that as soon as Lear realises the ingratitude of his daughters, his language becomes more and more simple and pathetic. Shakespeare's kings are apt to rant and mouth when first introduced; he seems to have thought pomp of speech went with royal robes; but when the action is engaged even his monarchs speak naturally.

The truth is, that just as the iambics of Greek drama were lifted above ordinary conversation, so Shakespeare's language, being the language mainly of poetic and romantic drama, is a little more measured and, if you will, more pompous than the small talk of everyday life, which seems to us, accustomed as we are to prose plays, more natural. Shakespeare, however, in his blank verse, reaches heights which are not often reached by prose, and when he pleases, his verse becomes as natural-easy as any prose, even that of Tolstoy himself. Tolstoy finds everything Lear says 'pompous', 'artificial', 'unnatural', but Lear's words:

> Pray do not mock me,
> I am a very foolish-fond old man
> Fourscore and upward, not an hour more nor less,
> And, to deal plainly
> I fear I am not in my perfect mind.

touch us poignantly, just because of their childish simplicity; we feel as if Lear, in them, had reached the heart of pathos. Tolstoy, I am afraid, has missed all the poetry of Lear, all the deathless phrases. Lear says:

> I am a man,
> More sinn'd against than sinning,

and the new-coined phrase passed at once into the general currency. Who, too, can ever forget his description of the poor?

> Poor naked wretches, wheresoe'er you are,
> That bide the pelting of this pitiless storm,
> How shall your houseless heads and unfed sides,
> Your looped and windowed raggedness, defend you
> From seasons such as these?

The like of that 'looped and windowed raggedness' is hardly to be found in any other literature. In the fourth and fifth acts Lear's language is simplicity itself, and even in that third act which Tolstoy condemns as 'incredibly pompous and artificial', we find him talking naturally:

Ha! here's three on's are sophisticated: thou art the thing itself, unaccommodated man is no more but such a poor, bare, forked animal as thou art.

There is still another reason why some of us cannot read *Lear* with the cold eyes of reason, contemptuously critical. *Lear* marks a stage in Shakespeare's agony. We who know the happy ingenuousness of his youth undimmed by doubts of man or suspicions of woman, cannot help sympathising with him when we see him cheated and betrayed, drinking the bitter cup of disillusion to the dregs. In *Lear* the angry brooding leads to madness; and it is only fitting that the keynote of the tragedy, struck again and again, should be the cry.

> O, let me not be mad, not mad, sweet Heaven!
> Keep me in temper: I would not be mad.

Lear is the first attempt in all literature to paint madness, and not the worst attempt.

In *Lear*, Shakespeare was intent on expressing his own disillusion and naked misery. How blind Lear must have been, says Tolstoy; how incredibly foolish not to know his daughters better after living with them for twenty years; but this is just what Shakespeare wishes to express: How blind I was, he cries to us, how inconceivably trusting and foolish! How could I have imagined that a young noble would be grateful, or a wanton true? *Lear* is a page of Shakespeare's autobiography, and the faults of it are the stains of his blistering tears.

Lear is badly constructed, but worse was to come. The next tragedy, *Timon*, is merely a scream of pain, and yet it, too, has a deeper than artistic interest for us as marking the utmost limit of Shakespeare's suffering. The mortal malady of perhaps the finest spirit that has ever appeared among men has an interest for us profounder than any tragedy. And to find that in Shakespeare's agony and bloody sweat he ignores the rules of artistry is simply what might have been expected, and, to some of us, deepens the personal interest in the drama.

In *Lear* Edgar is peculiarly Shakespeare's mouthpiece, and to Edgar Shakespeare gives some of the finest words he ever coined:

> The gods are just, and of our pleasant vices
> Make instruments to plague us.

Here, too, in what Edgar says of himself, is the moral of all passion: it is manifestly Shakespeare's view of himself:

> A most poor man, made tame to Fortune's blows,
> Who by the art of knowing and feeling sorrows
> Am pregnant to good pity.

Then we find the supreme phrase – perhaps the finest ever written:

> Men must endure
> Their going hence even as their coming hither.
> Ripeness is all.

Shakespeare speaks through Lear in the last acts as plainly as through Edgar. In the third scene of the fifth act Lear talks to Cordelia in the very words Shakespeare gave to the saint Henry VI at the beginning of his career. Compare the extracts on pages 99–100 with the following passage, and you will see the similarity and the astounding growth in his art.

> . . . Come, let's away to prison:
> We two alone will sing like birds i' the cage:
> When thou dost ask me blessing, I'll kneel down
> And ask of thee forgiveness: so we'll live,
> And pray, and sing, and tell old tales, and laugh
> At gilded butterflies, and hear poor rogues
> Talk of court news; . . .

More characteristic still of Shakespeare is the fact that when Lear is at his bitterest in the fourth act, he shows the erotic mania which is the source of all Shakespeare's bitterness and misery; but which is utterly out of place in Lear. The reader will mark how 'adultery' is dragged in:

> . . . Ay, every inch a king:
> When I do stare, see how the subject quakes.
> I pardon that man's life. What was thy cause?
> Adultery?
> Thou shalt not die: die for adultery! No:
> The wren goes to 't, and the small gilded fly
> Does lecher in my sight.
> Let copulation thrive;
> [. . .]
> Down from the waist they are Centaurs,
> Though women all above;
> But to the girdle do the gods inherit,
> Beneath is all the fiends; . . .

Thus Lear raves for a whole page: Shakespeare on his hobby: in the same erotic spirit he makes both Goneril and Regan lust after Edmund.

The note of this tragedy is Shakespeare's understanding of his insane blind trust in men; but the passion of it springs from erotic mania and from the consciousness that he is too old for love's lists. Perhaps his imagination never carried him higher than when Lear appeals to the heavens because they too are old:

> ... O heavens,
> If you do love old men, if your sweet sway
> Allow obedience, if yourselves are old,
> Make it your cause.

12

The Drama of Despair: *Timon of Athens*

Timon marks the extremity of Shakespeare's suffering. It is not to be called a work of art, it is hardly even a tragedy; it is the causeless ruin of a soul, a ruin insufficiently motived by complete trust in men and spendthrift generosity. If there was ever a man who gave so lavishly as Timon, if there was ever one so senseless blind in trusting, then he deserved his fate. There is no gradation in his giving, and none in his fall; no artistic crescendo. The whole drama is, as I have said, a scream of suffering, or rather, a long curse upon all the ordinary conditions of life. The highest qualities of Shakespeare are not to be found in the play. There are none of the magnificent phrases which bejewel *Lear*; little of high wisdom, even in the pages which are indubitably Shakespeare's, and no characterisation worth mentioning. The honest steward, Flavius, is the honest Kent again of *Lear*, honest and loyal beyond nature; Apemantus is another Thersites. Words which throw a high light on Shakespeare's character are given to this or that personage of the play without discrimination. One phrase of Apemantus is as true of Shakespeare as of Timon and is worth noting:

The middle of humanity thou never knewest, but the extremity of both ends.

The tragic sonnet-note is given to Flavius:

> What viler thing upon the earth than friends
> Who can bring noblest minds to basest ends!

In so far as Timon is a character at all he is manifestly Shakespeare, Shakespeare who raves against the world, because he finds no honesty in men, no virtue in women, evil everywhere – 'boundless thefts in limited professions'. This Shakespeare-Timon swings round characteristically as soon as he finds that Flavius is honest:

> Had I a steward
> So true, so just, and now so comfortable?
> It almost turns my dangerous nature mild.
> Let me behold thy face. Surely this man
> Was born of woman.
> *Forgive my general and exceptless rashness,*
> *You perpetual-sober gods!* I do proclaim
> One honest man – mistake me not – but one . . .

I cannot help putting the great and self-revealing line* in italics; a line Tolstoy would, no doubt, think stupid-pompous. Timon ought to have known his steward, one might say in Tolstoy's spirit, as Lear should have known his daughters; but this is still the tragedy, which Shakespeare wishes to emphasise, that his hero was blind in trusting.

Towards the end Shakespeare speaks through Timon quite unfeignedly: Richard II said characteristically:

> Nor I nor any man that but man is
> With nothing shall be pleased, till he be eased
> With being nothing:

And Timon says to Flavius:

> My long sickness
> Of health and living now begins to mend
> And nothing brings me all things.

Then the end:

> Timon hath made his everlasting mansion
> Upon the beached verge of the salt flood . . .

We must not leave this play before noticing the overpowering erotic strain in Shakespeare which suits Timon as little as it suited Lear. The long discussion with Phrynia and Timandra is simply dragged in: neither woman is characterised: Shakespeare-Timon eases himself in pages of erotic raving:

> . . . Strike me the counterfeit matron;
> It is her habit only that is honest,
> Herself's a bawd: . . .

---

* This passage is among those rejected by the commentators as un-Shakespearean: 'it does not stand the test,' says the egregious Gollancz.

And then:

> Consumptions sow
> In hollow bones of man
>   . . . Down with the nose,
> Down with it flat; take the bridge quite away . . .

The 'damned earth' even is 'the common whore of mankind'.

Timon is the true sequel to *The Merchant of Venice*. Antonio gives lavishly, but is saved at the crisis by his friends. Timon gives with both hands, but when he appeals to his friends, is treated as a bore. Shakespeare had travelled far in the dozen years which separate the two plays.

All Shakespeare's tragedies are phases of his own various weaknesses, and each one brings the hero to defeat and ruin. Hamlet cannot carry revenge to murder and fails through his own irresolution. Othello comes to grief through mad jealousy. Antony fails and falls through excess of lust; Lear through trust in men, and Timon through heedless generosity. All these are separate studies of Shakespeare's own weaknesses; but the ruin is irretrievable, and reaches its ultimate in Timon. Trust and generosity, Shakespeare would like to tell us, were his supremest faults. In this he deceived himself. Neither *Lear* nor *Timon* is his greatest tragedy; but *Antony and Cleopatra*, for lust was his chief weakness, and the tragedy of lust his greatest play.

Much of *Timon* is not Shakespeare's, the critics tell us, and some of it is manifestly not his, though many of the passages rejected with the best reason have, I think, been touched up by him. The second scene of the first act is as bad as bad can be; but I hear his voice in the line:

> Methinks, I could deal kingdoms to my friends,
> And ne'er be weary.

At any rate, this is the keynote of the tragedy, which is struck again and again. Shakespeare probably exaggerated his generosity out of aristocratic pose; but that he was careless of money and freehanded to a fault, is, I think, certain from his writings, and can be proved from the facts known to us of his life.

13

The Last Romances – All Copies:
The Winter's Tale, Cymbeline, The Tempest

The wheel has swung full circle: Timon is almost as weak as *Titus Andronicus*; the pen falls from the nerveless hand. Shakespeare wrote nothing for some time. Even the critics make a break after *Timon*, which closes what they are pleased to call his third period; but they do not seem to see that the break was really a breakdown in health. In *Lear* he had brooded and raged to madness; in *Timon* he had spent himself in futile, feeble cursings. His nerves had gone to pieces. He was now forty-five years of age, the forces of youth and growth had left him. He was prematurely old and feeble.

His recovery, it seems certain, was very slow, and he never again, if I am right, regained vigorous health, I am almost certain he went down to Stratford at this crisis and spent some time there, probably a couple of years, trying, no doubt, to staunch the wound in his heart, and win back again to life. The fear of madness had frightened him from brooding: he made up his mind to let the dead past bury its dead; he would try to forget and live sanely. After all, life is better than death.

It was probably his daughter who led him back from the brink of the grave. Almost all his latest works show the same figure of a young girl. He seems now, for the first time, to have learned that a maiden can be pure, and in his old idealising way which went with him to the end, he deified her. Judith became a symbol to him, and he lent her the ethereal grace of abstract beauty. In *Pericles* she is Marina; in *The Winter's Tale* Perdita; in *The Tempest* Miranda. It is probable when one comes to think of it, that Ward was right when he says that Shakespeare spent his 'elder years' in Stratford; he was too broken to have taken up his life in London again.

The assertion that Shakespeare broke down in health, and never won back to vigorous life, will be scorned as my imagining. The critics who have agreed to regard *Cymbeline*, *The Winter's Tale*, and *The Tempest* as his finest works are all against me on this point, and they will call for 'Proofs, proofs. Give us proofs', they will cry, 'that the man who went mad and raved with Lear, and screamed and cursed in *Timon* did really break down, and was not imagining madness and despair.' The proofs are to be found in these works themselves, plain for all men to read.

The three chief works of his last period are romances and are all copies; he was too tired to invent or even to annex; his own story is the only one that interests him. The plot of *The Winter's Tale* is the plot of *Much Ado about Nothing*. Hero is Hermione. Another phase of *Much Ado About Nothing* is written out at length in *Cymbeline*; Imogen suffers like Hero and Hermione, under unfounded accusation. It is Shakespeare's own history turned from this world to fairyland: what would have happened, he asks, if the woman whom I believed false, had been true? This, the theme of *Much Ado*, is the theme also of *The Winter's Tale* and of *Cymbeline*. The idealism of the man is inveterate: he will not see that it was his own sensuality which gave him up to suffering, and not Mary Fitton's faithlessness. *The Tempest* is the story of *As You Like it*. We have again the two dukes, the exiled good Duke, who is Shakespeare, and the bad usurping Duke, Shakespeare's rival, Chapman, who has conquered for a time. Shakespeare is no longer able or willing to discover a new play: he can only copy himself, and in one of the scenes which he wrote into *Henry VIII* the copy is slavish.

I allude to the third scene in the second act; the dialogue between Anne Bullen and the Old Lady is extraordinarily reminiscent. When Anne Bullen says –

> 'Tis better to be lowly born,
> And range with humble livers in content,
> Than to be perk'd up in a glistering grief
> And wear a golden sorrow.

I am reminded of Henry VI. And the contention between Anne Bullen and the Old Lady, in which Anne Bullen declares that she would not be a queen, and the Old Lady scorns her:

> Beshrew me, I would,
> And venture maidenhead for't; and so would you,
> For all this spice of your hypocrisy.

is much the same contention, and is handled in the same way as the contention between Desdemona and Emilia in *Othello*.

There are many other proofs of Shakespeare's weakness of hand throughout this last period, if further proofs were needed. The chief characteristics of Shakespeare's health are his humour, his gaiety, and wit – his love of life. A correlative characteristic is that all his women are sensuous and indulge in coarse expressions in and out of season. This is said to be a fault of his time; but only professors could use an argument which shows such ignorance of life. Homer was clean enough, and Sophocles, Spenser, too; sensuality is a quality of the individual man. Still another characteristic of Shakespeare's maturity is that his characters, in spite of being idealised, live for us a vigorous, pulsing life.

All these characteristics are lacking in the works after *Timon*. There is practically no humour, no wit, the clowns even are merely boorish-stupid with the solitary exception of Autolycus, who is a pale reflex of one or two characteristics of Falstaff. Shakespeare's humour has disappeared, or is so faint as scarcely to be called humour; all the heroines, too, are now vowed away from sensuality: Marina passes through the brothel unsoiled; Perdita might have milk in her veins, and not blood, and Miranda is but another name for Perdita. Imogen, too, has no trace of natural passion in her: she is a mere washing-list, so to speak, of sexless perfections. In this last period Shakespeare will have nothing to do with sensuality, and his characters, and not the female characters alone, are hardly more than abstractions; they lack the blood of emotion; there is not one of them could cast a shadow. How is it that the critics have mistaken these pale, bloodless silhouettes for Shakespeare's masterpieces?

In his earliest works he was compelled, as we have seen, to use his own experiences perpetually, not having had any experience of life, and in these, his latest plays, he also uses when he can his own experiences to give his pictures of the world from which he had withdrawn, some sense of vivid life. For example, in *Winter's Tale* his account of the death of the boy Mamillius is evidently a reflex of his own emotion when he lost his son, Hamnet, an emotion which at the time he pictured deathlessly in Arthur and the grief of the Queen-mother Constance. Similarly, in *Cymbeline*, the joy of the brothers in finding the sister is an echo of his own pleasure in getting to know his daughter.

I have an idea about the genesis of these last three plays as regards their order which may be wholly false, though true, I am sure, to

Shakespeare's character. I imagine he was asked by the author to touch up *Pericles*. On reading the play, he saw the opportunity of giving expression to the new emotion which had been awakened in him by the serious sweet charm of his young daughter, and accordingly he wrote the scenes in which Marina figures. Judith's modesty was a perpetual wonder to him.

His success induced him to sketch out *The Winter's Tale*, in which tale he played sadly with what might have been if his accused love, Mary Fitton, had been guiltless instead of guilty. I imagine he saw that the play was not a success, or supreme critic as he was, that his hand had grown weak, and seeking for the cause he probably came to the conclusion that the comparative failure was due to the fact that he did not put himself into *The Winter's Tale*, and so he determined in the next play to draw a full-length portrait of himself again, as he had done in *Hamlet*, and accordingly he sketched Posthumus, a staider, older, idealised Hamlet, with lymph in his veins, instead of blood. In the same idealising spirit, he pictured his rose of womanhood for us in Imogen, who is, however, not a living woman at all, any more than his earliest ideal, Juliet, was a woman. The contrast between these two sketches is the contrast between Shakespeare's strength and his weakness. Here is how the fourteen-year-old Juliet talks of love:

> Spread thy close curtain, love-performing night,
> That runaways' eyes may wink, and Romeo
> Leap to these arms, untalk'd of and unseen.
> Lovers can see to do their amorous rites
> By their own beauties.

And here what Posthumus says of Imogen:

> Me of my lawful pleasure she restrain'd,
> And pray'd me oft forbearance: did it with
> A pudency so rosy, the sweet view on't
> Might well have warmed old Saturn.

Neither of these statements is very generally true: but the second is out of character. When Shakespeare praises restraint in love he must have been very weak; in full manhood he prayed for excess of it, and regarded a surfeit as the only rational cure.

I think Shakespeare liked Posthumus and Imogen; but he could not have thought *Cymbeline* a great work, and so he pulled himself together for a masterpiece. He seems to have said to himself, 'All that fighting of Posthumus is wrong; men do not fight at forty-eight; I will paint myself simply in the qualities I possess now; I will tell the truth about myself so far as I can.' The result is the portrait of Prospero in *The Tempest.*

Let me just say before I begin to study Prospero that I find the introduction of the Masque in the fourth act extraordinarily interesting. Ben Jonson had written classic masques for this and that occasion; masques which were very successful, we are told; they had 'caught on', in fact, to use our modern slang. Shakespeare will now show us that he, too, can write a masque with classic deities in it, and better Jonson's example. It is pitiful, and goes to prove, I think, that Shakespeare was but little esteemed by his generation.

Jonson answered him conceitedly, as Jonson would, in the Introduction to his *Bartholomew Fair* (1612–14), 'If there be never a *Servant monster* i' the Fayre, who can help it, he sayes; nor a nest of *Antiques.* He is loth to make nature afraid in his *Playes,* like those that beget *Tales, Tempests,* and such like *Drolleries.'*

At the very end, the creator of Hamlet, the finest mind in the world, was eager to show that he could write as well in any style as the author of *Every Man in his Humour.* To me the bare fact is full of interest, and most pitiful.

Let us now turn to *The Tempest,* and see how our poet figures in it. It is Shakespeare's last work, and one of his very greatest; his testament to the English people; in wisdom and high poetry a miracle.

The portrait of Shakespeare we get in Prospero is astonishingly faithful and ingenuous, in spite of its idealisation. His life's day is waning to the end; shadows of the night are drawing in upon him, yet he is the same bookish, melancholy student, the lover of all courtesies and generosities, whom we met first as Biron in *Love's Labour's Lost.* The gaiety is gone and the sensuality; the spiritual outlook is infinitely sadder – that is what the years have done with our gentle Shakespeare.

Prospero's first appearance in the second scene of the first act is as a loving father and magician; he says to Miranda:

> I have done nothing but in care of thee,
> Of thee, my dear one! thee, my daughter.

He asks Miranda what she can remember of her early life, and reaches magical words:

> What seest thou else
> In the dark backward and abysm of time?

Miranda is only fifteen years of age. Shakespeare turned Juliet, it will be
remembered, from a girl of sixteen into one of fourteen; now, though
the sensuality has left him, he makes Miranda only fifteen; clearly he is
the same admirer of girlish youth at forty-eight as he was twenty years
before. Then Prospero tells Miranda of himself and his brother, the
'perfidious' Duke:

> And Prospero, the prime Duke, being so reputed
> In dignity, and for the liberal arts
> Without a parallel; those being all my study.

He will not only be a Prince now, but a master 'without a parallel' in the
liberal arts. He must explain, too, at undue length, how he allowed
himself to be supplanted by his false brother, and speaks about himself
in Shakespeare's very words:

> I thus neglecting worldly ends, all dedicate
> To closeness, and the bettering of my mind
> With that, which, but by being so retired,
> O'erprized all popular rate, in my false brother
> Awaked an evil nature: and my trust,
> Like a good parent, did beget of him,
> A falsehood, in its contrary as great
> As my trust was; which had, indeed, no limit,
> A confidence sans bound.

Shakespeare, too, 'neglecting worldly ends', had dedicated himself to
'bettering of his mind', we may be sure. Prospero goes on to tell us
explicitly how Shakespeare loved books, which we were only able to
infer from his earlier plays:

> Me, poor man, my library
> Was dukedom large enough.

And again, Gonzalo (another name for Kent and Flavius) having given
him some books, he says:

> Of his gentleness,
> Knowing I loved my books, he furnished me
> From my own library, with volumes that
> I prize above my dukedom.

His daughter grieves lest she had been a trouble to him: forthwith Shakespeare-Prospero answers:

> O, a cherubim
> Thou wast, that did preserve me. Thou didst smile
> Infused with a fortitude from heaven,
> When I have deck'd the sea with drops full salt
> Under my burden groan'd; which raised in me
> An undergoing stomach, to bear up
> Against what should ensue.

But why should the magician weep or groan under a burden? had he no confidence in his miraculous powers? All this is Shakespeare's confession. Every word is true; his daughter did indeed 'preserve' Shakespeare, and enable him to bear up under the burden of life's betrayals.

No wonder Prospero begins to apologise for this long-winded confession, which indeed is 'most impertinent' to the play, as he admits, though most interesting to him and to us, for he is simply Shakespeare telling us his own feelings at the time. The gentle magician then hears from Ariel how the shipwreck has been conducted without harming a hair of anyone.

The whole scene is an extraordinarily faithful and detailed picture of Shakespeare's soul. I find significance even in the fact that Ariel wants his freedom 'a full year' before the term Prospero had originally proposed. Shakespeare finished *The Tempest*, I believe, and therewith set the seal on his life's work a full year earlier than he had intended; he feared lest death might surprise him before he had put the pinnacle on his work. Ariel's torment, too, is full of meaning for me; for Ariel is Shakespeare's 'shaping spirit of imagination', who was once the slave of 'a foul witch', and by her 'imprisoned painfully' for 'a dozen years'.

That 'dozen years' is to me astonishingly true and interesting: it shows that my reading of the duration of his passion-torture was absolutely correct – Shakespeare's 'delicate spirit' and best powers bound to Mary Fitton's 'earthy' service from 1597 to 1608.

We can perhaps fix this latter date with some assurance. Mistress Fitton married for the second time a Captain or Mr Polwhele late in 1607, or some short time before March, 1608, when the fact of her recent marriage was recorded in the will of her great uncle. It seems to me probable, or at least possible, that this event marks her complete separation from Shakespeare; she may very likely have left the Court and London on ceasing to be a Maid of Honour.

Shakespeare is so filled with himself in this last play, so certain that he is the most important person in the world, that this scene is more charged with intimate self-revealing than any other in all his works. And when Ferdinand comes upon the stage Shakespeare lends him, too, his own peculiar qualities. His puppets no longer interest him; he is careless of characterisation. Ferdinand says:

> This music crept by me upon the waters
> Allaying both their fury and my passion
> With its sweet air.

Music, it will be remembered, had precisely the same peculiar effect upon Duke Orsino in *Twelfth Night*. Ferdinand, too, is extraordinarily conceited:

> I am the best of them that speak this speech
> . . . Myself am Naples.

Shakespeare's natural aristocratic pride as a Prince reinforced by his understanding of his own real importance. Ferdinand then declares he will be content with a prison if he can see Miranda in it:

> Space enough
> Have I in such a prison.

Which is Hamlet's:

> I could be bounded in a nutshell, and count myself a king of infinite space.

The second act, with its foiled conspiracy, is wretchedly bad, and the meeting of Caliban and Trinculo with Stephanio does not improve it much. Shakespeare has little interest now in anything outside himself: age and greatness are as self-centred as youth.

In the third act the courtship of Ferdinand and Miranda is pretty, but hardly more. Ferdinand is bloodless, thin, and Miranda swears 'by her modesty', as the jewel in her dower, which takes away a little from the charming confession of girl-love:

> I would not wish
> Any companion in the world but you.

The comic relief which follows is unspeakably dull; but the words of Ariel, warning the King of Naples and the usurping Duke that the wrong they have done Prospero is certain to be avenged unless blotted out by 'heart-sorrow and a clear life ensuing', are most characteristic and memorable.

In the fourth act Prospero preaches, as we have seen, self-restraint to Ferdinand in words which, in their very extravagance, show how deeply he regretted his own fault with his wife before marriage. I shall consider the whole passage when treating of Shakespeare's marriage as an incident in his life. Afterwards comes the masque, and the marvellous speech of Prospero, which touches the highest height of poetry:

> These our actors,
> As I foretold you, were all spirits, and
> Are melted into air, into thin air:
> And, like the baseless fabric of this vision,
> The cloud-capped towers, the gorgeous palaces,
> The solemn temples, the great globe itself,
> Yea, all which it inhabit, shall dissolve
> And, like this insubstantial pageant faded,
> Leave not a rack behind. We are such stuff
> As dreams are made of; and our little life
> Is rounded with a sleep. Sir, I am vex'd;
> Bear with my weakness; my old brain is troubled:
> Be not disturb'd with my infirmity:
> If you be pleased, retire into my cell,
> And there repose: a turn or two I'll walk,
> To still my beating mind.

I have given the verses to the very end, for I find the insistence on his age and weakness (which are not in keeping with the character of a magician), a confession of Shakespeare himself: the words 'beating mind' are extraordinarily characteristic, proving as they do that his thoughts and emotions were too strong for his frail body.

In the fifth act Shakespeare-Prospero shows himself to us at his noblest: he will forgive his enemies:

> Though with their high wrongs I am struck to the quick,
> Yet with my nobler reason 'gainst my fury

Do I take part: the rarer action is
In virtue than in vengeance: they being penitent,
The sole drift of my purpose doth extend
Not a frown further.

In *The Two Gentlemen of Verona* we saw how Shakespeare-Valentine
forgave his faithless friend as soon as he repented: here is the same
creed touched to nobler expression.

And then, with all his wishes satisfied, his heart's desire accomplished,
Prospero is ready to set out for Milan again and home. We all expect
some expression of joy from him, but this is what we get:

And thence retire me to my Milan, where
Every third thought shall be my grave.

The despair is wholly unexpected and out of place, as was the story of
his weakness and infirmity, his 'beating mind'. It is evidently Shakespeare's own confession. After writing *The Tempest* he intends to retire
to Stratford, where 'every third thought shall be my grave'.

I have purposely drawn special attention to Shakespeare's weakness
and despair at this time, because the sad, rhymed Epilogue which has to
be spoken by Prospero has been attributed to another hand by a good
many scholars. It is manifestly Shakespeare's, out of Shakespeare's very
heart indeed; though Mr Israel Gollancz follows his leaders in saying
that the 'Epilogue to the play is evidently by some other hand than
Shakespeare's': 'evidently' is good. Here it is:

Now my charms are all o'erthrown,
And what strength I have's mine own,
Which is most faint: now, 'tis true,
I must be here confined by you,
Or sent to Naples. Let me not
Since I have my dukedom got,
And pardon'd the deceiver, dwell
In this bare island by your spell;
But release me from my bands
With the help of your good hands:
Gentle breath of yours my sails
Must fill, or else my project fails,
Which was to please. Now I want,
Spirits to enforce, art to enchant;

> And my ending is despair,
> Unless I be relieved by prayer,
> Which pierces so that it assaults
> Mercy itself, and frees all faults.
> As you from crimes would pardon'd be,
> Let your indulgence set me free.

From youth to age Shakespeare occupied himself with the deepest problems of human existence; again and again we find him trying to pierce the darkness that enshrouds life. Is there indeed nothing beyond the grave – nothing? Is the noble fabric of human thought, achievement and endeavour to fade into nothingness and pass away like the pageant of a dream? He will not cheat himself with unfounded hopes, nor delude himself into belief; he resigns himself with a sigh – it is the undiscovered country, from whose bourn no traveller returns. But Shakespeare always believed in repentance and forgiveness, and now, world-weary, old and weak, he turns to prayer,* prayer that –

> assaults
> Mercy itself and frees all faults.

Poor, broken Shakespeare! 'My ending is despair': the sadness of it, and the pity, lie deeper than tears.

What a man! to produce a masterpiece in spite of such weakness. What a play is this *Tempest*! At length Shakespeare sees himself as he is, a monarch without a country; but master of a very 'potent art', a great magician, with imagination as an attendant spirit, that can conjure up shipwrecks, or enslave enemies, or create lovers at will; and all his powers are used in gentle kindness. Ariel is a higher creation, more spiritual and charming than any other poet has ever attempted; and Caliban, the earth-born, half-beast, half-man – these are the poles of Shakespeare's genius.

---

* Hamlet, too, after speaking with his father's ghost, cries: 'I'll go pray.'

14

Shakespeare's Life – Part One

Our long travail is almost at an end. We have watched Shakespeare painting himself at various periods of his life, and at full length in twenty dramas, as the gentle, sensuous poet-thinker. We have studied him when given over to wild passion in the sonnets and elsewhere, and to insane jealousy in *Othello*; we have seen him as Hamlet brooding on revenge and self-murder, and in *Lear*, and *Timon* raging on the verge of madness, and in these ecstasies, when the soul is incapable of feigning, we have discovered his true nature as it differed from the ideal presentments which his vanity shaped and coloured. We have corrected his personal estimate by that 'story of faults conceal'd' which Shakespeare himself referred to in sonnet 88. It only remains for me now to give a brief account of his life and the incidents of it to show that my reading of his character is borne out by the known facts, and thus put the man in his proper setting, so to speak.

On the other hand, our knowledge of Shakespeare's character will help us to reconstruct his life-story. What is known positively of his life could be given in a couple of pages; but there are traditions of him, tales about him, innumerable scraps of fact and fiction concerning him which are more or less interesting and authentic; and now that we know the man, we shall be able to accept or reject these reports with some degree of confidence, and so arrive at a credible picture of his life's journey, and the changes which Time wrought in him. In all I may say about him I shall keep close to the facts as given in his works. When tradition seems consonant with what Shakespeare has told us about himself, or with what Ben Jonson said of him, I shall use it with confidence.

Shakespeare was a common name in Warwickshire; other Shakespeares besides the poet's family were known there in the sixteenth century, and at least one other William Shakespeare in the neighbourhood of Stratford. The poet's father, John Shakespeare, was of farmer stock, and seems to have had an adventurous spirit: he left Snitterfield, his birthplace, as a young man, for the neighbouring town of Stratford, where he set up in business for himself. Aubrey says he was a butcher; he certainly dealt in meat, skins, and leather, as well as in corn, wool, and malt – an adaptable, quick man, who turned his hand to anything – a Jack-of-all-trades. He appears to have been successful at first, for in 1556, five years after coming to Stratford, he purchased two freehold tenements, one with a garden in Henley Street, and the other in Greenhill Street, with an orchard. In 1557 he was elected burgess, or town councillor, and shortly afterwards did the best stroke of business in his life by marrying Mary Arden, whose father had been a substantial farmer. Mary inherited the fee simple of Asbies, a house with some fifty acres of land at Wilmcote, and an interest in property at Snitterfield; the whole perhaps worth some £80 or £90, or, say, £600 of our money. His marriage turned John Shakespeare into a well-to-do citizen; he filled various offices in the borough, and in 1568 became a bailiff, the highest position in the corporation. During his year of office, we are told, he entertained two companies of actors at Stratford.

Mary Arden seems to have been her father's favourite child, and though she could not sign her own name, must have possessed rare qualities; for the poet, as we learn from *Coriolanus*, held her in extra-ordinary esteem and affection, and mourned her after her death as 'the noblest mother in the world'.

William Shakespeare, the first son and third child of this couple, was born on the 22nd or 23rd April, 1564, no one knows which day; the Stratford parish registers prove that he was baptised on 26th April. And if the date of his birth is not known, neither is the place of it; his father owned two houses in Henley Street, and it is uncertain which he was born in.

John Shakespeare had, fortunately, nothing to pay for the education of his sons. They had free tuition at the Grammar School at Stratford. The poet went to school when he was seven or eight years of age, and received an ordinary education together with some grounding in Latin. He probably spent most of his time at first making stories out of the frescoes on the walls. There can be no doubt that he learned easily all he was taught, and still less doubt that he was not taught much. He mastered Lyly's *Latin Grammar*, and was taken through some con-versation books like the *Sententiae Pueriles*, and not much further, for he puts Latin phrases in the mouth of the schoolmasters, Holofernes in *Love's Labour's Lost*, and Hugh Evans in *The Merry Wives of Windsor*, and all these phrases are taken word for word either from Lyly's *Grammar* or from the *Sententiae Pueriles*. In *Titus Andronicus*, too, one of Tamora's sons, on reading a Latin couplet, says it is a verse of Horace, but he 'read it in the grammar', which was probably the author's case. Ben Jonson's sneer was well-founded, Shakespeare had 'little Latine and lesse Greeke'. His French, as shown in his *Henry V*, was anything but good, and his Italian was probably still slighter.

It was lucky for Shakespeare that his father's increasing poverty withdrew him from school early, and forced him into contact with life. Aubrey says that 'when he was a boy he exercised his father's trade [of butcher]; but when he kill'd a calfe he would doe it in high style and make a speech'. I dare say young Will flourished about with a knife and made romantic speeches; but I am pretty sure he never killed a calf. Killing a calf is not the easiest part of a butcher's business; nor a task which Shakespeare at any time would have selected. The tradition is simply sufficient to prove that the town folk had already noticed the eager, quick, spouting lad.

Of Shakespeare's life after he left school, say from thirteen to eighteen, we know almost nothing. He probably did odd jobs for his father from time to time; but his father's business seems to have run rapidly from bad to worse; for in 1586 a creditor informed the local Court that John Shakespeare had no goods on which distraint could be levied, and on 6th September of the same year he was deprived of his alderman's gown. During this period of steadily increasing poverty in the house it was only to be expected that young Will Shakespeare would run wild.

The tradition as given by Rowe says that he fell 'into low company, and amongst them some that made a frequent practice of deer-stealing engaged him with them more than once in robbing the park of Sir Thomas Lucy of Charlecot, near Stratford. For this he was prosecuted by that gentleman, as he then thought somewhat too severely, and in order to revenge that ill-usage he made a ballad upon him.'

Another story has it that Sir Thomas Lucy got a lawyer from Warwick to prosecute the boys, and that Shakespeare stuck his satirical ballad to the park gates at Charlecot. The ballad is said to have been lost, but certain verses were preserved which fit the circumstances and suit Shakespeare's character so perfectly that I for one am content to accept them. I give the first and the last verses as most characteristic:

SONG

A parliament member, a Justice of peace,
At home a poor scarecrow, in London an asse,
If Lowsie is lucy, as some volke miscalle it
Then Lucy is lowsie, whatever befalle it.
    He thinks himself greate
    Yet an asse in his state,
We allowe by his ears but with asses to mate.
If Lucy is lowsie, as some volke miscalle it
Sing lowsie Lucy whatever befalle it.
[. . .]
'If a juvenile frolick he cannot forgive,
We'll sing lowsie Lucy as long as we live,
And Lucy, the lowsie, a libel may calle it
Sing lowsie Lucy whatever befalle it.
    He thinks himself greate
    Yet an asse in his state,
We allowe by his ears but with asses to mate.
If Lucy is lowsie, as some volke miscalle it
Sing lowsie Lucy, whatever befalle it.

The last verse, so out of keeping in its curious impartiality with the scurrilous refrain, appears to me to carry its own signature. There can be no doubt that the verses give us young Shakespeare's feelings in the matter. It was probably reading ballads and tales of 'Merrie Sherwood' that first inclined him to deer-stealing; and we have already seen from his *Richard II* and *Henry IV* and *Henry V* that he had been led astray by low companions.

In his idle, high-spirited youth, Shakespeare did worse than break bounds and kill deer; he was at a loose end and up to all sorts of mischief. At eighteen he had already courted and won Anne Hathaway, a farmer's daughter of the neighbouring village of Shottery. Anne was nearly eight years older than he was. Her father had died a short time before and left Anne, his eldest daughter, £6 13*s*. 4*d*., or, say, £50 of our money. The house at Shottery, now shown as Anne Hathaway's cottage, once formed part of Richard Hathaway's farmhouse, and there, and in the neighbouring lanes, the lovers did their courting. The wooing on Shakespeare's side was nothing but pastime, though it led to marriage.

His marriage is perhaps the first serious mistake that Shakespeare made, and it certainly influenced his whole life. It is needful, therefore, to understand it as accurately as may be, however we may judge it. A man's life, like a great river, may be limpid-pure in the beginning, and when near its source; as it grows and gains strength it is inevitably sullied and stained with earth's soilure.

The ordinary apologists would have us believe that the marriage was happy; they know that Shakespeare was not married in Stratford, and, though a minor, his parents' consent to the marriage was not obtained; but they persist in talking about his love for his wife, and his wife's devoted affection for him. Mr Halliwell-Phillipps, the bell-wether of the flock, has gone so far as to tell us how on the morning of the day he died 'his wife, who had smoothed the pillow beneath his head for the last time, felt that her right hand was taken from her'. Let us see if there is any foundation for this sentimental balderdash. Here are some of the facts.

In the Bishop of Worcester's register a licence was issued on 27th November, 1582, authorising the marriage of William Shakespeare with Anne Whately, of Temple Grafton. On the very next day in the register of the same Bishop there is a deed, wherein Fulk Sandells and John Richardson, farmers of Shottery, bound themselves in the Bishop's court under a surety of £40 to free the Bishop of all liability should a lawful impediment – 'by reason of any pre-contract or consanguinity' – be subsequently disclosed to imperil the validity of the marriage, then in contemplation, of William Shakespeare with Anne Hathaway.

Dryasdust, of course, argues that there is no connection whatever between these two events. He is able to persuade himself easily that the William Shakespeare who got a licence to marry Anne Whately, of Temple Grafton, on 27th November, 1582, is not the same William Shakespeare who is being forced to marry Anne Hathaway on the next day by two friends of Anne Hathaway's father. Yet such a coincidence as two William Shakespeares seeking to be married by special licence in the same court at the same moment of time is too extraordinary to be admitted. Besides, why should Sandells and Richardson bind them- selves as sureties in £40 to free the Bishop of liability by reason of any pre-contract if there were no pre-contract? The two William Shake- speares are clearly one and the same person. Sandells was a supervisor of the will of Richard Hathaway, and was described in the will as 'my trustie friende and neighbour'. He showed himself a trusty friend of the usual sort to his friend's daughter, and when he heard that loose Will

Shakespeare was attempting to marry Anne Whately, he forthwith went to the same Bishop's court which had granted the licence, pledged himself and his neighbour, Richardson, as sureties that there was no pre-contract, and so induced the Bishop, who no doubt then learned the unholy circumstances for the first time, to grant a licence in order that the marriage with Anne Hathaway could be celebrated, 'with once asking of the bannes' and without the consent of the father of the bridegroom, which was usually required when the bridegroom was a minor.

Clearly Fulk Sandells was a masterful man; young Will Shakespeare was forced to give up Anne Whately, poor lass, and marry Anne Hathaway, much against his will. Like many another man, Shakespeare married at leisure, and repented in hot haste. Six months later a daughter was born to him, and was baptised in the name of Susanna at Stratford Parish Church on the 26th of May, 1583. There was, therefore, an importunate reason for the wedding, as Sandells, no doubt, made the Bishop understand.

The whole story, it seems to me, is in perfect consonance with Shakespeare's impulsive, sensual nature; is, indeed, an excellent illustration of it. Hot, impatient, idle Will got Anne Hathaway into trouble, was forced to marry her, and at once came to regret. Let us see how far these inferences from plain facts are borne out from his works.

The most important passages seem to have escaped critical scholarship. I have already said that the earliest works of Shakespeare, and the latest, are the most fruitful in details about his private life. In the earliest works he was compelled to use his own experience, having no observation of life to help him, and at the end of his life, having said almost everything he had to say, he again went back to his early experience for little vital facts to lend a colour to the fainter pictures of age. In *The Winter's Tale*, a shepherd finds the child Perdita, who has been exposed; one would expect him to stumble on the child by chance and express surprise; but this shepherd of Shakespeare begins to talk in this way:

I would there were no age between ten and three-and-twenty, or that youth would sleep out the rest; for there is nothing in the between but getting wenches with child, wronging the ancientry, stealing, fighting. Hark you now! Would any but these boiled brains of nineteen and two-and-twenty hunt this weather?

Now this passage has nothing to do with the play, nor with the shepherd's occupation; nor is it at all characteristic of a shepherd boy. Between ten and three-and-twenty a poor shepherd boy is likely to be kept hard at work; he is not idle and at a loose end like young Shakespeare, free to rob the ancientry, steal, fight, and get wenches with child. That, in my opinion, is Shakespeare's own confession.

Of course, everyone has noticed how Shakespeare again and again in his plays declares that a woman should take in marriage an 'elder than herself', and that intimacy before marriage is productive of nothing but 'barren hate and discord'. In *Twelfth Night* he says:

> Let still the woman take
> An elder than herself: so wears she to him,
> So sways she level in her husband's heart.

In *The Tempest* he writes again:

> If thou dost break her virgin knot before
> All sanctimonious ceremonies may
> With full and holy rite be minister'd,
> No sweet aspersions shall the heavens let fall
> To make this contract grow; but barren hate,
> Sour-ey'd disdain, and discord, shall bestrew
> The union of your bed with weeds so loathly
> That you shall hate it both.

These admonitions are so far-fetched and so emphatic that they plainly discover personal feeling. We have, besides, those quaint, angry passages in *The Comedy of Errors*, to which we have already drawn attention, which show that the poet detested his wife.

The known facts, too, all corroborate this inference: let us consider them a little. The first child was born within six months of the marriage; twins followed in 1585; a little later Shakespeare left Stratford not to return to it for eight or nine years, and when he did return there was probably no further intimacy with his wife; at any rate, there were no more children. Yet Shakespeare, one fancies, was fond of children. When his son Hamnet died his grief showed itself in his work – in *King John* and in *The Winter's Tale*. He was full of loving kindness to his daughters, too, in later life; it was his wife alone for whom he had no affection, no forgiveness.

There are other facts which establish this conclusion. While Shakespeare was in London he allowed his wife to suffer the extremes of poverty. Sometime between 1585 and 1595 she appears to have borrowed forty shillings from Thomas Whittington, who had formerly been her father's shepherd. The money was still unpaid when Whittington died, in 1601, and he directed his executor to recover the sum from the poet, and distribute it among the poor of Stratford. Now Shakespeare was rich when he returned to Stratford in 1595, and always generous. He paid off his father's heavy debts; how came it that he did not pay this trifling debt of his wife? The mere fact proves beyond doubt that Shakespeare disliked her and would have nothing to do with her.

Even towards the end of his life, when he was suffering from increasing weakness, which would have made most men sympathetic, even if it did not induce them completely to relent, Shakespeare shows the same aversion to his poor wife. In 1613, when on a short visit to London, he bought a house in Blackfriars for £140; in the purchase he barred his wife's dower, which proceeding seems even to Dryasdust 'pretty conclusive proof that he had the intention of excluding her from the enjoyment of his possessions after his death'.

In the first draft of his will Shakespeare did not mention his wife. The apologists explain this by saying that, of course, he had already given her all that she ought to have. But if he loved her he would have mentioned her with affection, if only to console her in her widowhood. Before the will was signed he inserted a bequest to her of his 'second-best bed', and the apologists have been at pains to explain that the best bed was kept for guests, and that Shakespeare willed to his wife the bed they both occupied. How inarticulate poor William Shakespeare must have become! Could the master of language find no better word than the contemptuous one? Had he said 'our bed' it would have been enough; 'the second-best bed' admits of but one interpretation. His daughters, who had lived with their mother, and who had not been afflicted by her jealousy and scolding tongue, begged the dying man to put in some mention of her, and he wrote in that 'second-best bed' – bitter to the last. If his own plain words and these inferences, drawn from indisputable facts, are not sufficient, then let us take one fact more, and consider its significance; one fact, so to speak, from the grave.

When Shakespeare died he left some lines to be placed over his tomb. Here they are:

Good friend for Jesus sake forbeare
To Digg the dust enclosed heare.
Blessed be ye man yt spares thes stones
And Curst be ye yt moves my bones.

Now, why did Shakespeare make this peculiar request? No one seems to have seen any meaning in it. It looks to me as if Shakespeare wrote the verses in order to prevent his wife being buried with him. He wanted to be free of her in death as in life. At any rate, the fact is that she was not buried with him, but apart from him; he had seen to that. His grave was never opened, though his wife expressed a desire to be buried with him. The man who needs further proofs would not be persuaded though one came from the dead to convince him.

The marriage was an unfortunate one for many reasons, as an enforced marriage is apt to be, even when it is not the marriage of a boy in his teens to a woman some eight years his senior. Shakespeare takes trouble to tell us in *The Comedy of Errors* that his wife was spitefully jealous, and a bitter scold. She must have injured him, poisoned his life with her jealous nagging, or Shakespeare would have forgiven her. There is some excuse for him, if excuse be needed. At the time the marriage must have seemed the wildest folly to him, seething as he was with inordinate conceit. He was wise beyond his years, and yet he had been forced to give hostages to fortune before he had any means of livelihood, before he had even found a place in life. What a position for a poet – penniless, saddled with a jealous wife and three children before he was twenty-one. And this poet was proud, and vain, and in love with all distinctions.

But why did Shakespeare nurse such persistent enmity all through his life to jealous, scolding Anne Hathaway? Shakespeare had wronged her; the keener his moral sense, the more certain he was to blame his partner in the fault, for in no other way could he excuse himself.

It was overpowering sensuality and rashness which had led Shakespeare into the noose, and now there was nothing for it but to cut the rope. He had either to be true to his higher nature or to the conventional view of his duty; he was true to himself and fled to London, and the world is the richer for his decision. The only excuse he ever made is to be found in the sonnet-line:

Love is too young to know what conscience is.

For my part I do not see that any excuse is needed: if Shakespeare had married Anne Whately he might never have gone to London or written a play. Shakespeare's hatred of his wife and his regret for having married her were alike foolish. Our brains are seldom the wisest part of us. It was well that he made love to Anne Hathaway; well, too, that he was forced to marry her; well, finally, that he should desert her. I am sorry he treated her badly and left her unsupplied with money; that was needlessly cruel; but it is just the kindliest men who have these extraordinary lapses; Shakespeare's loathing for his wife was measureless, was a part of his own self-esteem, and his self-esteem was founded on snobbish non-essentials for many years, if not, indeed, throughout his life.

There is a tradition preserved by Rowe that before going to London young Shakespeare taught school in the country; it may be; but he did not teach for long, we can be sure, and what he had to teach there were few scholars in the English country then or now capable of learning. Another tradition asserts that he obtained employment as a lawyer's clerk, probably because of the frequent use of legal phrases in his plays. But these apologists all forget that they are speaking of men like themselves, and of times like ours. Politics is the main theme of talk in our day; but in the time of Elizabeth it was rather dangerous to show one's wisdom by criticising the government: law was then the chief staple of conversation: every educated man was therefore familiar with law and its phraseology, as men are familiar in our day with the jargon of politics.

When did Shakespeare fly to London? Some say when he was twenty-one, as soon as his wife presented him with twins, in 1585. Others say as soon as Sir Thomas Lucy's persecution became intolerable. Both causes no doubt worked together, and yet another cause, given in *The Two Gentlemen of Verona*, was the real *causa causans*. Shakespeare was naturally ambitious; eager to measure himself with the best and try his powers. London was the arena where all great prizes were to be won: Shakespeare strained towards the Court like a greyhound in leash. But when did he go? Again in doubt I take the shepherd's words in *The Winter's Tale* as a guide. Most men would have said from fourteen to twenty was the dangerous age for a youth; but Shakespeare had perhaps a personal reason for the peculiar 'ten to twenty-three'. He was, no doubt, astoundingly precocious, and probably even at ten he had learned everything of value that the grammar school had to teach, and his thoughts had begun to play truant. Twenty-three, too, is a significant date in his life; in 1587, when he was twenty-three, two companies of actors, under the nominal patronage of the Queen and Lord Leicester, returned to London from a provincial tour, during which they visited Stratford. In Lord Leicester's company were Burbage and Heminge, with whom we know that Shakespeare was closely connected in later life. It seems to me probable that he returned with this company to London, and arrived in London, as he tells us in *The Comedy of Errors*, 'stiff and weary with long travel', and at once went out to view the town and 'peruse the traders'.

There is a tradition that when he came to London in 1587 he held horses outside the doors of the theatre. This story was first put about by the compiler of *The Lives of the Poets*, in 1753. According to the author the story was related by D'Avenant to Betterton; but Rowe, to whom Betterton must have told it, does not transmit it. Rowe was perhaps right to forget it or leave it out; though the story is not in itself incredible. Such work must have been infinitely distasteful to Shakespeare, but necessity is a hard master, and Greene, who talks of him later as 'Shake-scene', also speaks in the same connection of these 'grooms'. The curious amplified version of the story that Shakespeare organised a service of boys to hold the horses is hardly to be believed. The great Doctor was anything but a poet, or a good judge of the poetic temperament.

The Shakespeares of this world are not apt to take up menial employs, and this one had already shown that he preferred idle musings and parasitic dependence to uncongenial labour. Whoever reads the second scene of the second act of *The Comedy of Errors*, will see that Shakespeare, even at the beginning, had an uncommonly good opinion of himself. He plays gentleman from the first, and despises trade; he snubs his servant and will not brook familiarity from him. In *The Two Gentlemen of Verona*, he tells us that he left the country and came to London seeking 'honour', intending, no doubt, to make a name for himself by his writings. He had probably *Venus and Adonis* in his pocket when he first reached London. This would inspire a poet with the self-confidence which a well-filled purse lends to an ordinary man.

I am inclined to accept Rowe's statement that Shakespeare was received into an actor-company at first in a very mean rank. The parish clerk of Stratford at the end of the seventeenth century used to tell the visitors that Shakespeare entered the playhouse as a servitor; but, however he entered it, it is pretty certain he was not long in a subordinate position.

What manner of man was William Shakespeare when he first fronted life in London somewhere about 1587? Aubrey tells us that he was 'a handsome, well-shap't man, very good company, and of a very readie and pleasant smooth witt'. The bust of him in Stratford Church was coloured; it gave him light hazel eyes, and auburn hair and beard. Rowe says of him that 'besides the advantages of his witt, he was in himself a good-natured man, of too great sweetness in his manners, and a most agreeable companion'.

I picture him to myself very like Swinburne – of middle height or below it, inclined to be stout; the face well-featured, with forehead domed to reverence and quick, pointed chin; a face lighted with hazel-clear vivid eyes and charming with sensuous-full mobile lips that curve easily to kisses or gay ironic laughter; an exceedingly sensitive, eager speaking face that mirrors every fleeting change of emotion . . .

I can see him talking, talking with extreme fluency in a high tenor voice, the reddish hair flung back from the high forehead, the eyes now dancing, now aflame, every feature quick with the 'beating mind'.

And such talk – the groundwork of it, so to speak, very intimate-careless; but gemmed with thoughts, diamonded with wit, rhythmic with feeling: don't we know how it ran – 'A hundred and fifty tattered prodigals . . . No eye hath seen such scarecrows, . . . discarded, unjust serving-men, younger sons to younger brothers, revolted tapsters, and ostlers trade-fallen: the cankers of a calm world and a long peace'. And after the thought the humour again – 'food for powder, food for powder'.

Now let us consider some of his other qualities. In 1592 he published his *Venus and Adonis*, which he had no doubt written in 1587 or even earlier, for he called it 'the first heir of my invention' when he dedicated it to Lord Southampton. This work is to me extremely significant. It is all concerned with the wooing of young Adonis by Venus, an older woman. Now, goddesses have no age, nor do women, as a rule, woo in this sensual fashion. The peculiarities point to personal experience. 'I, too,' Shakespeare tells us practically, 'was wooed by an older woman against my will.' He seems to have wished the world to accept this version of his untimely marriage. Young Shakespeare in London was probably a little ashamed of being married to someone whom he could hardly introduce or avow. The apologists who declare that he made money very early in his career give us no explanation of the fact that he never brought his wife or children to London. Wherever we touch Shakespeare's intimate life, we find proof upon proof that he detested his wife and was glad to live without her.

Looked at in this light *Venus and Adonis* is not a very noble thing to have written; but I am dealing with a young poet's nature, and the majority of young poets would like to forget their Anne Hathaway if they could; or, to excuse themselves, would put the blame of an ill-sorted union upon the partner to it.

There is a certain weakness, however, shown in the whole story of his marriage; a weakness of character, as well as a weakness of *morale* which it is impossible to ignore; and there were other weaknesses in Shakespeare, especially a weakness of body which must necessarily have had its correlative delicacies of mind.

I have pointed out in the first part of this book that sleeplessness was a characteristic of Shakespeare, even in youth; he attributes it to Henry IV in old age, and to Henry V, a youth at the time, who probably never knew what a sleepless night meant. Shakespeare's *alter ego*, Valentine, in *The Two Gentlemen of Verona*, suffers from it, and so do Macbeth and Hamlet, and a dozen others of his chief characters, in particular his impersonations – all of which shows, I think, that from the beginning the mind of Shakespeare was too strong for his body. As we should say today, he was too emotional, and lived on his nerves. I always think of him as a ship over-engined; when the driving-power is working at full speed it shakes the ship to pieces.

One other weakness is marked in him, and that is that he could not drink, could not carry his liquor like a man – to use our accepted phrase. Hamlet thought drinking a custom more honoured in the breach than in the observance; Cassio, Shakespeare's incarnation in *Othello*, confessed that he had 'poor unhappy brains for drinking': tradition informs us that Shakespeare himself died of a 'feavour' from drinking – all of which confirms my opinion that Shakespeare was delicate rather than robust. He was, also, extraordinarily fastidious: in drama after drama he rails against the 'greasy' caps and 'stinking' breath of the common people. This overstrained disgust suggests to me a certain delicacy of constitution.

But there is still another indication of bodily weakness which in itself would be convincing to those accustomed to read closely; but which would carry little or no weight to the careless. In sonnet 129

Shakespeare tells us of lust and its effects, and the confession seems to me purely personal. Here are four lines of it:

> Enjoy'd no sooner but despised straight;
> Past reason hunted; and no sooner had,
> Past reason hated, as a swallowed bait,
> On purpose laid to make the taker mad.

Now, this is not the ordinary man's experience of passion and its effects. 'Past reason hunted', such an one might say, but he would certainly not go on 'No sooner had, Past reason hated'. He is not moved to hate by enjoyment, but to tenderness; it is your weakling who is physically exhausted by enjoyment who is moved to hatred. This sonnet was written by Shakespeare in the prime of manhood at thirty-four or thirty-five at latest.

Shakespeare was probably healthy as a young man, but intensely sensitive and highly strung; too finely constituted ever to have been strong. One notices that he takes no pleasure in fighting; his heroes are, of course, all 'valiant', but he shows no loving interest in the game of fighting as a game. In fact, we have already seen that he found no wonderful phrase for any of the manly virtues; he was a neuropath and a lover, and not a fighter, even in youth, or Fulk Sandells might have rued his interference.

The dominating facts to be kept ever in mind about Shakespeare are that he was delicate in body, and over-excitable; yielding and irresolute in character; with too great sweetness of manners and inordinately given to the pleasures of love.

How would such a man fare in the world of London in 1587? It was a wild and wilful age; eager English spirits were beginning to take a part in the opening up of the new world; the old, limiting horizons were gone; men dared to think for themselves and act boldly; ten years before Drake had sailed round the world – the adventurer was the characteristic product of the time. In ordinary company a word led to a blow, and the fight was often brought to a fatal conclusion with dagger or sword or both. In those rough days actors were almost outlaws; Ben Jonson is known to have killed two or three men; Marlowe died in a tavern brawl. Courage has always been highly esteemed in England, like gentility and a university training. Shakespeare possessed none of these passports to public favour. He could not shoulder his way through the throng. The wild adventurous life of the time was not to his liking, even in early manhood; from the beginning he preferred 'the life removed' and his books; all given over to the 'bettering of his mind' he could only have been appreciated at any time by the finer spirits.

Entering the theatre as a servitor he no doubt made such acquaintances as offered themselves, and spent a good deal of his leisure perforce with second-rate actors and writers in common taverns and studied his Bardolph and Pistol, and especially his Falstaff at first hand. Perhaps Marlowe was one of his *ciceroni* in rough company. Shakespeare had almost certainly met Marlowe very early in his career, for he worked with him in the *Third Part of Henry VI*, and his *Richard III* is a conscious imitation of Marlowe, and Marlowe was dissipated enough and wild enough to have shown him the wildest side of life in London in the 1580s. It was the very best thing that could have happened to delicate Shakespeare, to come poor and unknown to London, and be soused in common rowdy life like this against his will by sheer necessity; for if left to his own devices he would probably have grown up a bookish poet – a second Coleridge. Fate takes care of her favourites.

It was all in his favour that he should have been forced at first to win his spurs as an actor. He must have been too intelligent, one would think, ever to have brought it far as a mummer; he looked upon the half-art of acting with disdain and disgust, as he tells us in the sonnets, and if in Hamlet he condescends to give advice to actors, it is to admonish them not to outrage the decencies of nature by tearing a passion to tatters. He had at hand a surer ladder to fame than the mummer's art. As soon as he felt his feet in London he set to work adapting plays, and writing plays, while reading his own poetry to all and sundry who would listen, and I have no doubt that patrons of the stage, who were also men of rank, were willing to listen to Shakespeare from the beginning. He was of those who require no introductions.

In 1592, four or five years after his arrival in London, he had already come to the front as a dramatist, or at least as an adapter of plays, for Robert Greene, a scholar and playwright, attacked him in his *Groatsworth of Wit* in this fashion:

There is an upstart Crow, beautified in our feathers that, with his tiger's heart wrapt in a player's hide, supposes he is as well able to bombast out a blank verse as the best of you, and, being an absolute Johannes fac totum, is, in his own conceit, the only Shakescene in a country. Oh, that I might intreat your rare wits to be employed in more profitable courses, and let these apes imitate your past excellence, and never more acquaint them with your admired inventions.

It is plain from this weird appeal that Shakespeare had already made his mark.

There are further proofs of his rapid success. One of Chettle's references to Shakespeare (I take Chettle to be the original of Falstaff) throws light upon the poet's position in London in these early days. Shortly after Greene had insulted Shakespeare as 'Shake-scene' Chettle apologised for the insult in these terms:

I am as sorry [Chettle wrote] as if the original fault had beene my fault, because myselfe have seen his [i.e., Shakespeare's] demeanour no less civill than he [is] exelent in the qualitie he professes. Besides, divers of worship have reported his uprightnes of dealing, which argues his honesty, and his facetious grace in writing that aprooves his art.

In 1592, then, Shakespeare was most 'civill in demeanour', and had won golden opinions from people of importance.

Actors and poets of that time could not help knowing a good many of the young nobles who came to the theatre and sat round the stage listening to the performances. And Shakespeare, with his aristocratic sympathies and charming sweetness of nature, must have made friends with the greatest ease. Chettle's apology proves that early in his career he had the art or luck to win distinguished patrons who spoke well of him. While still new to town he came to know Lord Southampton, to whom he dedicated *Venus and Adonis*; the fulsome dedication of *Lucrece* to the same nobleman two years later shows that deference had rapidly ripened into affectionate devotion; no wonder Rowe noticed the 'too great sweetness in his manners'. Thinking of his intimacy with Southampton on the one hand and Bardolph on the other, one is constrained to say of Shakespeare what Apemantus says of Timon:

> The middle of humanity thou never knewest,
> But the extremity of both ends.

In the extremes characters show themselves more clearly than they do in the middle classes; at both ends of society speech and deed are unrestrained. Falstaff and Bardolph and the rest were free of convention by being below it, just as Bassanio and Mercutio were free because they were above it, and made the rules. The young lord did what he pleased, and spoke his mind as plainly as the footpad. Life at both ends was the very school for quick, sympathetic Shakespeare. But even in early manhood, as soon as he came to himself and found his work, one other quality is as plain in Shakespeare as even his humour – high impartial intellect with sincere ethical judgement. He judges even Falstaff severely, to the point of harshness, indeed; as he judged himself later in Enobarbus. This high critical faculty pervades all his work. But it must not be thought that his conduct was as scrupulous as his principles, or his will as sovereign as his intelligence. That he was a loose-liver while in London is well attested. Contemporary anecdotes generally hit off a man's peculiarities, and the only anecdote of Shakespeare that is known to have been told about him in his lifetime illustrates this master trait of his character. Burbage, we are told, when playing Richard III, arranged with a lady in the audience to visit her after the performance. Shakespeare overheard the rendezvous, anticipated his fellow's visit, and met Burbage on his arrival with the jibe that 'William the Conqueror came before Richard III.' The lightness is no doubt as characteristic of Shakespeare as the impudent humour.

There is another fact in Shakespeare's life which throws almost as much light on his character as his marriage. He seems to have come to riches very early and very easily. As we have seen, he was never able to paint a miser, which confirms Jonson's testimony that he was 'of an open and free nature'. In 1597 he went down to Stratford and bought New Place, then in ruinous condition, but the chief house in the town, for £60; he spent at least as much more between 1597 and 1599 in rebuilding the house and stocking the barns with grain. In 1602 we find that he purchased from William and John Combe, of Stratford, a hundred and seven acres of arable land near the town, for which he paid £320; in 1605, too, he bought for £440 a moiety of the tithes of Stratford for an unexpired term of thirty-one years, which investment seems to have brought him in little except a wearisome lawsuit.

Now, how did the poet obtain this thousand pounds or so? English apologists naturally assume that he was a 'good business man'; with delicious unconscious irony they one and all picture the man who hated tradesmen as himself a sort of thrifty tradesman-soul – a master of practical life who looked after the pennies from the beginning. These commentators all treat Shakespeare as the Hebrews treated God; they make him in their own likeness. In Shakespeare's case this practice leads to absurdity. Let us take the strongest advocate of the accepted view.

Dryasdust is at pains to prove that Shakespeare's emoluments, even as an actor in the 1590s, were not likely to have fallen below a hundred a year; but even Dryasdust admits that his large earnings came after 1599, from his shares in the Globe Theatre, and is inclined 'to accept the tradition that Shakespeare received from the Earl of Southampton a large gift of money'. As Southampton came of age in 1595, he may well out of his riches have helped the man who had dedicated his poems to him with servile adulation. Moreover, the statement is put forward by Rowe, who is certainly more trustworthy than the general run of gossip-mongers, and his account of the matter proves that he did not accept the story with eager credulity, but as one compelled by authority. Here is what he says:

> There is one story so singular in magnificence of this patron of Shakespeare that if I had not been assured that the story was handed down by Sir Wm. D'Avenant, who was probably very well acquainted with his affairs, I should not have ventured to insert that my lord Southampton, at one time, gave him a thousand pounds to enable him to go through with a purchase to which he heard he had a mind. A bounty very great, and very rare at any time, almost equal to that profuse generosity the present age has shown to French dancers and Italian Eunuchs.

It seems to me a great deal more likely that this munificent gift of Southampton was the source of Shakespeare's wealth than that he added coin to coin in saving, careful fashion. It may be said at once that all the evidence we have is in favour of Shakespeare's extravagance, and against his thrift. As we have seen, when studying *The Merchant of Venice*, the presumption is that he looked upon saving with contempt, and was himself freehanded to a fault. The Revd John Ward, who was Vicar of Stratford from 1648 to 1679, tells us 'that he spent at the rate of a thousand a year, as I have heard'.

It is impossible to deny that Shakespeare got rid of a great deal of money even after his retirement to Stratford; and men accustomed to save are not likely to become prodigal in old age.

On the 10th March, 1613, Shakespeare bought a house in Black-friars for £140; the next day he executed another deed, now in the British Museum, which stipulated that £60 of the purchase-money was to remain on mortgage until the following Michaelmas; the money was unpaid at Shakespeare's death, which seems to me to argue a certain carelessness, to say the least of it.

Dryasdust makes out that Shakespeare, in the years from 1600 to 1612, was earning about six hundred a year in the money of the period, or nearly five thousand a year of our money, and yet he was unable or unwilling to pay off a paltry £60.

After passing the last five years of his life in village Stratford, where he could not possibly have found many opportunities of extravagance, he was only able to leave a little more than one year's income. He willed New Place to his elder daughter, Susanna Hall, together with the land, barns, and gardens at and near Stratford (except the tenement in Chapel Lane), and the house in Blackfriars, London, all together equal, at the most, to five or six hundred pounds; and to his younger daughter, Judith, he bequeathed the tenement in Chapel Lane, £150 in money, and another £150 to be paid if she was alive three years after the date of the will. Nine hundred pounds, or so, of the money of the period, would cover all he possessed at death. When we consider these things, it becomes plain, I think, that Shakespeare was extravagant to lavishness even in cautious age. While in London he no doubt earned and was given large sums of money; but he was free-handed and careless, and died far poorer than one would have expected from an ordinarily thrifty man. The loose-liver is usually a spendthrift.

There are worse faults to be laid to his account than lechery and extravagance. Everyone who has read his works with any care must admit that Shakespeare was a snob of the purest English water. Aristocratic tastes were natural to him; inherent, indeed, in the delicate sensitiveness of his beauty-loving temperament; but he desired the outward and visible signs of gentility as much as any podgy millionaire of our time, and stooped as low to get them as man could stoop. In 1596, his young son, Hamnet, died at Stratford, and was buried on 11th August in the parish church. This event called Shakespeare back to his village, and while he was there he most probably paid his father's debts, and certainly tried to acquire for himself and his successors the position of gentlefolk. He induced his father to make application to the College of Heralds for a coat of arms, on the ground not only that his father was a man of substance, but that he had also married into a 'worshipful' family. The draft grant of arms was not executed at the time. It may have been that the father's pecuniary position became known to the College, or perhaps the profession of the son created difficulties; but in any case nothing was done for some time. In 1597, however, the Earl of Essex became Earl Marshal and Chief of the

Heralds' College, and the scholar and antiquary, William Camden, joined the College as Clarenceux King of Arms. Shakespeare must have been known to the Earl of Essex, who was an intimate friend of the Earl of Southampton; he was indeed almost certainly a friend and admirer of Essex. The Shakespeares' second application to be admitted to the status of gentlefolk took a new form. They asserted roundly that the coat as set out in the draft of 1596 had been assigned to John Shakespeare while he was bailiff, and the heralds were asked to give him a 'recognition' of it. At the same time John Shakespeare asked for permission to quarter on his 'ancient coat of arms' that of the Ardens of Wilmscote, his wife's family. But this was going too far, even for a friend of Essex. To grant such a request might have got the College into trouble with the influential Warwickshire family of Arden, and so it was refused; but the grant was 'recognised', and Shakespeare's peculiar ambition was satisfied.

Every single incident in his life bears out what we have learned from his works. In all his writings he praises lords and gentlemen, and runs down the citizens and common people, and in his life he spent some years, a good deal of trouble, and many impudent lies in getting for his father a grant of arms and recognition as a gentleman – a very pitiful ambition, but peculiarly English. Shakespeare, one fancies, was a gentleman by nature, and a good deal more.

But his snobbishness had other worse results. Partly because of it he never got to know the middle classes in England. True, even in his time they were excessively Puritanical, which quality hedged them off, so to speak, from the playwright-poet. With his usual gentleness or timidity, Shakespeare never tells us directly what he thought of the Puritans, but his half-averted, contemptuous glance at them in passing, is very significant. Angelo, the would-be Puritan ruler, was a 'false seemer', Malvolio was a 'chough'. The peculiar virtues of the English middle class, its courage and sheepishness; its good conduct and respect for duties; its religious sense and cocksure narrow-mindedness, held no attraction for Shakespeare, and, armoured in snobbishness, he utterly missed what a knowledge of the middle classes might have given him.

Let us take one instance of his loss. Though he lived in an age of fanaticism, he never drew a fanatic or reformer, never conceived a man as swimming against the stream of his time. He had but a vague conception of the few spirits in each age who lead humanity to new and higher ideals; he could not understand a Christ or a Muhammad, and it seems as if he took but small interest in Jeanne d'Arc, the noblest being that came within the ken of his art. For even if we admit that he did not write the first part of *Henry VI*, it is certain that it passed through his hands, and that in his youth, at any rate, he saw nothing to correct in that vile and stupid libel on the greatest of women. Even the English fanatic escaped his intelligence; his Jack Cade, as I have already noticed, is a wretched caricature; no Cade moves his fellows save by appealing to the best in them, to their sense of justice, or what they take for justice. The Cade who will wheedle men for his own gross ambitions may make a few dupes, but not thousands of devoted followers. These elementary truths Shakespeare never understood. Yet how much greater he would have been had he understood them; had he studied even one Puritan lovingly and depicted him sympathetically. For the fanatic is one of the hinges which swing the door of the modern world. Shakespeare's 'universal sympathy' – to quote Coleridge – did not include the plainly-clad tub-thumper who dared to accuse him to his face of serving the Babylonish Whore. Shakespeare sneered at the Puritan instead of studying him; with the result that he belongs rather to the Renaissance than to the modern world, in spite even of his Hamlet. The best of a Wordsworth or a Turgenev is outside him; he would never have understood a Marianna or a Bazarof, and the noble faith of the sonnet to 'Toussaint l'Ouverture' was quite beyond him. He could never have written:

> Thou hast left behind
> Powers that will work for thee, air, earth and skies;
> There's not a breathing of the common wind
> That will forget thee; thou hast great allies;
> Thy friends are exultations, agonies,
> And love, and man's unconquerable mind.

It is time to speak of him frankly; he was gentle, and witty; gay, and sweet-mannered, very studious, too, and fair of mind; but at the same time he was weak in body and irresolute, hasty and wordy, and took habitually the easiest way out of difficulties; he was ill-endowed in the virile virtues and virile vices. When he showed arrogance it was always of intellect and not of character; he was a parasite by nature. But none of these faults would have brought him to ruin; he was snared again in full manhood by his master-quality, his overpowering sensuality, and thrown in the mire.

15
Shakespeare's Life – Part Two

Shakespeare's life seems to fall sharply into two halves. Till he met Mistress Fitton, about 1597, he must have been happy and well content, I think, in spite of his deep underlying melancholy. According to my reckoning he had been in London about ten years, and no man has ever done so much in the time and been so successful even as the world counts success. He had not only written the early poems and the early plays, but in the last three or four years half a dozen masterpieces: *A Midsummer's Night's Dream*, *Romeo and Juliet*, *Richard II*, *King John*, *The Merchant of Venice*, *The Two Parts of Henry IV*. At thirty-three he was already the greatest poet and dramatist of whom Time holds any record.

Southampton's bounty had given him ease, and allowed him to discharge his father's debts, and place his dearly loved mother in a position of comfort in the best house in Stratford.

He had troops of friends, we may be sure, for there was no gentler, gayer, kindlier creature in all London, and he set store by friendship. Ten years before he had neither money, place, nor position; now he had all these, and was known even at Court. The Queen had been kind to him. He ended the epilogue to the *Second Part of Henry IV*, which he had just finished, by kneeling 'to pray for the Queen'. Essex or Southampton had no doubt brought his work to Elizabeth's notice: she had approved his 'Falstaff' and encouraged him to continue. Of all his successes, this royal recognition was surely the one which pleased him most. He was at the topmost height of happy hours when he met the woman who was to change the world for him.

In the lives of great men the typical tragedies are likely to repeat themselves. Socrates was condemned to drain many a poisoned cup before he was given the bowl of hemlock: Shakespeare had come to grief with many women before he fell with Mary Fitton. It was his ungovernable sensuality which drove him in youth to his untimely and unhappy marriage; it was his ungovernable sensuality, too, which in his maturity led him to worship Mary Fitton, and threw him into those twelve years of bondage to earthy, coarse service which he regretted so bitterly when the passion-fever had burned itself out.

One can easily guess how he came to know the self-willed and wild-living maid-of-honour. Like many of the courtiers, Mistress Fitton affected the society of the players. Kemp, the clown of his company, knew her, and dedicated a book to her rather familiarly. I have always thought that Shakespeare resented Kemp's intimacy with Mistress Fitton, for when Hamlet advises the players to prevent the clown from gagging, he adds, with a snarl of personal spite:

> a most pitiful ambition in the fool that uses it.

Mary Fitton's position, her proud, dark beauty, her daring of speech and deed took Shakespeare by storm. She was his complement in every failing; her strength matched his weakness; her resolution his hesitation, her boldness his timidity; besides, she was of rank and place, and out of pure snobbery he felt himself her inferior. He forgot that humble worship was not the way to win a high-spirited girl. He loved her so abjectly that he lost her; and it was undoubtedly his overpowering sensuality and snobbishness which brought him to his knees, and his love to ruin. He could not even keep her after winning her; desire blinded him. He would not see that Mary Fitton was not a wanton through mere lust. As soon as her fancy was touched she gave herself; but she was true to the new lover for the time. We know that she bore a son to Pembroke and two illegitimate daughters to Sir Richard Leveson. Her slips with these men wounded Shakespeare's vanity, and he persisted in underrating her. Let us probe to the root of the secret sore. Here is a page of *Troilus and Cressida*, a page from that terrible fourth scene of the fourth act, when Troilus, having to part from Cressida, warns her against the Greeks and their proficience in the arts of love:

TROILUS   I cannot sing
        Nor heel the high lavolt, nor sweeten talk,
        Nor play at subtle games; fair virtues all,
        To which the Grecians are most prompt and pregnant:
        But I can tell thee in each grace of these
        There lurks a still and dumb-discoursive devil
        That tempts most cunningly: but be not tempted.

CRESSIDA Do you think I will?
TROILUS *No: but something may be done that we will not.*

The first lines show that poor Shakespeare often felt out of it at Court. The suggestion, I have put in italics, is unspeakable. Shakespeare made use of every sensual bait in hope of winning his love, liming himself and not the woman. His vanity was so inordinate that instead of saying to himself, 'it's natural that a high-born girl of nineteen should prefer a great lord of her own age to a poor poet of thirty-four': he strives to persuade himself and us that Mary Fitton was won away from him by 'subtle games', and in his rage of wounded vanity he wrote that tremendous libel on her, which he put in the mouth of Ulysses:

> Fie, fie upon her!
> There's language in her eye, her cheek, her lip,
> Nay, her foot speaks; her wanton spirits look out
> At every joint and motive of her body.
> O, these encounterers, so glib of tongue,
> That give accosting welcome ere it comes,
> And wide unclasp the tables of their thoughts
> To every ticklish reader! set them down
> For sluttish spoils of opportunity
> And daughters of the game.

His tortured sensuality caricatures her: that 'ticklish reader' reveals him. Mary Fitton was finer than his portraits; we want her soul, and do not get it even in Cleopatra. It was the consciousness of his own age and physical inferiority that drove him to jealous denigration of his mistress.

Mary Fitton did not beguile Shakespeare to 'the very heart of loss', as he cried; but to the innermost shrine of the temple of Fame. It was his absolute abandonment to passion which made Shakespeare the supreme poet. If it had not been for his excessive sensuality, and his mad passion for his 'gypsy', we should never have had from him *Hamlet*, *Macbeth*, *Othello*, *Antony and Cleopatra*, or *Lear*. He would still have been a poet and a dramatic writer of the first rank; but he would not have stood alone above all others: he would not have been Shakespeare.

His passion for Mary Fitton lasted some twelve years. Again and again he lived golden hours with her like those Cleopatra boasted of and regretted. Life is wasted quickly in such orgasms of passion; lust whipped to madness by jealousy. Mary Fitton was the only woman

Shakespeare ever loved, or at least, the only woman he loved with such intensity as to influence his art. She was Rosaline, Cressid, Cleopatra, and the 'dark lady' of the sonnets. All his other women are parts of her or reflections of her, as all his heroes are sides of Hamlet, or reflections of him. Portia is the first full-length sketch of Mary Fitton, taken at a distance: Beatrice and Rosalind are mere reflections of her high spirits, her aristocratic pride and charm: her strength and resolution are incarnate in Lady Macbeth. Ophelia, Desdemona, Cordelia, are but abstract longings for purity and constancy called into life by his mistress's faithlessness and passion.

Shakespeare admired Mary Fitton as intensely as he desired her, yet he could not be faithful to her for the dozen years his passion lasted. Love and her soft hours drew him irresistibly again and again: he was the ready spoil of opportunity. Here is one instance: it was his custom, Aubrey tells us, to visit Stratford every year, probably every summer: on his way he was accustomed to put up at an inn in Oxford, kept by John D'Avenant. Mrs D'Avenant, we are told, was 'a very beautiful woman, and of a very good witt and of conversation extremely agreeable'. No doubt Shakespeare made up to her from the first. Her second son, William, who afterwards became the celebrated playwright, was born in March, 1605, and according to a tradition long current in Oxford, Shakespeare was his father. In later life Sir William D'Avenant himself was 'contented enough to be thought his (Shakespeare's) son'. There is every reason to accept the story as it has been handed down. Shakespeare, as Troilus, brags of his constancy; talks of himself as 'plain and true'; but it was all boasting: from eighteen to forty-five he was as inconstant as the wind, and gave himself to all the 'subtle games' of love with absolute abandonment, till his health broke under the strain.

In several of the Sonnets, notably in 36 and 37, Shakespeare tells us that he was 'poor and despised . . . made lame by fortune's dearest spite'. He will not even have his friend's name coupled with his for fear lest his 'bewailed guilt' should do him shame:

> Let me confess that we two must be twain,
> Although our undivided loves are one:
> So shall those blots that do with me remain
> Without thy help, by me be borne alone . . .

Spalding and other critics believe that this 'guilt' of Shakespeare refers to his profession as an actor, but that stain should not have prevented Lord Herbert from honouring him with 'public kindness'. It is clear, I think, from the words themselves, that the guilt refers to the fact that both Herbert and he were in love with the same woman. Jonson, as we have seen, had poked fun at their connection, and this is how Shakespeare tries to take the sting out of the sneer.

Shakespeare had many of the weaknesses of the neurotic and artistic temperament, but he had assuredly the noblest virtues of it: he was true to his friends, and more than generous to their merits.

If his ethical conscience was faulty, his aesthetical conscience was of the very highest. Whenever we find him in close relations with his contemporaries we are struck with his kindness and high impartial intelligence. Were they his rivals, he found the perfect word for their merits and shortcomings. How can one better praise Chapman than by talking of 'The proud full sail of his great verse'? How can one touch his defect more lightly than by hinting that his learning needed feathers to lift it from the ground? And if Shakespeare was fair even to his rivals, his friends could always reckon on his goodwill and his unwearied service. All his fine qualities came out when as an elder he met churlish Ben Jonson. Jonson did not influence him as much as Marlowe had influenced him; but these were the two greatest of living men with whom he was brought into close contact, and his relations with Jonson show him as in a glass. Rowe has a characteristic story which must not be forgotten:

His acquaintance with Ben Jonson began with a remarkable piece of humanity and good-nature; Mr Jonson, who was at that time altogether unknown, had offered one of his playes to the Players, in order to have it acted; but the persons into whose hands it was put, after having turned it carelessly and superciliously over, were just upon returning it to him, with an ill-natured answer, that it would be of no service to their company, when Shakespeare luckily cast his eye upon it, and found something so well in it as to encourage him to read through and afterwards to recommend Ben Jonson and his writings to the publick. After this they were professed friends; though I don't know whether the other ever made him an equal return of gentleness and sincerity. Ben was naturally proud and indolent, and in the days of his reputation did so far take upon him the premier in witt that he could not but look with an evil eye upon anyone that seemed to stand in competition with him. And if at times he has affected to commend him, it has always been with some reserve, insinuating his incorrectness, a careless manner of writing and a want of judgement; the praise of seldom altering or blotting out what he writt which was given him by the players over the first publish of his works after his death was what Jonson could not bear . . .

The story reads exactly like the story of Goethe and Schiller. It was Schiller who held aloof and was full of fault-finding criticism: it was Goethe who made all the advances and did all the kindnesses. It was Goethe who obtained for Schiller that place as professor of history at Jena which gave Schiller the leisure needed for his dramatic work. It is always the greater who gives and forgives.

I believe, of course, too, in the traditional account of the unforgettable evenings at the Mermaid. 'Many were the wit-combats', wrote Fuller of Shakespeare in his *Worthies* (1662),

betwixt him and Ben Jonson, which too I behold like a Spanish great galleon and an English man of war. Master Jonson (like the former) was built far higher in learning, solid but slow in his performances. Shakespeare, with the English man-of-war, lesser in bulk, but lighter in sailing, could turn with all sides, tack about, and take advantage of all winds by the quickness of his wit and invention.

It was natural for the onlooker to compare Ben Jonson and his 'mountainous belly' to some Spanish galleon, and Shakespeare, with his quicker wit, to the more active English ship. It was Jonson's great size – a quality which has always been too highly esteemed in England – his domineering temper and desperate personal courage that induced the gossip to even him with Shakespeare.

Beaumont described these meetings, too, in his poetical letter to his friend Jonson:

> What things have we seen
> Done at the Mermaid? Heard words that have been
> So nimble and so full of subtle flame,
> As if that everyone from whence they came
> Had meant to put his whole wit in a jest,
> And had resolved to live a fool the rest
> Of his dull life.

In one respect at least the two men were antitheses. Jonson was exceedingly combative and quarrelsome, and seems to have taken a chief part in all the bitter disputes of his time between actors and men of letters. He killed one actor in a duel and attacked Marston and Dekker in *The Poetaster*; they replied to him in the *Satiromastix*. More than once he criticised Shakespeare's writings; more than once jibed at Shakespeare, unfairly trying to wound him; but Shakespeare would not retort. It is to Jonson's credit that though he found fault with Shakespeare's *Julius Caesar* and *Pericles*, he yet wrote of him in the *Poetaster* as a peacemaker, and, under the name of Virgil, honoured him as the greatest master of poetry.

Tradition gives us one witty story about the relations between the pair which seems to me extraordinarily characteristic. Shakespeare was godfather to one of Ben's children, and after the christening, being in a deep study, Jonson came to cheer him up, and asked him why he was so melancholy. 'No, faith, Ben,' says he; 'not I, but I have been considering a great while what should be the fittest gift for me to bestow upon my godchild and I have resolved at last.' 'I pr'ythee, what?' sayes he. 'I'faith, Ben, I'll e'en give him a dozen good Lattin spoons, and thou shalt translate them.' Lattin, as everybody knows, was a mixed metal resembling brass: the play upon words and sly fun poked at Jonson's scholarship are in Shakespeare's best manner. The story must be regarded as Shakespeare's answer to Jonson's sneer that he had 'little Latine and lesse Greeke'.

Through the mist of tradition and more or less uncertain references in his poetry, one sees that he had come, probably through Southampton, to admire Essex, and the fall and execution of Essex had an immense effect upon him. It is certain, I think, that the noble speech on mercy put into Portia's mouth in *The Merchant of Venice*, was primarily an appeal to Elizabeth for Essex or for Southampton. It is plainly addressed to the Queen, and not to a Jew pariah:

> ... It becomes
> The throned monarch better than his crown;
> His sceptre shows the force of temporal power,
> The attribute to awe and majesty,
> Wherein doth sit the dread and fear of kings;
> But mercy is above this scepter'd sway,
> It is enthroned in the heart of kings.

It is an attribute of God Himself,
And earthly power doth then show likest God's,
When Mercy seasons Justice.

All this must have seemed the veriest irony when addressed to an outcast Jew. It was clearly intended as an appeal to Elizabeth, and shows how far gentle Shakespeare would venture in defence of a friend. Like a woman, he gained a certain courage through his affections.

I feel convinced that he resented the condemnation of Essex and the imprisonment of Southampton very bitterly, for though he had praised Elizabeth in his salad days again and again, talked about her in *A Midsummer Night's Dream* as a 'fair vestal throned by the west'; walking in 'maiden meditation, fancy-free'; yet, when she died, he could not be induced to write one word about her. His silence was noticed, and Chettle challenged him to write in praise of the dead sovereign, because she had been kind to him; but he would not: he had come to realise the harsh nature of Elizabeth, and he detested her ruthless cruelties. Like a woman, he found it difficult to forgive one who had injured those he loved.

Now that I have discussed at some length Shakespeare's character, its powers and its weaknesses, let us for a moment consider his intellect. All sorts and conditions of men talk of it in superlatives; but that does not help us much. It is as easy to sit in Shakespeare's brain and think from there, as it is from Balzac's. If we have read Shakespeare rightly, his intelligence was peculiarly self-centred; he was wise mainly through self-knowledge, and not, as is commonly supposed, through knowledge of others and observation; he was assuredly anything but worldly-wise. Take one little point. In nearly every play he discovers an intense love of music and of flowers; but he never tells you anything about the music he loves, and he only mentions a dozen flowers in all his works. True, he finds exquisite phrases for his favourites; but he only seems to have noticed or known the commonest. His knowledge of birds and beasts is similarly limited. But when Bacon praises flowers he shows at once the naturalist's gift of observation; he mentions hundreds of different kinds, enumerating them month by month; in April alone he names as many as Shakespeare has mentioned in all his writings. He used his eyes to study things outside himself, and memory to recall them; but Shakespeare's eyes were turned inward; he knew little of the world outside himself.

Shakespeare's knowledge of men and women has been overrated.

With all his sensuality he only knew one woman, Mary Fitton, though he knew her in every mood, and only one man, himself, profoundly apprehended in every accident and moment of growth.

He could not construct plays or invent stories, though he selected good ones with considerable certainty. He often enriched the characters, seldom or never the incidents; even the characters he creates are usually sides of himself, or humorous masks without a soul. He must have heard of the statesman Burleigh often enough; but nowhere does he portray him; no hint in his works of Drake, or Raleigh, or Elizabeth, or Sidney. He has no care either for novelties; he never mentions forks or even tobacco or potatoes. A student by nature if ever there was one, all intent, as he tells us, on bettering his mind, he passes through Oxford a hundred times and never even mentions the schools: Oxford men had disgusted him with their *alma mater*.

The utmost reach of this self-student is extraordinary; the main puzzle of life is hidden from us as from him; but his word on it is deeper than any of ours, though we have had three centuries in which to climb above him.

> Men must abide
> Their going hence even as their coming hither.
> Ripeness is all.

And if it be said that the men of the Renaissance occupied themselves more with such questions than we do, and therefore show better in relation to them, let us take another phrase which has always seemed to me of extraordinary insight. Antony has beaten Caesar, and returns to Cleopatra, who greets him with the astounding words:

> Lord of lords,
> O, infinite virtue, com'st thou smiling from
> The world's great snare uncaught?

This is all more or less appropriate in the mouth of Cleopatra; but it is to me Shakespeare's own comment on life; he is conscious of his failure; he has said to himself: 'if I, Shakespeare, have failed, it is because everyone fails; life's handicap searches out every weakness; to go through life as a conqueror would require "infinite virtue"'. This is perhaps the furthest throw of Shakespeare's thought.

But his worldly wisdom is to seek. After he had been betrayed by Lord Herbert he raves of man's ingratitude, in play after play. Of course men are ungrateful; it is only the rarest and noblest natures who can feel thankful for help without any injury to vanity. The majority of men love their inferiors, those whom they help; to give flatters self-esteem; but they hate their superiors, and lend to the word 'patron' an intolerable smirk of condescension. Shakespeare should have understood that at thirty.

When his vanity was injured, his blindness was almost inconceivable. He should have seen Mary Fitton as she was and given us a deathless-true portrait of her; but the noble side of her, the soul-side a lover should have cherished, is not even suggested. He deserved to lose her, seeking only the common, careless of the 'silent, silver lights' she could have shown him. He was just as blind with his wife; she had been unwillingly the ladder to his advancement; he should have forgiven her on that ground, if not on a higher.

He was inordinately vain and self-centred. He talked incontinently, as he himself assures us, and as Ben Jonson complains. He was exceedingly quick and witty and impatient. His language shows his speed of thought; again and again the images tumble over each other, and the mere music of his verse is breathlessly rapid, just as the movement of Tennyson's verse is extremely slow.

More than once in his works I have shown how, at the crisis of fate, he jumps to conclusions like a woman. He seems often to have realised the faults of his own haste. His Othello says:

> How poor are they that have not patience.

With this speed of thought and wealth of language and of wit, he naturally loved to show off in conversation; but as he wished to get on and make a figure in the world, he should have talked less and encouraged his patrons to show off. Poor heedless, witty, charming Shakespeare! One threat which he used again and again, discovers all his world-blindness to me. Gravely, in sonnet 140, he warns Mary Fitton that she had better not provoke him or he will write the truth about her – just as if the maid of honour who could bear bastard after bastard, while living at court, cared one straw what poor Shakespeare might say or write or sing of her. And Hamlet runs to the same weapon: he praises the players to Polonius as

> Brief chronicles of the time; after your death you were better have a bad epitaph than their ill report while you live.

It is all untrue; actors were then, as now, only mummers without judgement. Shakespeare was thinking of himself, the dramatist-poet, who was indeed a chronicle of the time; but the courtier Lord Polonius would not care a dam for a rhymester's praise or blame. Posthumus, too, will write against the wantons he dislikes. Shakespeare's weapon of offence was his pen; but though he threatened, he seldom used it maliciously; he was indeed a 'harmless opposite', too full of the milk of human kindness to do injury to any man. But these instances of mis-apprehension in the simple things of life, show us that gentle Shakespeare is no trustworthy guide through this rough all-hating world. The time has now come for me to consider how Shakespeare was treated by the men of his own time, and how this treatment affected his character. The commentators, of course, all present him as walking through life as a sort of uncrowned king, feted and reverenced on all sides during his residence in London, and in the fullness of years and honours retiring to Stratford to live out the remainder of his days in the bosom of his family as 'a prosperous country gentleman', to use Dowden's unhappy phrase. As I have already shown, his works give the lie to this flattering fiction, which in all parts is of course absolutely incredible. It is your Tennyson, who is of his time and in perfect sympathy with it; Tennyson, with his May Queens, prig heroes and syrupy creed, who passes through life as a conqueror, and after death is borne in state to rest in the great Abbey.

The Shakespeares, not being of an age, but for all time, have another guess sort of reception. From the moment young Will came to London, he was treated as an upstart, without gentle birth or college training: to Greene he was 'Maister of Artes in Neither University'. He won through, and did his work; but he never could take root in life; his children perished out of the land. He was in high company on sufferance. On the stage he met the highest, Essex, Pembroke, South-ampton, on terms of equality; but at court he stood among the menials and was despitefully treated. Let no one misunderstand me: I should delight in painting the other picture if there were any truth in it: I should have joyed in showing how the English aristocracy for this once threw off their senseless pride and hailed the greatest of men at least as an equal. Frederick the Great would have done this, for he put Voltaire at his own table, and told his astonished chamberlains that 'privileged spirits rank with sovereigns'. Such wisdom was altogether above the English aristocracy of that or any time. Yet they might have risen above the common in this one instance. For Shakespeare had not only supreme genius to commend him, but all the graces of manner, all the sweetness of disposition, all the exquisite courtesies of speech that go to ensure social success. His imperial intelligence, however, was too heavy a handicap. Men resent superiority at all times, and there is nothing your aristocrat so much dislikes as intellectual superiority, and especially intellect that is not hallmarked and accredited: the Southamptons and the Pembrokes must have found Shakespeare's insight and impartiality intolerable. It was Ben Jonson whom Pembroke made Poet Laureate; it was Chapman the learned, and not Shakespeare, who was regarded with reverence. How could these gentlemen appreciate Shakespeare when it was his *Venus and Adonis* and his *Lucrece* that they chiefly admired. *Venus and Adonis* went through seven editions in Shakespeare's lifetime, while *Othello* was not thought worthy of type till the author had been dead six years.

But badly as the aristocrats treated Shakespeare they yet treated him better than any other class. The shopkeepers in England are infinitely further removed from art or poetry than the nobles; now as in the time of Elizabeth they care infinitely more for beef and beer and broadcloth than for any spiritual enjoyment; while the masses of the people prefer a dog-fight to any masterpiece in art or letters.

Some will say that Shakespeare was perhaps condemned for dissolute living, and did not come to honour because of his shortcomings in character. Such a judgement misapprehends life altogether. Had Shakespeare's character been as high as his intellect he would not have been left contemptuously on one side; he would have been hated and persecuted, pilloried or thrown into prison as Bunyan was. It was his dissolute life that commended him to the liking of the loose-living Pembroke and Essex. Pembroke, we know from Clarendon, was 'immoderately given to women'. Four maids of honour, we learn, were *enceintes* to Essex at the same time. Shakespeare was hardly as dissolute as his noble patrons. The truth was they could not understand his genius; they had no measure wherewith to measure it, for no one can see above his own head; and so they treated him with much the same condescending familiarity that nobles nowadays show to a tenor or a ballet dancer. In March, 1604, after he had written *Hamlet* and *Macbeth*, Shakespeare and some other actors walked from the Tower of London to Westminster in the procession which accompanied King James on his formal entry into London. Each of the actors received four and a half yards of scarlet cloth to wear as a cloak on the occasion. The scarlet cloak to Shakespeare must have been a sort of Nessus' shirt, or crown of thorns – the livery of derision.

Shakespeare, who measured both enemies and friends fairly, measured himself fairly, too. He usually praises his impersonations: Hamlet is 'a noble heart', Brutus 'the noblest Roman of them all'; and speaking directly he said of himself in a sonnet:

> I am that I am, and they that level
> At my abuses reckon up their own;
> I may be straight though they themselves be bevel.

He knew his own greatness, none better, and as soon as he reached middle age and began to take stock of himself, he must have felt bitterly that he, the best mind in the world, had not brought it far in the ordinary estimation of men. No wonder he showed passionate sympathy with all those who had failed in life; he could identify himself with Brutus and Antony, and not with the Caesars.

Shakespeare's view of England and of Englishmen was naturally affected by their treatment of him. He is continually spoken of as patriotic, and it is true that he started in youth with an almost lyrical love of country. His words in *Richard II* are often quoted; but they were written before he had any experience or knowledge of men.

> GAUNT This royal throne of kings, this scepter'd isle,
> [. . .]
> This happy breed of men, this little world;
> This precious stone set in the silver sea,
> Which serves it in the office of a wall,
> Or as a moat, defensive to a house,
> Against the envy of less happier lands;
> This blessed plot, this earth, this realm, this England.

The apologists who rejoice in his patriotism never realise that Shakespeare did not hold the same opinions throughout his life; as he grew and developed, his opinions developed with him. In *The Merchant of Venice* we find that he has already come to saner vision; when Portia and Nerissa talk of the English suitor, Portia says:

You know I say nothing to him; for he understands not me, nor I him: he hath neither Latin, French, nor Italian; and you will come

into the court and swear that I have a poor pennyworth in the
Englishman. He is a proper man's picture; but, alas, who can converse
with a dumb show? How oddly he is suited! I think he bought his
doublet in Italy, his round hose in France, his bonnet in Germany,
and his behaviour everywhere.

What super-excellent criticism it all is; true, now as then, 'a proper
man's picture but . . . a dumb show'. It proves conclusively that Shakespeare was able to see around and over the young English noble of his
day. From this time on I find no praise of England or of Englishmen in
any of his works, except *Henry V*, which was manifestly written to catch
applause on account of its jingoism. In his maturity Shakespeare saw his
countrymen as they were, and mentioned them chiefly to blame their
love of drinking. Imogen says:

> Hath Britain all the sun that shines? Day, night,
> Are they not but in Britain?
>   . . . prithee, think
> There's livers out of Britain.

Whoever reads *Coriolanus* carefully will see how Shakespeare loathed
the common Englishman; there can be no doubt at all that he in-
corporated his dislike of him once for all in Caliban. The qualities he
lends Caliban are all characteristic. Whoever will give him drink is to
Caliban a god. The brutish creature would violate and degrade art
without a scruple, and the soul of him is given in the phrase that if he
got the chance he would people the world with Calibans. Sometimes
one thinks that if Shakespeare were living today he would be inclined to
say that his prediction had come true.

One could have guessed without proof that in the course of his life
Shakespeare, like Goethe, would rise above that parochial vanity which
is so much belauded as patriotism. He was in love with the ideal and
would not confine it to any country.

There is little to tell of his life after he met Mary Fitton, or rather the
history of his life afterwards is the history of his passion and jealousy
and madness as he himself has told it in the great tragedies. He appears
to have grown fat and scant of breath when he was about thirty-six or
seven. In 1608 his mother died, and *Coriolanus* was written as a sort of
monument to the memory of 'the noblest mother in the world'. His
intimacy with Mary Fitton lasted, I feel sure, up to his breakdown in

1608 or thereabouts, and was probably the chief cause of his infirmity and untimely death.

It only remains for me now to say a word or two about the end of his life. Rowe says that 'the latter part of his life was spent as all men of good sense will that theirs may be, in ease, retirement, and the conversation of his friends. He had the good fortune to gather an estate equal to his occasion, and, in that, to his wish, and is said to have spent some years before his death at his native Stratford.' Rowe, too, tells us that it is a story 'well remembered in that country, that he had a particular intimacy with Mr Combe, an old gentleman noted thereabouts for his wealth and usury; it happened that in a pleasant conversation amongst their common friends Mr Combe told Shakespeare, in a laughing manner, that he fancied he intended to write his epitaph, if he happened to outlive him; and since he did not know what might be said of him when he was dead, he desired it might be done immediately; upon which Shakespeare gave him these four verses:

> Ten in the Hundred lies here ingrav'd
> 'Tis a Hundred to Ten his soul is not sav'd:
> If any Man ask, "Who lies in this tomb",
> Oh! ho! quoth the Devil, 'tis my John-a-Combe.

But the sharpness of the Satyr is said to have stung the man so severely that he never forgave him.'

I have given all this because I want the reader to have the sources before him, and because the contempt of tradesman-gain and usury, even at the very end, is so characteristic.

It appears, too, from the Stratford records, and is therefore certain, that as early as the year 1614 a preacher was entertained at New Place – 'Item, one quart of sack, and one quart of claret wine, given to a preacher at the New Place, twenty pence.' The Reverend John Ward, who was vicar of Stratford, in a manuscript memorandum book written in the year 1664, asserts that 'Shakespeare, Drayton and Ben Jhonson had a merie meeting, and itt seems drank too hard, for Shakespeare died of a feavour there contracted.'

Shakespeare, as we have seen from *The Tempest*, retired to Stratford – 'where every third thought shall be my grave' – in broken health and in a mood of despairing penitence. I do not suppose the mood lasted long; but the ill-health and persistent weakness explain to me as nothing else could his retirement to Stratford. It is incredible to me that Shakespeare should leave London at forty-seven or forty-eight years of age, in good health, and retire to Stratford to live as a 'prosperous country gentleman'! What had Stratford to offer Shakespeare – village Stratford with a midden in the chief street and the charms of the village usurer's companionship tempered by the ministrations of a wandering tub-thumper?

There is abundant evidence, even in *The Winter's Tale* and *Cymbeline*, to prove that the storm which wrecked Shakespeare's life had not blown itself out even when these last works were written in 1611–12; the jealousy of Leontes is as wild and sensual as the jealousy of Othello; the attitude of Posthumus towards women as bitter as anything to be found in *Troilus and Cressida*:

> Could I find out
> The woman's part in me! For there's no motion
> That tends to vice in man but I affirm
> It is the woman's part: be it lying, note it,
> The woman's; flattering, hers; deceiving, hers;
> Lust and rank thoughts, hers, hers; revenges, hers;
> Ambitions, covetings, change of prides, disdain,
> Nice longing, slanders, mutability,
> All faults that may be named, nay, that hell knows,
> Why, hers, in part or all, but rather all;
> For even to vice
> They are not constant, but are changing still
> One vice, but of a minute old, for one
> Not half so old as that.

The truth is, that the passions of lust and jealousy and rage had at length worn out Shakespeare's strength, and after trying in vain to win to serenity in *The Tempest*, he crept home to Stratford to die.

In his native air, I imagine, his health gradually improved; but he was never strong enough to venture back to residence in London. He probably returned once or twice for a short visit, and during his absence his pious daughter, Mrs Hall, entertained the wandering preacher in New Place.

As Shakespeare grew stronger he no doubt talked with Combe, the usurer, for want of anyone better.

It is probable, too, that on one of his visits to London he took up Fletcher's *Henry VIII* and wrote in some scenes for him and touched up others, or Fletcher may have visited him in Stratford and there have begged his help.

His youngest daughter, Judith, was married early in 1616; it seems probable to me that this was the occasion of the visit of Jonson and Drayton to Stratford. No doubt Shakespeare was delighted to meet them, talked as few men ever talked before or since, and probably drank too much with those 'poor unhappy brains for drinking' which his Cassius deplored. Thus fanned, the weak flame of his life wasted quickly and guttered out. It is all comprehensible enough, and more than likely, that the greatest man in the world, after the boredom of solitary years spent in Stratford, died through a merry meeting with his friends; in his joy and excitement he drank a glass or so of wine, which brought on a fever. It is all true, true to character, and pitiful beyond words.

Shakespeare to me is the perfect type of the artist, and the artist is gradually coming to his proper place in the world's esteem. In the introduction to one of his *Lives*, Plutarch apologises for writing about a painter, a mere artist, instead of about some statesman or general, who would be a worthy object of ambition for a well-born youth. But since Plutarch's time our view of the relative merits of men has changed and developed: today we put the artist higher even than the saint. Indeed, it seems to us that the hero or statesman, or saint, only ranks in proportion to the artist-faculty he may possess. The winning of a battle is not enough to engage all our admiration; it must be won by an artist. In every department of life this faculty is beginning to be appreciated as the finest possession of humanity, and Shakespeare was an almost perfect example of the self-conscious artist.

People talk as if his masterpieces were produced at haphazard or by unconscious fruition; but masterpieces are not brought forth in this happy-go-lucky fashion. They are of the sort that only come to flower with perfect tendance. Even if we did not know that Shakespeare corrected his finest verses again and again with critical care, we should have to assume it. But we know that he spared no pains to better his finer inspirations, and he has told us in a sonnet how anxiously he thought about his art and the art of his rivals:

> Desiring this man's art, and that man's scope,
> With what I most enjoy contented least.

He has all the qualities and all the shortcomings of the reflective, humane, sensuous artist temperament, intensified by the fact that he had not had the advantage of a middle-class training.

In a dozen ways our Puritan discipline and the rubs and buffets one gets in this workaday world where money is more highly esteemed than birth or sainthood or genius, have brought us beyond Shakespeare in knowledge of men and things. The courage of the Puritan, his self-denial and self-control, have taught us invaluable lessons; Puritanism tempered character as steel is tempered with fire and ice, and the necessity of getting one's bread not as a parasite, but as a fighter, has had just as important results on character. Shakespeare is no longer an ideal to us; no single man can now fill our mental horizon; we can see around and above the greatest of the past: the overman of today is only on the next round of the ladder, and our children will smile at the fatuity of his conceit.

But if we can no longer worship Shakespeare, it is impossible not to honour him, impossible not to love him. All men – Spenser as well as Jonson – found him gentle and witty, gay and generous. He was always willing to touch up this man's play or write in an act for that one. He never said a bitter or cruel word about any man. Compare him with Dante or even with Goethe, and you shall find him vastly superior to either of them in loving kindness. He was more contemptuously treated in life than even Dante, and yet he never fell away to bitterness as Dante did: he complained, it is true; but he never allowed his fairness to be warped; he was of the noblest intellectual temper.

It is impossible not to honour him, for the truth is he had more virtue in him than any other son of man. 'By their fruits ye shall know them.' He produced more masterpieces than any other writer, and the finest sayings in the world's literature are his. Think of it: Goethe was perfectly equipped; he had a magnificent mind and body and temperament: he was born in the better middle classes; he was well off; splendidly handsome; thoroughly educated; his genius was recognised on all hands when he was in his teens; and it was developed by travel and princely patronage. Yet what did Goethe do in proof of his advantages? *Faust* is the only play he ever wrote that can rank at all with a dozen of Shakespeare's. Poor Shakespeare brought it further in the sixteenth century than even Goethe at full strain could bring it in the nineteenth. I find Shakespeare of surpassing virtue. Cervantes ranks with the greatest because he created Don Quixote and Sancho Panza; but Hamlet and Falstaff are more significant figures, and take

Hamlet and Falstaff away from Shakespeare's achievement, and more is left than any other poet ever produced.

Harvest after harvest Shakespeare brought forth of astounding quality. Yet he was never strong, and he died at fifty-two, and the last six years of his life were wasted with weakness and ill-health. No braver spirit has ever lived. After *Hamlet* and *Antony and Cleopatra* and *Lear* and *Timon* he broke down: yet as soon as he struggled back to sanity, he came to the collar again and dug *The Winter's Tale* out of himself, and *Cymbeline*, and seeing they were not his best, took breath, and brought forth *The Tempest* – another masterpiece, though written with a heart of lead and with the death-sweat dank on his forehead. Think of it; the noblest autumn fruit ever produced; all kindly-sweet and warm, bathed so to speak in love's golden sunshine; his last word to men:

> The rarer action is
> In virtue than in vengeance . . .

And then the master of many styles, including the simple, wins to a childlike simplicity, and touches the source of tears:

> We are such stuff as dreams are made of,
> And our little life is rounded with a sleep.

True, Shakespeare was not the kind of man Englishmen are accustomed to admire. By a curious irony of fate Jesus was sent to the Jews, the most unworldly soul to the most material of peoples, and Shakespeare to Englishmen, the most gentle sensuous charmer to a masculine, rude race. It may be well for us to learn what infinite virtue lay in that frail, sensual singer.

This dumb struggling world, all in travail between Thought and Being, longs above everything to realise itself and become articulate, and never has it found such width of understanding, such melody of speech, as in this Shakespeare. 'I have often said, and will often repeat,' writes Goethe, 'that the final cause and consummation of all natural and human activity is dramatic poetry.' Englishmen do not appear yet to understand what arrogance and what profound wisdom there is in this saying; but in a dull, half-conscious way they are beginning dimly to realise that the biggest thing they have done in the world yet is to produce Shakespeare. When I think of his paltry education, his limiting circumstances, the scanty appreciation of his contemporaries, his indifferent health, and recall his stupendous achievement, I am fain to apply to him, as most appropriate, the words he gave to his *alter ego*, Antony, Antony who, like himself, was world-worn and passion-weary:

> A rarer spirit never
> Did steer humanity; but you, gods, will give us
> Some faults to make us men.